# SAINT
# WOODY

# SAINT
# WOODY

## The History and Fanaticism
## of Ohio State Football

BOB HUNTER

University of Nebraska Press | Lincoln

The University of Nebraska Press is part of a land-grant institution with campuses and programs on the past, present, and future homelands of the Pawnee, Ponca, Otoe-Missouria, Omaha, Dakota, Lakota, Kaw, Cheyenne, and Arapaho Peoples, as well as those of the relocated Ho-Chunk, Sac and Fox, and Iowa Peoples.

First Nebraska paperback printing: 2022

**Library of Congress Cataloging-in-Publication Data**
Hunter, Bob, 1951–
   Saint Woody : the history and fanaticism of Ohio State football / Bob Hunter.
      p. cm.
   Includes bibliographical references and index.
   ISBN 978-1-61234-200-9 (hardcover : alk. paper)
   ISBN 978-1-4962-3309-7 (paperback)
   ISBN 978-1-61234-201-6 (electronic)
   1. Ohio State University—Football—History. 2. Ohio State Buckeyes
(Football team)—History. 3. Hayes, Woody, 1913–1987. 4. Football
coaches—Ohio—Biography. I. Title.
   GV958.O35H86 2012
   796.332'630977156—dc23

                              2012018887

# CONTENTS

# ACKNOWLEDGMENTS

This book has been years in the making, and hence, it would be nearly impossible to thank all of those who have had some hand in its creation.

My early education on Ohio State football came from veteran newspaper writers who had covered the program in one form or another for years: Dick Otte, Paul Hornung, and Dick Fenlon from the *Columbus Dispatch*; Kaye Kessler, Tom Pastorius, and Tom Keys from the *Columbus Citizen-Journal*; Si Burick from the *Dayton Daily News*; George Strode from the Associated Press (and later the *Dispatch*); and countless others.

Since then, the stories have come from many different directions. While the Ohio State football program has never been among the most open in terms of news media access, most former players, former coaches, and former administrators have been willing to share their experiences and their memories over the years. It's primarily because of them that the school's football history is as rich and detailed as it is.

A special thanks is owed to Linda Deitch, archive and collection manager of the *Columbus Dispatch* library, who always offered her able assistance with the newspaper's photo archive. Linda and *Dispatch* library director Julie Albert helped me find and choose many of the subjects in this book, and I'm grateful for that. They are efficient and competent, and the *Dispatch* is lucky to have them.

Bertha Ihnat and Michelle Drobik at the Ohio State University Archives were also helpful, as always, and also deserve my thanks.

# INTRODUCTION

B etween the time this book was conceived and the time it was finished, the smooth, straight road the turbocharged Ohio State University football machine had traveled for most of Jim Tressel's ten years as head coach came to a sharp and potentially deadly right turn. A painful crash ensued, followed by a messy cleanup.

At other less football-obsessed institutions, Tattoogate—as it came to be known because of the free and discounted tattoos several players received from Columbus tattoo parlor owner Edward Rife in exchange for jerseys and memorabilia, which was in violation of NCAA rules—could be a program killer. The scandal that eventually sacked Tressel for failing to report what he knew about the incidents sent quarterback Terrelle Pryor to the NFL early, took a healthy bite out of the Buckeyes' 2011 season, and handed them a post-season ban for 2012; it proved to be the program's most serious setback in the past fifty years.

What's remarkable is that some of other scandals that have dragged college football through the mud during the past two years make Ohio State's problems seem almost tame by comparison.

In December 2010, everyone wondered whether Auburn quarterback/Heisman Trophy favorite Cam Newton would even be eligible for the award because his father had been accused of offering Newton's services to Mississippi State for $180,000 before his son went to Auburn University. After Newton won the Heisman and the Tigers won the national championship, everyone waited to see whether the flashy quarterback and the program he represented would be allowed to keep what they won after the NCAA investigation concluded. They were—because the NCAA had no proof that Newton knew anything about his father's actions or that Auburn had given the former Florida quarterback anything other than a scholarship to go there. But skeptics recalled the example of the University of Southern California's Reggie Bush, who voluntarily gave up his 2005 Heisman later because of persistent allegations that he received improper benefits while in school.

In August 2011, an eleven-month investigation by Yahoo! Sports alleged that University of Miami Hurricanes booster Nevin Shapiro "provided thousands of impermissible benefits to at least 72 athletes from 2002 through 2010." These benefits included cash, prostitutes, entertainment in his multimillion-dollar homes and yacht, paid trips to expensive restaurants and nightclubs, jewelry, bounties for on-field play, travel, and an abortion.

The scandal at Penn State University even trumped that. Legendary head coach Joe Paterno's longtime assistant coach Jerry Sandusky was charged with forty counts of child sexual abuse over a fifteen-year period, including at least one instance in the school's football locker room. The school fired Paterno—a much-beloved figure and the winningest coach in college football history—for relaying only to the athletic director and another school official a grad assistant coach's admission that he had witnessed the crime. The school also fired the athletic director and school president for failing to alert the proper authorities, an act that seemed to show that they valued the Penn State football program's reputation over the safety of boys who may still be in harm's way. Sadly, Paterno died of complications from lung cancer a little over two months after he was fired.

While those were the worst of the worst, college football's problems seemed to ooze to the surface during that time period like pus from an open wound. The NCAA stripped Southern California of its 2004 national title because of the Bush incidents; meanwhile, the organization pressed new USC coach, Lane Kiffin, to explain NCAA violations he committed while he coached at Tennessee. Longtime Fiesta Bowl president and CEO John Junker lost his job in a corruption scandal that included an expense report on his corporate credit-card bill for $1,200 to a gentlemen's club. As the epidemic of rules violations and ugly incidents spread—the football programs at Michigan, Oregon, Boise State, LSU, Texas Tech, Georgia Tech, and North Carolina made the news for the wrong reasons during this period—

a concerned NCAA president Mark Emmert hosted fifty-four university presidents and chancellors to discuss "systemic change" in college sports.

The religion and fanaticism of Ohio State football, which inspired this interpretive history, is clearly emblematic of what is occurring in the sport in many other places. If the intensity of interest in football isn't quite as strong at most schools as it is at OSU, it's clear from the daily news reports that there are many places where feeding this frenzy sometimes takes precedence over practicing common sense.

Because of this growing fanaticism, college football has become a huge business and perspective is in increasingly short supply. In 1995, Florida State's Bobby Bowden became college football's first coach to earn $1 million per year. Today, University of Alabama coach Nick Saban makes nearly $5.6 million annually, and salaries for him and his staff have increased from the $6.24 million they made when he arrived in 2007 to $9.11 million now. The average annual compensation for head football coaches at public universities, according to research conducted by Duke economist Charles Clotfelter, is more than $2 million. Current Ohio State coach Urban Meyer, hired last November after he spent a year out of coaching due to health concerns created in part by the pressure to succeed at the University of Florida, signed a six-year contract for $4 million annually, even more than the $3.7 million Tressel made in 2011 before he stepped down. His nine assistants' salaries are up from the roughly $2.26 million that Luke Fickell's assistants made in 2011 to $3.22 million in 2012.

The program Meyer took over doesn't hold the same dominant national position today that it did during most of Tressel's ten years as coach. Saddled with the Tattoogate suspensions, an ongoing NCAA investigation, and additional player suspensions because of their alleged overpayment for part-time work, the Buckeyes saw their string of six consecutive Big Ten championships end in 2011 during an atypical 6–7 regular season, their first non-winning campaign since 1999. Then in December 2011, the NCAA hit the program with additional sanctions beyond those that OSU had self-imposed. The school had self-imposed a loss of five scholarships; the NCAA imposed a nine-scholarship penalty, three during each of the next three years. The NCAA also added the 2012 post-season ban and three years' probation.

It's doubtful those struggles would have launched a football recession at OSU, however. Meyer's reputation as both a coach and recruiter—he won three national titles at Florida—generated a new surge of interest in the program. The laments over Tressel's departure and the lost season faded quickly when Meyer scored a few quick recruiting coups in the weeks following his hiring. When recruiting for OSU's 2012 class ended, three top recruiting websites (Scout, Rivals, and ESPN) ranked it No. 3, 4, and 6, and some fans suggested that the program might be even stronger than before.

This inveterate optimism, while another symptom of the fans' intense love affair with the Buckeyes, isn't without justification. Ohio State football has proved to be remarkably resilient over the years. The NCAA slapped the program with a year's probation in 1955 after then head coach Woody Hayes admitted to giving loans or gifts to some of his "needy" players out of the $4,000 he received for appearing on his local TV show. After a 6-3 season in 1956, the Buckeyes won a national championship in 1957. The Ohio State faculty council's decision to keep the Buckeyes home from the 1961 Rose Bowl started one of the program's rare recessions, which lasted six years. But in 1968 OSU went unbeaten and won the national championship. With the exception of an occasional so-so season, the Buckeyes have been among a small handful of top programs ever since.

Tattoogate and its fallout interrupted a remarkable run of fifteen years when the Buckeyes hogged the national spotlight. During those fifteen years, Ohio State football regularly made news. It produced two Heisman Trophy winners. One of its prominent players challenged the NFL draft rules in court and lost, and subsequently wound up in prison for armed robbery. A former player died of complications from heat stroke suffered during an NFL practice, and another was in and out of prison because of his gambling addiction. In 2004, NFL teams took fourteen Buckeyes in the NFL draft, the most ever by one school in one year. OSU played in three national championship games in six years and won one. When the scandal broke, it had been No. 1 at some point in three of the previous five seasons, had finished in the top five in seven of the previous nine, and had won or shared six consecutive Big Ten championships. At last count, it had more than forty players on current NFL rosters.

All of this success/tragedy/news coverage resulted in an unprecedented intensity of interest in a program where fanaticism is the norm. The ubiquity of the OSU fans is, too. In September 2011, the *New York Times* asked nationally known statistician Nate Silver to determine which college football teams were the most popular nationally—he ranked OSU No. 1. Silver extrapolated data from Google searches, television markets, and census information to produce an estimated number of fans by team. For Ohio State he came up with a figure of 3,167,263.

The numbers at least partially explain why the program's history and fanaticism make good starting points for any examination of college football's condition. Fans in their familiar scarlet and gray garb are heard shouting "Go Bucks" on planes, in restaurants, and on city streets. It's nothing to see four of them use their arms to mimic the spelling of O-H-I-O on a public beach or in a public park. They have become so pervasive in airports, bars, and shopping malls that the football team was voted as the "most hated" in a Yahoo! survey. It is the kind of status normally reserved for successful, free-spending professional sports teams such as the New York Yankees and colleges with a heavy national sports footprint such as Notre Dame. It is a sign of enthusiasm, overexposure, and even arrogance. It is also a sign of success.

Tattoogate's long-term effect on the program probably won't be clear for several years. Whatever happens, the causes and effects of the fanaticism with Ohio State football examined in these pages remain. The program's history is rich. Its success has been extraordinary. The passion for the program and the expectations it brings aren't likely to change.

"Win it all," Meyer said when asked what is expected of him shortly after he accepted the job. "This is a monster. Ohio State is a monster. I get that."

Meyer's handling of the situation will be watched closely from the far corners of a college football world that at times seems to have run amok. The Toledo native admits he lost his personal perspective when he tried to do just about everything while coaching the Gators. He was rushed to a hospital while suffering from chest pains and dehydration in 2009, and submitted his resignation. He turned that into a leave of absence, returned to coaching, and then finally quit again in 2010. For a guy who values time spent with his family, one who thought retiring from coaching would be the best way to maintain perspective, his is a dangerous mission. Heading up any major college football program is akin to wrestling with a powerful beast on a daily basis, and the football monster at Ohio State may be the biggest of all.

"It will eat you alive," OSU athletic director Gene Smith said on the day Meyer met the team's news media.

Smith thought about that for a few seconds and nodded. His face bore no trace of his familiar smile.

"Every large college athletic program can be like this," he said. "If you don't have balance, it will eat you alive."

# 1

# Religion?

S ports fanaticism isn't unusual. Some Boston Red Sox fans really couldn't hate the New York Yankees more if they were a team of serial killers. The sight of Brett Favre in a purple Minnesota Vikings jersey used to be enough to ruin the month for some Green Bay Packers fans. When the Philadelphia Phillies lose, many Phillies fans mean every hateful decibel of their boos. It's nothing to watch a college basketball game and see a pulsating mob of students in more face paint than a Broadway diva, acting as if they accidentally left their brains back in the dormitory. What's more important—self-respect or home court advantage?

A team jersey, sweater, or jacket is the signature item in many fans' wardrobe. Millions of eyes have been blackened because either the attacker or victim was wearing a certain team's t-shirt or hat. Even the woeful Cleveland Browns inspire some fans to profess loyalty by wearing dog masks and dog collars as they tailgate on a dead gray patch of lakefront asphalt on a sleepy Sunday morning, knowing they will likely soon see their heroes utterly hammered in that expansive torture chamber known as Cleveland Browns Stadium.

On the surface then, fanaticism for Ohio State football doesn't seem any different. Fifty-something Buckeyes fans like to wear "authentic" football jerseys, the same as fifty-something fans at Penn State, Florida, Alabama, Texas, and Nebraska. When the team is having a bad afternoon, i.e., beating Indiana by 14 instead of 44, OSU fans love the backup quarterback, even if coaches who see him every day in practice hope he will never take a real snap in a real game. The fanatics think all "true" fans should blindly support the head coach; or they think the head coach might be worth his $4 million annual salary if only he would throw to the tight ends more; or they think the moron should be fired for losing to USC, no matter how many conference championships he has won.

This is routine fanaticism. Kentucky basketball fans behave that way. So do college football fans in Austin (home of the University of Texas Longhorns) and Baton Rouge (where the Louisiana State University Tigers call home). So do hockey fans in Montreal and Toronto; baseball fans in St. Louis, New York, and Boston; and pro-football fans in New York, Dallas, Cleveland, and Green Bay. By normal standards, it seems pretty bizarre, but then again, fanaticism wouldn't be what it was if it wasn't a little strange.

And yet the fanaticism for Ohio State football goes beyond even that to reach a level of devotion that has religious overtones. It may not seem that way to those on the outside or seem that much different from fanaticism elsewhere, until you spend some time at ground zero and take a closer look.

The day that convinced me was December 21, 2002. It seemed a strange time and place to have this epiphany. The Buckeyes had finished an unbeaten regular season and were preparing for an appearance in the Bowl Championship Series game against Miami. Officials of the City Center Mall in downtown Columbus decided to try to capitalize on the team's chance to win the school's first national championship since 1968 by hosting a pre-Christmas autograph session—a stroke of marketing genius that presented a rare opportunity for those who were running a doomed downtown mall that has since been razed.

The organizers set up a table on the second level of the mall, and people began lining up in front of it, even though they had no idea who would actually be sitting there signing autographs when the event started. The session wouldn't start for at least an hour, and those empty seats at the table could have been filled by guys whose scrawls wouldn't be recognized by their own family members. Yet, one-by-one, people began to blindly line up after those lucky souls in front.

The line grew quickly. It snaked past dozens of City Center stores, and it wasn't long before it burst through the doors of the indoor mall and spilled out onto the street. In some places, the line grew to be wider than a college offensive line and it kept growing, consuming blocks of the downtown sidewalk. All this for a chance to get an autograph by a couple of Ohio State football players, regardless of their identities.

Meanwhile, one level below, similar lines had formed in various directions, beginning from the edge of identical tables where some mall official had promised that an Ohio State football gladiator or two would soon be holding that great magnet of the human race, the fountain pen.

I waded into this sea of people thinking there might be a column here. My experience had prepared me for a certain level of fanaticism, but this was off the charts. I was immersed in these human waters when I heard a quivering voice behind me mutter a phrase that bore a faint hint of derangement: "This is *unbelievable*." When I wheeled around, I saw that the exasperation came from a man in a Pittsburgh Steelers jersey, carrying a shopping bag.

He was clearly either in Columbus for the holidays, had just moved to town, or maybe—as difficult as this is to believe—just didn't appreciate the value of a B. J. Sander autograph.

The man had a look of murder in his eyes, so a change of venue seemed appropriate. I retraced my steps past hundreds of eager "shoppers," exited the mall, and followed the line down the street.

"Who's at the front of this line?" I heard a member of the autograph herd say.

"I don't know," another replied. "Somebody told me there were like ten players at some tables up there, but I don't know which ones."

This conversation occurred so far away from the tables that we might have been in Wyoming. On a normal day, a leisurely walk from one end of the mall to the other might consume the better part of a lunch hour, and we were too far away from the entrance to see the doors. But to those who were planted in line—the line hadn't moved an inch for maybe a half-hour—the identity of the players at the end didn't matter. Even if the only reward for all of their efforts wasn't the perfect signature from quarterback Craig Krenzel but the scribble from a second-team offensive lineman or a third-team cornerback, they believed in a pot of gold at the end of the rainbow. Their friends and neighbors would be impressed: those black smudges, be it on a photo, plain white paper, or a crumpled McDonald's napkin, came from the hand of an Ohio State football player.

By itself, that kind of zealotry bears only a tenuous resemblance to religion; for all we know, some of those idlers could have been mercenaries who were hoping to score a Krenzel autograph and make a not-so-fast $10 on eBay.

But every time I have replayed the scene in my mind, it has reminded me that this obsession with Ohio State football bears some study. When people proudly display a photo of a dead football coach they have never met above their fireplace or squat on a scarlet and gray toilet seat in their Ohio State football–themed bathroom, it's clear that whatever is going on here occupies a deadly serious place in their lives.

Religion?

Well, something.

## 2

# Genesis

A conversation in the Selby Field press box prior to an Ohio Wesleyan football game many years ago was the beginning of my quest to find the site of the first official Ohio State football game.

"Do you know where they played that game?" I asked an OWU publicity man whose name has been lost among my dead brain cells.

"No, no one knows exactly where it was," he said. "There are some theories about it, but no one really knows."

So ended my exhaustive research. I had read news accounts of that 1890 game, and since I was in Delaware, Ohio, with an expert standing before me, it couldn't hurt to ask. But if no one knew, no one knew. It would remain one of life's enduring mysteries.

Several years later, a column about that first game in which I casually mentioned the unknown location drew interest from one of my *Columbus Dispatch* buddies who lived in Delaware at the time.

"I know a guy who I bet knows where it is," Mike Arace said. "He's a real local history buff."

My response to Mike escapes me, but it's safe to say that I didn't pursue it any further. Hey, if some guy whose name I can't remember told me no one knows where it is, then obviously no one knows. End of story.

Except that a couple of years later in October 2006, another column appeared regarding the Schumacher Place Civic Association's plans to erect a historic marker in the parking lot of the Giant Eagle grocery store at Whittier and Jaeger Streets, just east of Columbus's German Village neighborhood, the site of Recreation Park and Ohio State's first *home* football game against Wooster. The celebration was even bigger than a sale on fresh

5

produce. Jim Tressel and OSU athletic director Gene Smith spoke. A pep band played "Hang on Sloopy" and other historic numbers. Hundreds of people—OSU fans and grocery shoppers—were on hand to celebrate.

As a way of demonstrating my deep knowledge about Ohio State history, I wrote that it was "too bad no one knows the exact location" of the first game, the one at Ohio Wesleyan. Seeing this again, Mike went to his Delaware historian/pal, retired middle school teacher Brent Carson, who had also seen my careless remark and gone to retired OWU athletic director Dick Gordin. Carson figured that if anyone knew where the site of that game was, Gordin did, and he was right. Or at least Gordin knew where he could find out.

"There's this letter, from a man named C. Rollin Jones, and it's in our archives," Gordin told him. "I've read it a hundred times. It has landmarks."

C. Rollin Jones played for Ohio Wesleyan on that red-letter day, May 3, 1890. He also participated in OWU's centennial celebration fifty-two years later in 1942. And just as Gordin had said, Jones had written a letter in 1948 that described exactly where the field had been, on the northern edge of the Ohio Wesleyan campus, not far from Selby Field.

Delaware Run, a creek students used to call Dishwater Run, marks the north side of the field. A monument on the site of the sulfur spring, a tourist destination before a hotel there sold out to the college-building Methodists, marks the south side of the field. On the east side, where one end zone was situated, there is a semicircular parking lot that runs on and off of Henry Street. To the west, the lawn climbs gently until it hits Sandusky Street.

The place doesn't look much different now than it did then. Truthfully, if you could pick a spot for the birthplace of Ohio State football, a lush, green meadow snuggled against the rushing waters of Delaware Run would be hard to beat. You could have spent a tranquil hour there and not even suspected that this is ground zero for Ohio State football.

Carson and the Delaware County Historical Society raised money for a plaque, and on May 3, 2008, Tressel and two-time Heisman Trophy winner Archie Griffin were among those who spoke to a crowd of about a thousand Ohio State and Ohio Wesleyan fans who came out on a rainy morning for the plaque's unveiling.

Amid all the nice speeches, the most intriguing voices came from the grave—excerpts from Jones's 1948 letter and a 1938 interview with Ohio

State player George Cole. The living witnesses said nothing. They just stood there tall and strong, waving their maple leaves in the soft breeze and probably wondering why it took so long for everybody to get there.

Gordin's reading of Jones's letter proved the most fascinating, like the unearthing of a rare artifact.

"It was a continuous playing game void of the present-day delays," Jones wrote. "The huddle had not been invented. All plays were run from signals given by the captain except when Old Hickory was called, which meant a desperate drive to shove the ball over the goal line. . . . After the down, play resumed just as soon as the team with the ball could align itself. The players had no pads, no headgears, and their heads were hard, and they had plenty of hair for protection. There was no forward passing, but the ball could be lateralled. The game was an outgrowth of British rugby and soccer . . . and a scrum took place on every play.

"Dropkicking was a big part of the game. At times, the ball was kicked into Delaware Run, and we had to retrieve the ball so the game could proceed."

If it all seems a little odd, so does this: at the time, Ohio State and Ohio Wesleyan were about the same size—approximately 700 students— and the Delaware school had been around thirty-one years longer. Traveling by horse and buggy on unpaved roads, the OSU team had to leave at 6 a.m. to get to Delaware, twenty-seven miles to the north, for the 9:30 a.m. start.

Ohio State won 20–14 in front of about 700 people, although the game was scored differently than it is today. Touchdowns were worth four points—Joseph H. Large, Charles B. Morrey, Charles W. Foulk, and Arthur H. Kennedy scored for OSU—and extra-point kicks counted for two.

"Anything went but brass knuckles," Cole said in that 1938 interview. "There was none of this fancy forward passing or razzle-dazzle. It was all power stuff and wedge work—the flying wedge, a sheer power play, was then in vogue. It was all right to step on a man's face, but you had to be careful how you did it."

In some small way, Cole could almost be credited with the formation of that first Ohio State team, although a little history is in order before we get to him and his big moment.

A few OSU students had tried their hand at the game of football as early as 1881 on the wide open spaces near the North and South dorms west of Neil Avenue. They probably did it out of curiosity as much as anything. The contest many historians regard as the first football game—a match between Princeton and Rutgers—had occurred just twelve years before.

They called that Princeton-Rutgers game football, but it was played with a small round rubber ball and was more of a cousin to modern soccer. The rugby version of the game, between Harvard and Montreal's McGill University, was first played in 1874. So when a handful of enterprising OSU students attempted to play the new game, the rules were in a state of flux.

The Princeton-Rutgers game was played with twenty-five players on each side, and the ball could be kicked or batted with the hands to advance it; Harvard and McGill played with fifteen players per team and were allowed only to run with the ball. There were no yard lines or downs in either version. Whenever a ball went out of bounds, the player who recovered it would carry it to the spot where it left the field of play and throw it out onto the field, where both sides scrambled to recover it. There was no neutral zone between the two scrimmage lines; the imaginary line of scrimmage was drawn through the center of the ball. Both sides rushed to the line to gain an advantage, and there was so much pushing and shoving, bickering about which side was trying to get an unfair advantage (they both were), and so many appeals to the referee for justice, that it often took more than a minute to put the ball back in play. It's debatable which delay the modern fan would find more annoying—all of the constant, game-interrupting arguments or today's commercial interruptions.

Yale joined with Harvard in adopting rugby-style rules two years later, and the sport gradually began to assume a familiar shape, although it would have been interesting to see how Ohio State students played when they engaged in those first pickup games in the evenings on the gently sloping dorm grounds east of the Olentangy River. There's a good chance a game they thought was football was really something else, an amalgamation of rules from various styles of play. It's just too bad there were no Internet message boards in those days for self-proclaimed experts to straighten those early players out. Whatever they were doing, it had to have been wrong.

But then outside of the players themselves, no one knew that Ohio State students were even playing football. Some people today still like to call Columbus a cow town, but in those days it really was. When you left the city limits, which didn't extend much more than a mile or so beyond the modern inner belt in *any* direction, you were swallowed by farms as far as the eye could see in most directions, and some city dwellers weren't ashamed to raise a few chickens if they had a big enough yard. Columbus was growing quickly but hadn't come close to growing up.

The school that had opened as the Ohio Agricultural and Mechanical College in 1873 comprised only a handful of widely scattered buildings. Open land still separated the city of Columbus and the campus in many places; local residents still referred to Ohio State as "the college farm," probably because that's what it had been less than fifteen years before—Billy Neil's farm. Neil Avenue once served as a private lane to his house, which stood where the William Oxley Thompson Library stands today. The Rickly home, a sprawling two-story brick house and accompanying barn on the west side of High Street at 15th Avenue dated from the 1850s, had passed from a local miller to the university and was designated as home to the school president. The OSU students who gave football a whirl might just as well have been playing on a cornfield in western Iowa. Outside of the participants, no one even knew they were there.

As a bow to those students, the school included some kind of football in its field day of athletic activities that year, but again this was more experimental than anything. Marietta College students challenged Ohio State students to a game in 1887, but it was apparently never played. That same year, some OSU students met a team from the Columbus Buggy Company; no score was recorded and it was apparently a one-time deal. It's probably a good thing: Ohio State football wouldn't be nearly as popular if the long-defunct Columbus Buggy Company had become the Buckeyes' biggest rival instead of the University of Michigan.

The game they played in 1887 probably looked a little more like football but not *Ohio State* football. Think of a pickup football game you once played with your friends and neighbors in an empty lot or city park while growing up, and you have a good point of reference to those early football games.

Ohio State students finally got serious about football—well, at least one of them did—in the spring of 1889. George Cole decided to take up a collection to buy a real football to replace the homemade one he and the other students were using for their pickup games. When it arrived in the mail, its elliptical shape so befuddled Cole and his buddies that they repacked the ball and prepared to send it back, thinking there had been a mistake. But before they could return it, another student slipped into Cole's dorm room and took the ball, and a gang of boys started playing with it. Cole retrieved the ball, but because it had been used, there was no sending it back, as he later said, "much to our disgust."

Cole had also written to the Spalding sporting goods company for a football rulebook, and when it arrived, he found that the weird ball was exactly as it was supposed to be. When this light finally dawned, a powerful college football factory and the religion that grew up around it were born.

A second major event occurred when Cole learned that one of his old Columbus schoolmates was back in town. Al Lilley had attended Princeton and played football there. Cole sought him out and asked him if he would be willing to coach an Ohio State team. While this request didn't quite rival those "national" searches the university would conduct later when it wanted to show that only the best coach in America could run its football machine, it served its purpose at the time.

Lilley enlisted the coaching aid of another former Princeton player who was living in the city at the time—former All-American K. L. "Snake" Ames—and for the first time, OSU had a real team and a real coaching staff. Since streetcar service from Columbus to the tiny campus was somewhat sporadic, Lilley rode an Indian pony to and from practice from his home at E. Main and Rose Streets, a tradition I think we can all agree should be revived just as soon as Urban Meyer can find a suitable pony.

Ohio Wesleyan had formed a team at about the same time and the two squads agreed to meet, although the game seems to have been rescheduled a couple of times before it finally was played on that May day next to Delaware Run. Ohio State's first official game was also its first spring game, an odd piece of history. OSU was supposed to play a game against Denison the following Saturday but didn't because of bad weather. A rematch with Ohio Wesleyan was proposed but never came about.

So that first OSU team played only one game, a fact that has also been obscured by that game's timing. For some reason, it has been lumped together—for recordkeeping purposes—with the second OSU team that played three games that following November. This might make sense for fans of the calendar but it shouldn't to football fans; several of the players who participated that spring weren't even around in the fall, including team captain Jesse Jones.

Jones didn't miss much. The first home game at Recreation Park wasn't much to celebrate at the time. That second Ohio State team played Wooster, which had been playing football a little longer than the boys from Columbus—and it looked that way on the south Columbus athletic field that day.

For mental images of the game, we are grateful for the memories of OSU player Hugh Fullerton, the Hillsboro, Ohio, native who would go on to sportswriting success in New York and Chicago before returning to Columbus late in his career as a columnist for the *Columbus Dispatch*. Fullerton is a reliable source; he is one of the founders of the Baseball Writers' Association of America and is the reporter credited with first having suspicions about the team that became known as the Chicago Black Sox, for conspiring with gamblers to throw the 1919 World Series.

But in 1890, he was just a mischievous college student.

"Wooster took the field all togged out in new sweaters and wearing pretty stocking caps in place of headgears," Fullerton said during a visit to Columbus in 1916. "I was playing halfback and we had a wonderful fullback in Dirty Mike Kennedy. He said 'Let's get 'em.' And we got 'em. Before the first half was over, each Ohio State man was wearing his opponent's stocking cap tucked in his belt.

"Well, the rest of the game developed into a fight on our part to hold the caps and on the part of the Wooster fellows to get them back. Wooster won the game, but we won the fight."

Wooster not only won the game, it won 64–0. That prompted not only criticism of the officiating, but also of the OSU players, whom the student newspaper *Ohio State Lantern* thought were out of shape. It suggested that "a run of two miles a day would give greater powers of endurance."

Some things obviously haven't changed.

# 3

# The Martyr

Nothing about Congress, Ohio, indicates that anything of significance has ever happened there. It isn't Cooperstown or Gettysburg. It's not colonial Williamsburg. It's not even Mayberry. It is a poor representative of small-town America, a crossroads of maybe forty weather-beaten houses and a few trailers—a place time obviously forgot, if it was ever known at all.

If this village were human, a priest would have performed last rites on it decades ago. This unremarkable settlement is framed by gently rolling farm fields; the enduring image is that of a homely face surrounded by a pretty hairdo. It lies a few miles to the east of I-71, eighty miles north of Columbus, and about seventy-five years from the twenty-first century. It's the kind of town that if you passed through once, you have almost certainly forgotten it. A traveler has to go out of his way to visit. Few surely do. Congress had 185 full-time residents in 2010. The question that nags on your first visit there is why.

There are no visible businesses, unless you count the Congress Community Church. It stands as the town's only imposing structure, at best a dubious distinction. The sprawling, odd-shaped, barn-like structure seems more like a visitor than a permanent resident. The building, with a triangular-shaped roof and matching triangular-shaped tower, looks like it should be perched on a street corner in Belgium or facing a dyke in Holland, but it doesn't project the fatigue that emanates from the rest of Congress. The village reminds you of a weary old-timer who dug ditches for forty years and can barely lift his legs and arms.

It's hard to believe that this frowning little parcel of real estate holds a notable spot in Ohio State football history. Less surprisingly, it guards this information as if it were a family secret. Probably no one who lives more than a dozen corn rows from Congress knows the story, and the same could doubtless be said of most of its residents. In a state that has planted commemorative plaques for everything from the Berea Triangle to the Tingle Tavern to the Van Wert Gazebo, the death of the only Ohio State player killed in a football game doesn't get so much as a hand-painted sign in his hometown.

Given the runaway passion for all things Buckeye, it seems remarkable that the program's only football martyr lies in a sleepy little cemetery on the hilly north end of a sleepy little village, without so much as a passing mention of the fact. John Sigrist is remembered with the same silent indifference as those who lived and died in Congress—with his name, birth and death years carved onto a granite monument in the Congress Cemetery. His marker also denotes the final resting place of his mother (Madeline), his father (Christian), and two of his sisters. There is no mention of Ohio State or the game that killed him. The grave isn't marked by an OSU flag. It isn't even adorned by a bouquet of plastic scarlet and gray flowers.

Not that Sigrist has been *totally* forgotten. In the small library of OSU football books released every year, he occasionally receives a brief mention. His name is in the Ohio State football media guide on the list of lettermen, although it is spelled "Segrist." The *Columbus Dispatch* did a story on him on the 110th anniversary of his death on October 28, 2011; before that, his name didn't come up until the third screen of entries on Google under a "this day in Big Ten history" listing posted by the Big Ten Network. His place on the Internet search engine's roll call fell behind another John Sigrist who is mentioned in an article on the Textile Influences on Wallpaper—that Sigrist made wallpaper in the 1770s—and another John Sigrist who finished in tenth place in a Rochester Yacht Club race in 2007. You can't help but wonder if Congress would give either of them more notice if they were buried there.

Granted, Sigrist died over a century ago, at a time when football deaths weren't as rare as they are now, but his apparent anonymity in a town this small is hard to believe.

When Sigrist broke his neck in an OSU home game against Western Reserve on October 26, 1901, it was big news. He was a good player, had been captain of the team four years before, and was in his fifth year on the roster (a Michigan player named Horace Prettyman once occupied a spot on the Wolverine roster for *nine* years, so there were no raised eyebrows over Sigrist playing another year of football while he tried to finish up his agriculture degree). He was twenty-seven years old and had two brothers on the team; his younger brother, Charles, started at tackle.

Ohio State football hadn't yet developed into a religion; for most of those who would eventually become part of the congregation, it wasn't even much of a hobby. There were 1,200 spectators at the pastoral spot at High and 16th Streets, which came to be known as Ohio Field, to see OSU and Western Reserve play what was regarded as a "50-cent game"—as opposed to one that couldn't demand such a large admission fee. Sigrist and the Buckeyes didn't even arrive on the field until ten minutes after the scheduled starting times. Even "50-cent games" weren't taken quite as seriously as the ones fans pay more than $70 to watch now.

Nonetheless, it was a fiercely contested game, which in those days meant just that. Safety wasn't one of the priorities. The "equipment" worn by the players consisted of light padding on the legs and shoulders; few if any players wore the rudimentary leather helmets that had been existence fewer than ten years. Broken bones, cuts, welts, deep bruises, and gouged eyes were common afflictions. Players had a somewhat different definition of "contact."

Sigrist was the team's starting center; in the ensuing eulogies, he was called the best center Ohio State football had produced in its eleven-year history. He was "coming low through the line with his head down," there was a pileup, and one or more—possibly all—of the Western Reserve players fell on him. The pile disassembled and Sigrist didn't. He was carried to the sidelines, where he complained of a severe pain in the area of the seventh vertical vertebrae.

At that point, Sigrist could still move his arms and legs, but it was clear he had suffered a serious injury. He was taken to the nearby armory, where Dr. J. A. McClure examined him about an hour after he was hurt.

Sigrist complained of numbness, particularly in his right leg. McClure could see this was no minor injury; unfortunately, he couldn't accompany the player to Grant Hospital because of a previous engagement. Instead, he telephoned Dr. J. F. Baldwin and asked him to meet Sigrist there. When McClure saw him the next morning, Sigrist was paralyzed "from the third rib down."

The next day, the local newspapers reported that Sigrist had been "very seriously injured" in the Buckeyes' 6–5 victory and that physicians in attendance refused to make any statement concerning his chances of recovery. His paralysis from the waist down was noted, but the possibility of death wasn't mentioned. It was called a severe injury to his spine. By Monday, the *Ohio State Journal* was reporting that Sigrist's neck was broken and that doctors were awaiting the arrival of his parents from Congress for approval for an operation on Tuesday. The reason they were waiting wasn't reported until later; his brothers weren't willing to take the responsibility for an operation doctors said might prove fatal.

His mother reached the hospital Monday morning—as Dr. Baldwin said, "over forty hours after the accident"—and immediately approved the procedure. Arrangements were made to operate at 2:30 p.m. At noon, Sigrist's breathing became labored. No pulmonary sounds were heard from the left lung. Dr. Baldwin allowed the physicians who had examined him previously to decide whether to go ahead when they arrived at 2 p.m., but at 1:30, Sigrist died unexpectedly. An autopsy discovered that his left lung was completely filled with blood and contained no air whatsoever. Dr. Baldwin surmised that had they been able to operate, Sigrist likely would have died from hemorrhaging. Further examination showed that the spinal cord had been fractured, crushed at the fifth cervical vertebrae. The heart was engorged with blood almost to the point of bursting. According to the *Columbus Dispatch*, he was conscious the entire time, up to a few moments before he died.

The OSU athletic board met that night and canceled the Ohio Wesleyan game scheduled for the following Saturday. Board members let the team decide whether the rest of the season would be canceled at a meeting in the armory the following afternoon. The players chose to finish the season, even with the loss of the Sigrists, Paul Hardy, and Laffy Bulen, who had been forbidden by their parents to continue playing.

That, if anything, indicates that keeping the program alive was no sure thing. Michigan, a team Ohio State had never beaten and which was one of the strongest in college football, followed Ohio Wesleyan on the schedule. The *State Journal* reported that after the meeting, one or two of the members of the first eleven said they didn't want to be overwhelmed by Michigan, and it might be just as well to cancel the rest of the games, despite the vote taken by the team.

School officials canceled classes that morning so students could attend a funeral service for Sigrist in the university chapel. The Ohio Medical University football team attended the service and offered to play out the rest of the Buckeyes' schedule, but the vote taken later made that unnecessary. After the funeral ended, a crowd of students and a detail of cadets accompanied Sigrist's body to Union Station. Head coach John Eckstrom and team captain J. M. Kittle were among those who traveled to Congress for the service there the following morning.

It would be an understatement to say this was a critical moment in the history of Ohio State football. Six days after Sigrist's fatal injury, a memorial service was held for him in the campus chapel. Several of the speakers called football "inhuman" and "brutal." Some favored canceling the rest of the season, and others the elimination of the sport on campus. One student who spoke on behalf of Sigrist's brother Charles said it was his wish that the schedule be completed and the program continue.

At a faculty meeting on November 4, Professor N. W. Lord offered a resolution calling for a cancellation of the remainder of the schedule. After a heated discussion, the proposal was voted down 18–8. When the schedule resumed, a depleted OSU squad lost to Michigan, 21–0.

In 1905, a year when there were so many deaths in the sport of football—eighteen overall, including three college players—then football-loving president Theodore Roosevelt called for a commission to reform the rules and "save" the sport. By then, talk of eliminating the sport at OSU had abated and John Sigrist lay all but forgotten in an isolated Congress cemetery.

4

# The Prophet

A random check of one hundred Ohio State football fans probably wouldn't find more than a half-dozen who could explain who Thomas French was and what, if anything, he had done to affect their favorite college program.

At least some of them could probably come up with the name French Field House, a building completed in 1956 that was designed for indoor track and field meets and still sits next to St. John Arena.

I actually tested this in a conversation with a friend of mine, and it played out pretty much the way I expected.

"Let me guess," he said. "If his name is on a track building, he was probably a famous old track coach, right?"

Nice try, but no, he wasn't a track coach, famous or otherwise. French managed to get his name attached to a track and field building because he was Ohio State's first and longest-serving faculty representative to what was then popularly known as the Western Conference. The Big Ten, as it came to be known, has always been governed by a board that consists of one faculty representative from each institution. When it was formed in 1895, it was actually called the Intercollegiate Conference of Faculty Representatives, and the name wasn't officially changed to the Big Ten until 1987. No one knows it, but what Woody Hayes technically won were thirteen ICFR football titles. For a long time, the league was like a guy who had a secret identity and was too embarrassed to tell anybody.

If French had come along sooner, he might have been the one who came up with the popular Western Conference or Big Nine designation for the league in 1899 (as there were only nine teams in the league then); he was

19

definitely smart enough to know a lousy name for a league when he saw one. But Ohio State wasn't part of the ICFR in those days and French had graduated only four years earlier. When OSU was admitted to the conference in 1912, French became the school's faculty representative for athletics, serving until his death in 1944.

So that's how he got his name on a track and field building. But it doesn't explain why he is important enough to have his own chapter in a book about the school's football program, even though he doubtless proposed and supported lots of conference rules that affected college football over the years. No, French is here because he envisioned a giant, horseshoe-shaped stadium at a time when the team sometimes drew crowds that weren't large enough to support a neighborhood flea market. French was more than a long-serving steward of conference athletic programs—French was a prophet.

The first evidence came in 1908, when French was a young engineering drawing professor who served on the school's athletic board. The board recommended improvements to Ohio Field that would raise seating capacity from 4,200—the program seldom drew 4,000 in those days—to 6,100. Meanwhile French was dreaming of a "magnificent concrete stadium." Michigan, the Midwest's oldest and most successful football power, had only recently expanded Ferry Field to seat 18,000, and its bleachers were still made of wood. Even major league baseball teams were still playing in wooden facilities; Philadelphia's Shibe Park and Pittsburgh's Forbes Field would start the trend toward concrete and steel the following year.

But in explaining the planned improvements to Ohio Field in the *Alumni Quarterly*, French made it plain that he was either a visionary or a dreamer:

It is hoped that this is only the beginning of the final Ohio Field. The fence will be continued around the entire enclosure, with perhaps behind the bleachers a concrete wall paneled for bronze tablets to be left by future classes; and with the continued splendid financial management and the support of the alumni the dream of a magnificent concrete stadium in horse-shoe shape may be realized sooner than anyone would expect.

This was a curious choice of words, since no one other than French could have seriously expected that. The Ohio State football program at that point was still small time; it had only recently started to have consistent success against Ohio teams such as Case and Oberlin. Membership in the Western Conference was still five years away. Jack Wilce, the school's first Hall of Fame football coach, was still playing football for Wisconsin. Lynn St. John, the athletic director who would help French realize his stadium dream, was still coaching and finishing up a bachelor's degree at Wooster College. Chic Harley, Pete Stinchcomb, Howard Yerges, Hap and Howard Courtney, and the other players who would bring the school its first real success on the football field were still a bunch of snot-nosed kids whose only athletic glory had come in their neighborhood parks, yards, and alleys.

If any of the people French passed on the Columbus streets had paid the least bit of attention to him—and there is no indication that any of them did—they would almost surely have judged him to be a few marbles short of a load. But the kind of football stadium he was dreaming about did exist in some places—just not in Midwestern college football backwaters.

The college game had gotten its start on the East Coast; all of the game's great powers were located there and so was its biggest fan base. Harvard had built a 50,000-seat, concrete, U-shaped stadium in 1903. Yale had topped that with a giant, bowl-shaped, 70,000-seat structure in 1908. Princeton had Palmer Stadium in mind, if not in concrete, and opened the 45,000-seat horseshoe-shaped stadium six years later. So it wasn't as if French was on a different planet with his stadium dreams; he just seemed to be at the wrong school, at the wrong time, in the wrong section of the country. Ohio Stadium was probably about fifteen or twenty years ahead of its time when it opened in 1922. To dream about it in 1908 seems just plain crazy.

Born in Mansfield, Ohio, in 1871, French had moved with his family to Dayton while he was still a boy. He worked as a draftsman there before entering Ohio State in 1891. He continued as a draftsman while he was in school, helped pay for his education by making patent drawings, and landed a teaching job upon graduation in 1895. His brother, Edward, had been captain of the football team in 1896, and Thomas devoted a significant amount of his time to the school's loosely organized athletic programs. He helped to recruit volunteer coaches. He helped to schedule games with other

Ohio schools. He was an advocate for all of the university's teams, and it wasn't long before he was called to serve on the university's athletic board.

It would be a serious mistake to think that French was just a sports advocate who liked to draw. He published a textbook, *A Manual of Engineering Drawing*, in 1911 that is now in its 13th edition with several coauthors and updates sixty-six years after his death. Anyone inclined to think that this poor guy spent his days doodling triangles, squares, and rectangles and staring out his campus window daydreaming about football would be shocked back to reality by a quick flip through his book.

"Different courses have been designed for different purposes," he wrote in the preface of his textbook, "and criticism is not intended, but it would seem that better unity of method might result if there were a better recognition of the conception that drawing is a real language to be studied and taught in the same way as any other language."

I know nothing about engineering drawing, but five minutes with this book convinced me that a) French was an extremely bright guy, and b) if he saw the still relatively young Ohio State football program someday playing in "a magnificent concrete stadium of horseshoe-shape" in 1908, it was no accident. Here was a man who designed the university seal and crest, designed bookplates as a hobby (an old university bio of him noted that sixteen of his bookplates were in use in university libraries around the country), and designed the building (Brown Hall) where he maintained his office.

It took many things to make his concrete horseshoe-shaped stadium idea happen; admission to the Western Conference in 1912 and championship teams in 1916 and 1917 created widespread interest in a team that had previously appealed to only a small core of devoted followers. But French was there during every step of the process, and there seems little doubt that the Ohio Stadium we know today wouldn't have existed without his vision, input, and support.

French gave a speech to the Columbus Chamber of Commerce in 1915, when Ohio State still hadn't won anything, in which he said he could foresee the day when more than 50,000 fans would attend the school's football games. This notion seemed bizarre even then—the school's record crowd (for the 1902 Michigan game) was 8,200 at that point—but it sounded a little more like simple exaggeration than it did in 1908, when it seemed like pure fantasy.

"It was in 1915 that the first preliminary notion of some kind of stadium began to develop," French wrote in the *Columbus Dispatch* stadium edition on Ohio Stadium dedication day in 1922. "The increasing interest in football and the demand for seats was overtaxing the capacity for Ohio Field and the temporary expedients were reaching their limit.

"We had bought circus seats, most uncomfortable things, as those who had to sit on them well remember, had rented movable stands and built standing platforms until all available space had been filled and Director St. John said in desperation, 'We've got to tear down this field and build a larger one.'"

What this doesn't explain is that the circus seats, movable stands, and standing platforms didn't come until 1916, a year after French gave that Chamber of Commerce speech. Again, he was ahead of the curve. The crowds did swamp Ohio Field in 1916, and the school's board of trustees did "look with favor" on building a 40,000-seat bowl-shaped stadium in the woods to the west of Ohio Field in February 1917, before the plan died. When the team had another championship season in 1917, French asked one of his colleagues, professor of architecture Howard Dwight Smith, to draw up plans for a horseshoe-shaped arena in 1918; in the midst of World War I, nothing came of it at that time. But when interest boomed again in 1919, French went back to Smith and had him work on the plans that eventually became Ohio Stadium.

He had lots of support now, most notably from St. John (whom he helped hire as an assistant football coach in 1912), OSU president William Oxley Thompson, and eventually the hundreds of fans who pledged over a million dollars to build the landmark stadium that opened in 1922.

Those who came to call French the "daddy of the stadium" in later years knew what they were talking about. Even if he didn't pay for it with his athletic skill or his own bank account, he was the first to see a giant concrete stadium on campus while his colleagues on that 1908 athletic board were congratulating themselves on spending $30,000 to replace an ugly, old wooden fence on the Ohio Field's south end with an iron railing.

Crazy?

Absolutely. But genius sometimes seems like a form of insanity.

# 5

# The Messiah

Charles "Chic" Harley wasn't born in a manger on the south side of Chicago in 1894, but he just as well might have been. As far as the Ohio State football program goes, Harley is the messiah, the savior, the kid at the center of the religion that is Ohio State football. He was the kid who made the Buckeyes relevant to seemingly every man, woman, and child—first in Columbus and then into much of Ohio. He was the player who raised the team to that next level today's athletes chatter endlessly about, and he did it with such force that it stuck there.

Everyone knew that story sixty years ago. Then for most of the next fifty years it was like no one remembered it. Harley went from being a larger-than-life hero who many thought deserved to have his name on Ohio Stadium, to a guy who seemed only vaguely familiar. This descent into relative anonymity halted about ten years ago, and since then, Harley has finally gotten some of his glory back. He has been the topic of two books and one DVD, had one of his numbers retired and hung on a façade inside the stadium, and has a memorial garden planned on the South Champion Avenue site of one of his Columbus homes. There is even talk of erecting a statue of him somewhere near the stadium, talk that went nowhere eight or nine years ago but seems to be gaining a little more credence now.

Harley still doesn't have the name recognition of, say, Mike Nugent or Santonio Holmes—hey, we're not talking miracles here—but at least when his name is mentioned, many Ohio State fans no longer look befuddled. They know he is a football hero, even if they aren't quite sure why.

I did an in-depth column on Harley in April 2000 that doubtless helped introduce Chic to many who were unaware of him; its research also heightened my concern about how cruel fate had been to him. Here was an immensely popular and wildly talented guy who had it all, and then had it snatched away from him by a mental illness. He might have become one of early pro football's biggest stars or even owned the Chicago Bears, might have one day become the Ohio State football coach, the mayor of Columbus, or a rich, successful businessman. But he never had a chance to do any of those things. The DVD about Harley's life, released by Dean Carnevale during the fall of 2009, was entitled *Lost Legend*, and the name was sadly appropriate. The Harley legend was clearly lost for decades to all but a small, devoted group of OSU football historians.

My introduction to Chic occurred in a rather bizarre scene in the *Columbus Dispatch* sports department in the late 1970s. I was aware of Harley because of my interest in sports history, but I had just learned that he had spent most of his life in a mental hospital before dying in 1974. That piqued my curiosity enough to ask one of the staff's senior members about him, and I was surprised when the guy lowered his voice to almost a whisper and looked around cautiously, as if he were about to try to sell me a fake Rolex.

"You know that his mental problems came from a case of syphilis, don't you?" he said.

I didn't, of course, and I carried this little "secret" around with me for years. Then in the 1990s, an interview I conducted with an elderly gentleman who had once served on the Ohio State board of trustees resulted in almost an identical experience—same hushed tone, same fear that someone other than me would find out, even though near as I can remember, no one else was even in the room. Obviously, this wasn't a "secret." Lots of people both knew about it and told other people about it, even if it wasn't true.

That was on my mind when I wrote that column in 2000; maybe school officials had subconsciously subverted Chic's legend because of this dirty little secret of his illness. Then I met Richard Wessell, Harley's seventy-eight-year-old nephew and retired editor and owner of a suburban Chicago newspaper chain, and interviewed him for the column. He loved his late uncle and couldn't have been happier to get the call.

"Time causes a lot of things to fade," Wessel said. "And I'm sorry to say I think he is one of the things that is fading."

When I asked Wessell if he had heard the syphilis rumors, he told me that he had not only heard them, but he was intent on disproving them. He was planning to write a book about Chic, and if it were at all possible, he would prove in the book that Chic never had syphilis. He had even gone to great lengths to get all of his uncle's medical records from the Veterans Administration hospital in Danville, Illinois, where Chic had spent the last thirty-six years of his life, and was going to have doctors analyze them. He saw these rumors as an ugly blotch on his uncle's life.

Twenty-five years after his death, the rumors didn't seem that important to me. Maybe this was in part because a case of syphilis no longer seems quite so scandalous today as it must have been in the 1920s, but mostly because it seemed like such a small part of the story. Anyone doing more than cursory research into Chic's life will find a terrific player who is more responsible for the immensely successful Ohio State football program than anyone else, a modest guy who was enormously popular with both his peers and his fans. As titillating as it must have been for some people to imagine this football star as a guy with a voracious sexual appetite and who paid for it with a lifetime in mental hospitals, and as intriguing as it was to think he may have been victimized by some cruel urban legend, it struck me that his legacy was so much more important.

For those who possess an almost religious devotion to Ohio State football, this ignorance is tantamount to having no knowledge of the basic tenets of their religion. In many ways, the program they worship started with him. To understand what Harley did and how he did it, the modern fan must first realize what OSU football was before he arrived. It is a remarkable story and one that somewhat parallels Thomas French's tale in the previous chapter.

At the time that Harley's Ohio-born parents moved back to Columbus from Chicago in 1907, Chic was twelve years old and Ohio State football was a minor player in town. The program was only a few years older than he was, having started in relative anonymity during the spring of 1890. It grew slowly, just like the "college in a cornfield" it represented, and by the time the Harley family arrived it was doing okay; OSU had started to routinely beat the other Ohio colleges it regularly competed against—teams such as Otterbein, Muskingum, Wittenberg, and Oberlin—and its games sometimes even drew 3,000 or 4,000 fans. This was not yet a big-time program, and it wasn't even the biggest game in town—that distinction belonged to the Columbus Senators of baseball's American Association.

Chic was a smallish kid who excelled at sports. He was one of the best baseball players on the east side sandlots, a fleet runner, and an excellent boxer. But he was only 5'6" and weighed only 125 pounds when he arrived at Columbus East High School as a sophomore, and had to be convinced by his buddies to go out for the football team.

"You fellows think I'm good," he told them. "But look at the size of those guys."

It quickly became apparent, though, that the size of the older players was more of a detriment than an advantage when it came to tackling little Chic. He flitted around the field like a football firefly, changing both his direction and speed so quickly that the other players were often left lunging at air, trying to tackle a body that was no longer there. By his junior and senior seasons, he was the city's biggest high school star, and college coaches other than those at the local colleges had noticed. Even in the days before widespread recruiting, both Notre Dame and Michigan tried to lure him away from Ohio State.

But even when he arrived on campus as a freshman in 1915, no one knew if he really was good enough to be a star on the college level. Ohio State had joined the Western Conference in 1912 and hired twenty-five-year-old University of Wisconsin assistant Jack Wilce—only one year removed from a job as athletic director and coach at a high school in La Crosse, Wisconsin—as coach in 1913; in three seasons so far, there had been no sign that the Buckeyes were ready to challenge the top teams in the league. Chicago and Minnesota wouldn't even deign to find a place for them on their schedules.

Even though the 1915 varsity team was a good one—it had a 5-1-1 record overall and 2-1-1 in the league—it still received only lukewarm interest from the public. Most of OSU's games still didn't draw as many fans as the games that Harley's East High School teams had drawn against city rival North High on Ohio Field, and even Chic's success on the freshman team was no guarantee of stardom on the varsity stage.

The *Chicago Tribune* summed up what the outside world thought of Harley in its 1916 preview of the conference: "Ohio coach Wilce is happy to welcome local boy Chas. Harley, who might find the going too much when he starts playing with the big boys." What the *Tribune* didn't know, what no one including Wilce and even the prophet who headed the OSU engineering drawing department knew, was that the Ohio State football program was about to undergo a profound change. The summer of 1916 would be the calm before Chic Harley, the last time OSU football would ever be more of a curiosity than an obsession, the last time Columbus would ever have an apathetic attitude toward OSU football.

Ohio Wesleyan, the one-time rival now turned schedule-filler, was OSU's opponent in the season opener. There was no buzz. The game drew 4,889 fans, less than half of Ohio Field's now 10,000 capacity, and the newspapers implied it was one of the biggest opening day crowds ever because of the local fans' curiosity about seeing Harley.

"I have not seen an Ohio State game in two years," a seventy-year-old man told the *Columbus Dispatch*. "But I saw Harley play in high school games and I want to see what he will do."

The old man's uncertainty about Harley's prospects put him in the same camp as the *Chicago Tribune*; he obviously saw the possibility of Chic's success but didn't count on it. The 12–0 win over the Ohio Wesleyan Bishops didn't prove much and neither did a school record 128–0 win over Oberlin the following week in which none of starters, including Harley, saw much action. The announced crowd of 3,300 showed that OSU football still wasn't a big deal, and no one including French had any idea what was about to happen.

Ohio State's next game was at Illinois, which was slowly becoming a conference power under coach Bob Zuppke. Local fans hoped for the best and expected the worst. It was a rainy, miserable day in Champaign and only 4,388 turned out, including 175 OSU rooters who made the trip from Columbus. The swampy ground made for poor traction. The OSU offense was going nowhere, in part because Harley couldn't get his footing and use his speed to run outside. The Illini were leading 6–0 with two minutes to go when the little halfback began chewing up yards through the center of the line. With 1:10 left and the Buckeyes in a 4th and 3 situation somewhere between the 13- and 20-yard lines—on the sloppy field, the rain had erased all the markings—Wilce called for what he called a "spot zone" pass play. It flooded one area of the defense with five receivers and left the other side open for Harley to perform his magic.

The Buckeyes' line shifted right. Harley went left. He faked a pass, then angled toward the northwest corner of the end zone. Harley straight-armed one tackler off him, eluded another, and then another. From about three yards out, he made a desperate dive for the end zone and made it. Impossible as it must have been for Illinois fans to believe, the score was tied.

The extra point rule was more complicated in those days. The scoring team had to kick the ball out of the end zone toward the field of play, and if a teammate fielded it cleanly, the team had a chance to make the conversion kick from there. Harley booted the ball to teammate Fred Norton, who caught it on the 22-yard line near the sidelines. It wasn't a good spot, particularly on a mushy field; a successful kick would win the game.

Harley looked at his shoe, which was caked with mud, and called time out. He walked to the sideline and called to trainer Doc Gurney.

"Gimme a shoe," he said.

Gurney handed him one, and while everyone in the stadium watched, the little sophomore calmly changed shoes, sauntered to the spot where Kelly Van Dyne was preparing to hold the ball, and in just his third college game, he kicked the extra point to beat Illinois, 7–6. No one knew it at the time, but this was the Big Bang of Ohio State football, the birth of the football behemoth that would still be alive almost a century later. It would never be the same again.

News of the upset gripped Columbus. By Monday, Ohio State officials were already making plans for Wisconsin's visit to Ohio Field, even though it was still two weeks away. By Wednesday, the newspapers were already reporting that the crowd would eclipse the school record 8,200 fans who had attended the 1902 Michigan game, and athletic director Lynn St. John announced that Ohio Field would be able to accommodate 12,000 fans due to the erection of bleachers at the south end and permanent boxes in front of the east bleachers. He said the athletic department was deluged with mail orders for tickets and would try to fill as many as it could.

Not everyone believed that the Buckeyes had suddenly become a Western Conference power, however. When the Wisconsin Badgers arrived in Columbus and checked into the Great Southern Hotel, their coach, Paul Withington,

wasn't with them. In probably one of the most blatant displays of disrespect in college football history, Withington had put assistant coach Ed
Soucy in charge for the OSU game and had instead gone to Minneapolis
to scout the Minnesota-Chicago game. He believed they were the teams
Wisconsin would have to beat in November to win the conference title and
apparently thought a win over upstart Ohio State was all but assured.

The Buckeyes won the game 14–13 on a remarkable 80-yard run from
scrimmage by Harley. Why Withington wasn't fired on the spot after the
loss is hard to figure; for all we know, he may have blamed the assistant
coach he left in charge for the loss. But afterward, few in Columbus were
concerned about Withington's arrogance. The 12,268 who had crammed
into Ohio Field proved that the Buckeyes were suddenly in style, and the
city had a sports hero unlike any it had known before. In two weeks, everyone in town and most of the state had come to know Chic Harley.

It's remarkable, really, that the Ohio State football world changed so
abruptly. "Only" 8,000 showed up to see the Buckeyes blast Indiana, the
conference doormat. A trip to Cleveland left Case officials sorry that they
didn't move the game to League Park, home of the Cleveland Indians, where
they were certain they could have sold more than 10,000 tickets. Cleveland,
after all, was suddenly going wild over the Buckeyes. The final home game
against Northwestern was played for the conference title and an unbeaten
season, and the newspapers called the crowd of 11,979 "disappointing."
After the Buckeyes won 23–3—Harley kicked a field goal and had touchdown runs of 61 and 16 yards—the fans celebrated as if they had won the
World Series.

The *Chicago Tribune*'s Walter Eckersall, a former Chicago star renowned
as one of the college football's leading authorities, covered the Northwestern
game, and he immediately placed Harley on his All-American ballot, declaring that "Harley is as great as Willie Heston," a legendary former Michigan
star. One by one, other experts weighed in with similar sentiments. Harley
was the real deal, and he had given the Buckeyes the kind of football cred-
ibility they had never known.

Harley and his teammates went undefeated again during the 1917 season and Chic was again an All-American, but the crowds were down
slightly, particularly for the tune-up games. The emotional drag of World

War I may have had something to do with it, even if it probably wasn't the whole story. Ohio Wesleyan and Denison wouldn't draw crowds anymore. Ohio State was one of the big boys now, and the smaller crowds for the nonconference games reflected that. The season came down to home games against Wisconsin and Illinois, and there was plenty of demand for tickets to those games. St. John added to the bleachers at both ends of Ohio Field, expanding seating to more than 14,000, and the crowd exceeded capacity at both games.

The war took a serious bite out of the program's momentum in 1918, with Harley and most his teammates in the service, but it picked back up again in 1919. Michigan, which had withdrawn from the conference in 1908 because of a disagreement over league rules, had returned in 1918. The Wolverines immediately became the focus, primarily because the Buckeyes had never beaten them in fifteen tries. But the fans sensed that things were different now, and the local newspapers regularly devoted space to the Michigan game, even though it was fourth on OSU's schedule.

True to form, Harley and the Buckeyes didn't disappoint. In fact, Chic played so well in OSU's 13–3 victory in Ann Arbor that famous Michigan coach Fielding Yost went into the Buckeyes' locker room afterward to congratulate the team, and specifically to applaud Chic.

"And you, Mr. Harley, I believe you are one of the finest little machines I have ever seen," Yost said.

Wins over Purdue and at Wisconsin followed, and the Buckeyes' chances to win a third consecutive conference title and close out Harley's three-year unbeaten streak came down to a home game against Illinois, which again hiked the ticket demand to unprecedented levels. The bleachers at both ends were expanded further until Ohio Field now looked like an uncomfortable, ill-fitted offspring of the famous Yale Bowl. It was a radical transformation of what had once been a pastoral setting; the little High Street football field wore the changes like a hobo who had been given a new suit.

That the Buckeyes lost this final game of the season seems almost inconsequential now. Harley played hurt and didn't play well; afterward, he broke down sobbing on the field and had to be helped to the locker room in what may have been a sign of the mental problems that would eventually institutionalize him. Demand for tickets had already caused school officials to discuss plans for a new stadium and the turnout for this game probably sealed their decision. An estimated 20,000 filled the stands, dozens more were perched in trees surrounding Ohio Field, and St. John commented that he might have sold 55,000 to 60,000 tickets if he had the seats. The board of trustees met three days later and passed a resolution giving him the go-ahead to build a new stadium. The new place would often be referred to as the "house that Harley built," at least until many of those who saw him play had died.

His contemporaries knew what he had done, however. In 1928, John Heisman, a prominent former player and coach who died in time to get his name on what would become college football's most famous trophy, pegged Harley's legacy in a piece for King Features Syndicate: "It's not too much to say that if one player ever pulled a football aggregation on its feet and put his college into a place in the sun, that player was Chic Harley."

It's intriguing to think of how Harley's legacy might have played out if he had been able to live a normal life. He played only one year of pro football with the Decatur/Chicago Staleys, which might have become *his* Chicago Bears. He and brother Bill had an agreement that guaranteed them a percentage of ownership of the Staleys, but after Chic got injured and seemed headed toward a mental breakdown, owners George Halas and Dutch Sternaman changed the team's name to the Bears, contended that it was a different team from the old Staleys, and reneged on the agreement. Eventually, both the other NFL owners and the courts sided with Halas and Sternaman, although by that time, Chic had bigger problems. He was exhibiting erratic behavior, suffering crying jags, and at times acting nothing at all like the humble, quiet man his friends knew.

For a while, he was in and out of various mental hospitals. He was diagnosed with dementia praecox and was told that it would get progressively worse over time and that there was no cure. His family took care of him for years, but he finally entered the Veterans Administration hospital in Danville, Illinois, in 1938, and except for an occasional trip outside the grounds to stay with his family, he lived there the rest of his life.

He wasn't initially forgotten, though. Insulin shock treatments in the 1940s improved his condition substantially, and in 1948 he returned to Columbus for the Ohio State–Michigan game in what turned out to be an amazing homecoming. An estimated crowd of 75,000—at the time, Columbus was a city of 375,000—cheered him as he rode in the back seat of an open convertible down High Street in a ticker-tape parade in his honor, which consisted of twenty-one floats and the OSU marching band. When the parade reached the Statehouse, the governor and mayor of Columbus were there to greet him, and he spent the next two days at the Deshler-Wallick Hotel receiving visits from former teammates and old friends.

He returned to Ohio State again in 1953 to be honored for his 1951 selection into the College Football Hall of Fame's first class, but by then, his fame was already fading. In a 1950 Associated Press poll designed to choose college football's all-star team for the first half of the twentieth century, Jim Thorpe was the top vote getter, followed by Red Grange and Bronko Nagurski. Only 2 of 391 sportswriters voted for Harley.

Still, if Harley had died in the 1940s or early 1950s, Ohio Stadium likely would have been named for him. The idea was bandied about in various Ohio newspapers for years; it never happened though because it was an accepted practice not to affix the names of living persons to public buildings out of fear the person might commit an embarrassing act later. There didn't seem to be much urgency to honor Harley again anyway. His friends and former teammates remembered what he had done for the Ohio State football program and many of them revered him. To those who had seen him play, there was no chance of him being forgotten. That he would always be credited for his accomplishments seemed like a certainty.

Unfortunately, Harley outlived many of his contemporaries, and when they died, so did their memories. By the time he died in 1974 at the age of seventy-eight, there was no talk about naming the stadium for anyone, and if there had been, the first name that probably would have come to mind was Woody Hayes.

But why didn't university administrators who should have known better do more to keep Harley's memory alive? Maybe because they were slightly embarrassed by his lifetime of mental illness and knew the dirty little secret about Harley's syphilis problems, which the Danville records would later prove wasn't true.

And even if there was no conscious effort to let Harley's memory fade, it gradually happened anyway. By the 1990s, Chic Harley was a name and not much more than that. His name didn't come up when it was first announced that the school would retire numbers of some of its star players and post them inside Ohio Stadium; the school planned to honor its Heisman Trophy winners first and might—*might*—consider others later. One of his numbers was finally retired in 2004, although even after recognition was slow in coming. A relief statue of Harley kicking the ball on the façade of the old University theater was still there in 2011, partially obscured by the sign for the submarine sandwich shop that now occupies the building; one of his former teammates, Leo Yassenoff, built the movie house across from the site of old Ohio Field in the late 1940s. The day I visited there, the statue was kicking a submarine sandwich. No one in the vicinity could identify the player as Harley.

But to those who saw Harley play, the memory never died. Famous humorist James Thurber attended both Columbus East High and Ohio State at the same time as Harley, and wrote about him for years afterward. His description of Harley's running style was so good that a Columbus newspaper columnist even plagiarized it later.

"If you never saw him run with a football, we can't describe it to you," Thurber wrote. "It wasn't like [Jim] Thorpe or [Red] Grange or [Tom] Harmon or anybody else. It was a kind of a cross between music and cannon fire, and it brought your heart up under your ears."

It also brought a football program from next to nowhere to a place among the football elite.

# 6

# The Shrine

Ohio Stadium is the best football facility in the United States of America, and that's not hyperbole.

In a nation that sometimes seems to love its football even more than God, country, and family, competition for that title is stiff. Every decade brings a bigger, prettier, and swankier football palace than the last one, and through it all, the venerable, concrete stadium that was born as a horseshoe is still the best of the best. Even millions of Shaq-sized high-def television monitors, dazzling luxury boxes, retractable roofs, cushioned seats, sushi-on-a-stick stands, children's petting zoos, and architectural brilliance can't change the fact.

There will always be at least one NFL owner eager to build a football stadium suitable for 60,000 Roman emperors. This egocentric tycoon thinks he can build the greatest stadium in the history of the world as long as he's willing to exceed the gross national product of Portugal in the construction of it. His goal, aside from the enrichment of his own ego, is to a) immerse his fans in the kind of Sybaritic luxury that would have embarrassed the bone-snapping, eye-gouging football gladiators who made the sport what it is, and b) get his investment back by charging the customers prices their grandparents once paid for a two-story house large enough to raise a growing family. But money can't demand reverence, and it's no guarantee of a stadium's character. Money can buy opulence. It can't buy history.

In 1995, I interviewed Mike Dolan, then superintendent of facilities for OSU athletics, for a column about Ohio Stadium. I never forgot the respectful way he spoke of it. His voice softened. His eyes twinkled. His words carried an unmistakable earnestness. It was almost as if he were speaking of a beloved grandfather.

Caring for the old horseshoe had been his most important responsibility for almost thirty years and he took it as seriously as if it were an aged relative or a disabled child. If he had been entrusted with the maintenance of Notre Dame Cathedral or Westminster Abbey, it couldn't have been any more important to him. He knew precisely what an awesome responsibility he had been given. Ohio Stadium was a landmark. It was a shrine. A temple. A football cathedral.

"This is the football facility for the state of Ohio," he said. "When people call it 'the 'Shoe,' to me that's disrespectful. I know it's not meant to be, but that's how I feel."

No blasphemy is intended by the nickname, of course. Many who routinely refer to this revered structure as the 'Shoe would doubtless thank Dolan for his sentiment, and they might even apologize for their insensitivity. They think of it as a close friend or a family member. To them, calling it the 'Shoe is no different than calling a good friend named William by the name of Billy. They mean no disrespect. It is a term of endearment.

Stadiums and ballparks have always been more than just places to watch games. They're places we once tagged along with Grandma, Grandpa, Mom, or Dad, where we enjoyed the best of times with the best of friends and where we met our future husbands or wives. There's a good chance a stadium marks a spot where we've laughed as hard as we've ever laughed, experienced exhilarating joy and intense fear, and maybe even cried. It can be a storehouse of memories and, yes, in rare cases such as this, a house of worship. Even some newspaper columnists who know and understand the sanctity of this particular building have probably gotten careless at times and referred to the sacred spot, just a fly pattern east of the Olentangy River, as the 'Shoe. Here's hoping that at least one of us doesn't burn in hell for it.

Dolan's feelings run deeper because he knows Ohio Stadium better than any of us; before he retired, he had an intimate daily relationship with it. His office was located at the north end of the old stadium near the rotunda. He lived with the ghosts, not only of the players and coaches who competed there, but of the millions of fans who have worshiped football within the confines of this shrine since it opened in 1922. If the dearly departed leave traces of their own energy behind for ghost-hunters, then the "house that Harley built" surely holds enough to power the campus for several years.

"This place means a lot to me," Dolan said. "You might think this sounds weird, but you almost become part of it."

Actually, it doesn't. A lot of fans have similar feelings for athletic facilities that don't have nearly this much magnetism. If a minor league baseball park can become the object of deep affection, if a high school football stadium can be seen as the most important building in town, it doesn't seem at all strange that this massive concrete edifice, a wonder of the sports world at the time it was built, could affect this kind of emotion from a man who cared for it like a doting parent.

Many people have a lot invested in the old horseshoe, starting with Thomas French, who envisioned it when Ohio State football was still in its infancy, and continuing through former OSU athletic director Andy Geiger, who undertook the expensive and somewhat risky move of expanding and modernizing it in 1999.

The story of how it came to be sounds like the work of a hack novelist. Chic Harley and his teammates created the need for a bigger stadium with their success in 1916, and for the first time, others began to see some of the potential that French did. After an explosion of interest in the team in the fall, the school's board of trustees met in February 1917 and "looked with favor" on building a 40,000-seat, bowl-shaped stadium. They even went so far as to mark the woods just to the west of Ohio Field, today a densely built area of labs and chemistry buildings, as the site. But when school president William Oxley Thompson realized that the stadium would be ten feet taller than the new library and cover ten times the area, he had second thoughts. It would be nice to give Thompson credit for showing more perspective than many of those who followed him. My guess is that more than anything, he understood the value of good and bad PR. One good season wouldn't be enough to quell the public outcry of having football lord over academics. But two or three? Thompson was a savvy guy.

After the Buckeyes went undefeated again in 1917 and drew overflow crowds, French had sensed an opportunity and asked colleague Howard Dwight Smith to draw up plans for a horseshoe-shaped stadium in 1918. And after the 1919 Illinois game drew an overflow crowd of 17,000 and then athletic director Lynn St. John said he could have sold 55,000 or 60,000 if he had had the seats to sell, it seemed that just about everybody, including the campus academics, wanted a bigger stadium. At that point, French asked Smith to get out those old plans and create a design for a 50,000-seat, horseshoe-shaped facility—probably 10,000 to 20,000 more seats than most thought were needed—that could also accommodate a 220-yard running track. St. John at first told him to increase the capacity to 60,000—the young assistant director must have had gonads the size of grapefruits—and finally asked him to build it as large as possible within the framework of the plans, which was finally determined to be 63,000 permanent seats.

From where we're sitting today, this seems like a stroke of genius. Viewed from a seat at a breakfast table in 1920, it was sheer lunacy. The University of Wisconsin had erected Camp Randall Stadium in 1917 with an initial capacity of 10,000. Michigan was planning to expand the seating capacity of Ferry Field from 21,000 to 42,000, which it did in 1921. By comparison, Ohio State was a football baby. To have a stadium with 63,000 seats? In the 1910 census, the entire city of Columbus had 181,511 residents—and baseball, not football, was the city's most popular sport. Try securing a loan on that business model today.

St. John and French knew the critics would try to derail this crazy idea before it made its way to the finance stage, so they hatched an ingenious plan: they just wouldn't tell anybody how big the new stadium was going to be until they were ready to raise the money for it. It would keep critics guessing and stop them from building momentum against the project. It was difficult to make a good case against a bad idea if they didn't know what it was. When the breadth of the project was finally announced by Simon Lazarus, owner of the local Lazarus department store, which grew into the Federated department store chain we now know as Macy's, the critics' voices were barely heard in accompanying din.

The public was asked to donate $1 million for the construction of the new Ohio Stadium that would seat 63,000; a comparison with the infamous Colosseum in Rome, which seated a measly 45,000, was offered as evidence that they weren't just building a stadium, but a landmark. The huge fund-raising campaign began with a parade of more than 3,000 Ohio State students dressed in athletic garb down High Street to the Statehouse, presumably to deliver the subliminal message that the physical fitness of all the school's students would be improved by the building of a gargantuan new football stadium. The parade drew an estimated 100,000 spectators. On another day, OSU infantry and artillery regiments marched downtown—can a horseshoe-shaped stadium make an entire nation safe?—and on yet another day, campus fraternities and sororities and independent campus organizations held a parade of fifty-one floats, all of which promoted the stadium campaign. Each day brought music, stunts, and short pep talks at noon and 5 p.m. on the west side of Statehouse and stories in the local newspapers. A large electronic horseshoe outside the Deshler Hotel showed how much money had been raised, and billboards on both the Statehouse lawn and other conspicuous spots around town begged for donations for the stadium. The campaign reached its goal of $1 million just over three months after it started.

It seems almost like a waste of space to say that this couldn't happen today, but this was a different public. It didn't know the taxman as well as we do. It didn't know how it felt to have a rich sports entrepreneur ask the public for a new facility when the old one still hadn't reached adulthood, all because the old one didn't have enough luxury boxes to sustain the latest spike in athletes' salaries. That public believed that a massive stadium could put Columbus, Ohio, on the world map, which would be a source of tremendous pride for both the city and the state. And besides, the football team was winning.

Yet the most vocal critics of the era weren't exactly dumb: it would be years before that many seats were needed on a regular basis. Temporary seats were erected at the south end for the "dedication game" against Michigan on October 21, 1922, and an estimated 72,500 fans attended that day, but the first game against Ohio Wesleyan on October 7 drew only 25,000 spectators. From 1922 to 1934, average attendance was mostly in the 25,000–40,000 range, so Dr. Thomas Corwin Mendenhall, an original member of the school's 1871 faculty and one of the university trustees, wasn't far wrong when he insisted that the new stadium not exceed 35,000 seats. But then again, ol' Dr. Stick-in-the-Mud wasn't all right either; he insisted that the stadium be made of brick because he doubted the reliability of concrete. He also said that it would "never" be filled at that size. It's too bad Doc Mendenhall can't see the place when it's jammed to capacity, now at more than 105,000. It would be interesting to see whether he was sickened or amazed by that development—and whether he would join some of his successors in trying to scalp his faculty-earned season tickets on eBay.

Regardless of whether it was ego or vision that prompted St. John to go for the largest stadium possible when it wasn't needed, it's the primary reason the old structure is still around today. Geiger is probably reason No. 2. By the 1990s, Ohio Stadium's capacity had been expanded to the low 90,000s by continually growing the temporary bleachers that became the South Stands and narrowing the width of the bleacher seats, never a popular move in an era of expanding butts. But even more seats were needed, and the concrete that Mendenhall was afraid wouldn't last had finally matured to the point where it needed work.

Expansion ideas proliferated over the years. Many involved putting another deck on top of C deck; that ignited discussions over whether the old structure would support it. Some even envisioned lowering the field, although because the site was near the Olentangy River it cast doubts about whether that was even possible. Getting beneath the water table and inadvertently turning the floor of Ohio Stadium into a lake might seem like a good idea to the school's rowing teams; unfortunately, rowing fans surely wouldn't fill the almost 100,000 seats that surrounded it. But Geiger came up with a plan in 1996 to reinforce the concrete—expand the stadium by approximately 10,000 seats by lowering the field fourteen feet (and surrounding it by a slurry wall that reaches from ground level to bedrock, almost fifty feet deep in places to keep it from flooding), adding nineteen more rows at the top of C deck, building a larger, permanent South Stands, and paying for it all by adding luxury boxes. This concept put to rest the demands for a new, larger stadium and preserved most of the old structure for future generations to enjoy.

Not everyone bought into this. First, Geiger's reputation as a buildaholic had been growing. He had already hatched plans to erect a new basketball arena and a baseball stadium, and removing the track from Ohio Stadium in this remodeling plan had him also envisioning construction of a new track and field/soccer facility. Some athletic department types were calling his vision "Andyland," which wasn't meant as a compliment. The idea of having luxury boxes in the "house that Harley built" also had some traditionalists wringing their hands over a money-making machine that had run amok.

Geiger was as unfazed by this as St. John had been eighty years before. He, too, had a vision, and he had no fear of spending the money that was required to sustain it.

"The goal of the project is not to put hospitality suites in," Geiger said at the time. "The goal of the project is to improve the stadium and enlarge the stadium and renovate it and preserve it. If we need to do hospitality suites as part of that, we're prepared to do so."

The original price of the renovation was set at $187 million and grew to $200 million by the time of the project's completion before the start of the 2001 season. John Peterkord, the architectural design chief for the Kansas City–based HNTB Corp. that did the work, called this "a very good bargain." Whether he would have felt that way about blowing his own money on such a project wasn't recorded, but he did have a point: a new 100,000-seat stadium might have cost $500 or $600 million, and it wouldn't have been Ohio Stadium. It would have been just another monument to the excesses of American football.

On the other hand, the first time I saw the place during construction in March 2000, I wasn't so sure there was going to be much of Ohio Stadium left. The bottom third of A deck had been gutted. The lush green field where Archie Griffin danced and Pete Johnson churned had been turned into a giant sinkhole. The locker rooms were gone and so was most of B deck. There were holes in C deck were people used to sit.

I closed my eyes and then opened them again. What was going on here? Had we lost the war?

As I stood there with an open mouth and aching stomach, I couldn't help but wonder if Geiger had lost his mind. It occurred to me that if some knucklehead had planted a stick of dynamite under a corner of A deck and blown out a chunk of concrete, he would have been charged with desecrating a shrine, and any jury in Ohio would have convicted him. Now men in bulldozers and cranes were doing the same thing, and everyone wanted to know why they couldn't do it a little quicker. There were games to be played in the fall. It sure would be nice if they could get some of those musty old walls out of the way so we could get things started.

My heart was pounding. There were beads of sweat on my brow. Then I saw Dolan and made an urgent plea for help.

"Isn't it exciting?" he said.

I studied Dolan's face for additional signs of lunacy. Poor guy. He had always been one of the university's most valuable employees, and now he was losing his mind.

"It's wonderful," Dolan said. "We're saving the stadium."

Saving the stadium? I looked around again. I looked back at Dolan. No one loved Ohio Stadium the way he did.

"Remember how they redid the concrete back in the '70s?" he said. "It was about ready to have it done again. It costs millions to have that done, and there have been discussions about whether it's worth it. . . . This is great. You get tired of seeing buildings get torn down all the time."

I took another look into the bowl, where the field used to be. If Eddie George had tried to run in there, he'd have probably been killed by a dump truck.

"I'll tell you," Dolan said, "it's been heaven for me to see this happening. I'm almost at the end of my time, and it's nice to know that we'll be leaving it in a little better shape than it was when we got it."

After a few more minutes with Dolan, I was breathing easier, although the view was still alarming. There were beams of concrete that had attached themselves to the outer walls of the stadium like the legs of a giant spider, beams that would create a new outer wall of the stadium and support those extra rows of seats on top of C deck. Since 1922, the old horseshoe had looked exactly the same. When Paul Brown was refused entrance as a new coach in 1941 because an usher didn't recognize him, it looked the same. When God threw a thick blanket of snow over it in 1950, it looked the same. Now, it didn't look the same.

"Once the walls are done, I don't think you'll feel that way," Dolan said. "The problem is right now everything is pretty raw. The outer wall will have all the arches. They will line up with the originals. If we lose our arches, we blew it. If we didn't live up to the original design of Howard Dwight Smith, I would have been upset. If I didn't feel good about this, I would have quit. I have deep, emotional feelings for this building."

The last thing I saw when I looked at Dolan were dollar signs. I knew he wasn't into luxury boxes, fund-raising, and million-dollar contracts; he was a bricks-and-mortar, grass-and-dirt kind of a guy.

Before he took the job at Ohio State, he was grounds superintendent for Crosley Field, the former home of the Cincinnati Reds, following in the footsteps of his maternal grandfather, Matty Schwab, and a great-grandfather of the same name. He had taken care of Ohio Stadium for the last thirty-two years and treated it as if he owned it. This was a man who lost a dear friend when Crosley Field met the bulldozer, and he desperately didn't want to lose another one.

"I'll say it, I cried," he said, of the old ballpark's demise. "That was sad. But this is the reverse of that. This is exciting. I can't wait to get to work every day. We're saving a monument."

Twenty-two years later, it's clear Dolan was right. The place looks a little different, but it's still the same football cathedral that it was in 1922, just a little bigger and a little less of a horseshoe, and as hard as it is to believe, it is a little more intimidating for opposing teams.

It hurts to think that the track where Jesse Owens ran, the field where Red Grange played his final college game, and the locker room Woody Hayes ruled have been remodeled out of existence, but anyone who enters it knows that the ghosts are still there, haunting in all their glory.

This is the place for football, all right. And if Geiger's vision was correct, it will be for the next fifty to seventy-five years.

# 7

# The Graveyard

One day during the John Cooper era, I noticed that a paragraph in my column about Ohio State's reputation as the graveyard of coaches was mysteriously missing the name of one of the victims.

At first, I thought it had been one of those accidental deletes. Maybe a hyperactive copyeditor had decided to bring order to my chaos by putting the names in alphabetical order or by listing them chronologically by birth-dates and had somehow overlooked Carroll Widdoes's name while retyping. Still, it couldn't hurt to check.

When I called the office and was told that the managing editor had deleted the name on purpose, a pent-up profanity may have escaped my lips.

"He said Widdoes didn't belong on the list," a copyeditor explained. "He said that he 'retired.'"

I was aghast. I wondered if this were simple ignorance or if the editor had purposely engaged in a little revisionist history.

"*Retired?*" I repeated. "He switched jobs with Paul Bixler and eventually became the head coach at Ohio University. He coached there for a long time after he left Ohio State."

Widdoes actually was the head coach at the Mid-American Conference school for nine years, from 1949 to 1957, so he didn't exactly turn into a Walmart greeter in his "retirement." Contrary to the editor's curious position—and he was a guy who didn't like to see anything negative about his beloved Buckeyes reach print—Widdoes wasn't looking for something to do in the evenings when his wife was playing bingo. No one "retired" to become the head coach of a major college football program.

In at least one sense, the editor had it right: Widdoes didn't get planted in the graveyard the way so many other OSU coaches had—he put himself there. After serving as the head coach for two years when Paul Brown left to serve during World War II, he owned an impressive 16-2 record when he voluntarily traded positions with Bixler, his offensive coordinator. Plenty of reasons are cited for this: that he was more of a family guy than a head coach, that he didn't relish the limelight, that he was deeply religious and thus had different priorities, and so on. But it seems clear the pressure of the job had more to do with his stepping aside than anything else. Brown once described him as "a very sensitive man," and the world knows how difficult the Ohio State job would be for any coach who isn't impervious to criticism. If that weren't the primary reason Widdoes decided to give up the job, how else to explain his nine-year stint as head coach at OU? It's doubtful his religion revealed that Athens, Ohio, is closer to heaven than Columbus. As beautiful as it is down there—I'm an OU grad and I love the place—in some of its un-pious ways, it may actually be closer to hell.

Whatever the reason for his switch/retirement/move, Widdoes is one of the guys who helped give Ohio State its well-deserved reputation as a coaching graveyard. It earned that stigma because it had seven different head coaches from 1928 to 1950, when Woody Hayes got there and finally gave the program some stability. And even that happened only after he was almost fired himself.

Some of the coaches were pretty good, which come to think of it really has nothing to do with anything. There was just no tolerance for losing, and we're not talking about losing seasons but losing *games*, particularly against Michigan. There were only two losing seasons during that twenty-four-year period, one of them during World War II when most of the players were off doing something a tad more important. Yet Ohio State coaches came and went like hotel guests, and a few of them, including Widdoes, fled from the job like terrified jackrabbits. The fanaticism for the program had a lot to do with it. The job was magnetic, prestigious, immensely attractive, and downright scary.

"Some men wrestle alligators for a living," *Look* magazine wrote, around the time Hayes was hired. "Others umpire baseball games. Still others munch on razor blades and wash them down with fire. And there are those, the supreme daredevils, who coach football at Ohio State."

John (Jack) Wilce is never included with the graveyard crowd because the Hall of Fame coach kept his job for sixteen years. But in his own way, he was the first Ohio State coach to be entombed there. Wilce helped shepherd the program into the Western Conference as a green twenty-five-year-old in 1913, brought Chic Harley to campus, and had a fine .688 winning percentage. But alas, he was the first coach to discover that OSU fans can turn on you in one afternoon—or less—and he coached his last few years under heavy fire from his detractors.

Wilce was considered a coaching genius when he won three league titles in his first eight seasons at OSU with a team that was considered undersized by Western Conference standards. He recognized that his players didn't have the size and strength of those they would have to compete against, so he became a proponent of the "open game" and embraced the then radical concept of the forward pass. Then, after a second-place finish in 1921, he experienced a run of four second-division finishes, and only a few years removed from "genius," the fans decided that the game had passed him by. After all that success, it only took two mediocre seasons for many to call for his head.

Wilce always insisted he would leave under his own terms and wouldn't be shoved out the door, and true to his word, he successfully orchestrated his departure. He announced his retirement from coaching in June 1928, saying that in order to concentrate on his medical practice, he would step down *after* the season. Even though his team put together a 5-2-1 campaign that included a 6–6 tie with Princeton and a 19–7 win over Michigan, many fans couldn't wait to get rid of him. He had earned his medical degree in 1919 so it wasn't as if he needed to coach football to make ends meet (he completed cardiology training at the University of Edinburgh in the 1930s and served as the director of student health services at OSU from 1934 to 1958). But the criticisms about his coaching clearly bothered him.

In a 1952 article in the *Columbus Citizen*, writer Chester Smith retold an old Wilce story that had circulated the city for years.

"When the doctor finally resigned, he was quoted as saying that if he ever coached again, it would only be on the team at the Ohio Penitentiary," Smith wrote, "because that was the one place that the alumni never wanted to go back."

Compared to some of those who followed him, Wilce was treated royally. Sam Willaman, an early football star at Ohio State, followed Wilce and lasted but five seasons. Willaman's downfall showed how quickly a football hero can lose his halo.

After he graduated from Ohio State in 1913, Willaman experienced stunning success as head coach at Cleveland East Tech High School while also playing pro football on Sundays with the Akron/Cleveland Indians and later the Canton Bulldogs, where he was a teammate of Jim Thorpe.

Willaman left to become Iowa State's head coach, and after four years there, he returned to Columbus to join Wilce's staff in 1926, presumably as Wilce's successor if and when he finally stepped down. Then when it finally happened, Notre Dame's Knute Rockne expressed interest in the job, and Ohio State negotiated with him while Willaman was left to squirm. Rockne seems to have been merely using OSU's interest as leverage to get a better deal at Notre Dame, however, and when Rockne decided to stay in South Bend, Willaman was hired.

If Rockne had taken the Ohio State job, maybe he would have had runaway success there. He had an 86-12-5 record during twelve years in South Bend, although he would coach there only two more years before being killed in a plane crash. But if Rockne had followed up Notre Dame's 5-4 season in 1928 with a few more of those at OSU, he might have joined the parade to the unemployment line. Rockne's previous record at Notre Dame notwithstanding, without those last two unbeaten seasons with the Irish—9-0 in 1929 and 10-0 in 1930—a couple of good but not great seasons might have gotten him a quick hook in Columbus that would have cost him his legacy. If that had happened, most fans today would probably guess that Sam Willaman was a journeyman golfer or an Indy-car driver, and Rockne might have been just another body in the potter's field of college coaches.

But Willaman did get the job, and in 1929, many people were happy about it. There were two reasons: he was a hero and he wasn't Wilce. His first team had an end named Wes Fesler who was destined to eventually have his own plot in the school's coaching graveyard, a guy who had been named first team All-American as a sophomore and would achieve the same honor the next two years. The Buckeyes won the first three games, including a 7–0 win over Michigan, then went 1-3-1 in the last five games.

Year Two wasn't bad—the Buckeyes posted a 5-2-1 record—but the seeds of discontent had been sown; it included a 13–0 loss to Michigan and a fourth-place finish in the Big Ten. The following year (1931), they were 6-3 and beat Michigan, but finished fourth again. You can probably see where this is going. In 1932, they were 4-1-3, but the loss was to Michigan. Conference finish: fourth. Average home attendance was dropping, from 37,867 in 1930 to 32,671 in 1931 to 22,743 in 1932, in a stadium that seated 65,000. The Great Depression didn't help, although it's likely some of the folks standing in long Columbus bread lines passed the time discussing how that dope Willaman should never have been given the job. Why in the hell hadn't the school hired Rockne?

The 1933 season was pretty good—the team went 7-1—but again the loss was to Michigan. The heat was turned up all the way now, and not just from the fans. The city's business titans, the people the school turned to when it needed money, had had enough of Willaman (no Big Ten championships, too many losses to Michigan, not Rockne) and applied so much pressure that Willaman resigned before he was tarred and feathered and escorted to the Ohio border. School officials wouldn't put so much stock in the OSU pedigree next time.

The big wigs wanted a coach who had won on a national stage and got what they wanted: forty-six-year-old Texas Christian coach Francis Schmidt, whose teams had won two Southwest Conference titles in his five seasons there. While Schmidt is such an intriguing character that he has his own chapter in this book, suffice it to say that the incredible highs of his initial four seasons weren't enough to save him when *he* started losing to Michigan.

That was well in the future though. After Willaman's team had lost to the Wolverines three of his last four seasons, Schmidt came in with a startling revelation: "They put their pants on one leg at a time, the same as we do," all the info that was apparently needed to beat Michigan four games in a row. Whether the Wolverines figured out a new way to put on their pants isn't known, but when Michigan then beat OSU three years in a row, Schmidt was history. His first six teams had two Big Ten titles and finished second three of the other four times.

Had World War II not intervened, OSU's coaching graveyard might have closed the gate, locked it, and thrown away the key. Schmidt's successor,

Massillon High School's Paul Brown, might have stayed at Ohio State into the '70s, beating Michigan, winning championships, and making everyone deliriously happy.

Brown, also the subject of his own chapter in this book, won a national championship in 1942 before his players began to drift away to war in 1943. At the end of that trying year, he accepted a commission at the Great Lakes Naval Training Center in Chicago.

That's when the traffic into Ohio State's coaching graveyard started backing up. Widdoes had been with Brown since his Massillon days and Brown chose him as his temporary successor. His only experience as a head coach had been at the junior high school level, but hey, there was a war going on, and if Brown said he could do it, the Ohio State Athletic Board wasn't about to disagree with him. Brown had compiled a 51-1-1 record in six years at Massillon and had won a national championship in his second year at OSU, so his word was gospel.

But after two seasons, Widdoes "retired" and Bixler immediately found himself living in a pressure chamber he hadn't anticipated. Bixler had been an assistant football coach and head basketball coach at Canton McKinley High School while Brown was at Massillon. He was a smart guy who was known for his comprehensive scouting reports and had never been a head football coach, much less at a major college where the alums expected perfect seasons.

With many players returning from the war, expectations were high, so a 13–13 tie with Missouri in the season opener wasn't the best way to start, particularly after the Tigers had lost 42–0 to Texas the week before. The Buckeyes posted an impressive 21–0 win over Southern California in the Los Angeles Memorial Coliseum the next week, but lost to Wisconsin 20–7 in Madison the following week. Impressions were already being set in stone: Bixler wasn't Paul Brown, not by a long shot. He wasn't even Carroll Widdoes.

After a tie with Purdue, OSU won three games in a row, but a loss at Illinois, followed by a 58–6 drubbing by Michigan created an uneasy situation. The fans were unhappy, but even they weren't prepared for what happened next: Bixler resigned as the Buckeyes' head coach on February 5, 1947, in order to accept the head coaching job at Colgate.

Colgate? That's what *everybody* thought. But it only seemed like a ridiculous move to those who had never held the OSU position; Bixler cited the "pressure of the Ohio State job" as his reason for moving.

Viewed from the safety of the twenty-first century, it's easy to see the central figure in this whole graveyard-of-the-coaches business: Paul Brown. For various reasons, Brown's expected return to Ohio State after the war didn't happen, which contributed to the head coaching job's constant turnover. OSU athletic director Lynn St. John had promised Brown his old job back, but when Brown was ready to take it in 1945, Widdoes was coming off an unbeaten season. St. John told him he would stand by his vow although it would be a "sticky" situation given Widdoes's success—not what Brown wanted to hear.

Brown later admitted that he wanted to be wanted and hadn't gotten that impression from St. John. So when *Chicago Tribune* sports editor Arch Ward offered him a chance to coach the Cleveland pro team in the new All-American Conference, a position that came with 5 percent ownership of the team and complete control over personnel matters, Brown took it. By the time Widdoes and Bixler switched jobs, Brown was considered a traitor by some for not only leaving Ohio State for the pros, but also for signing some of his former OSU players when they returned from the war.

When Bixler left, there was a campaign to bring Brown back, but the athletic department wasn't part of it. It took only nine days for St. John and incoming athletic director Dick Larkins (he would take over in five months) to hire former OSU teammate Wes Fesler, who had been head coach at Pittsburgh for only one year. Despite the 3-6-1 record Fesler's Panthers had in 1946, Ohio State gave him a five-year contract. He lasted four.

Before he even started, he lost a couple of his best players to professional football. He ran a single wing formation he had learned in a year as an assistant coach at Princeton, one that made extensive use of flankers and started from an unbalanced line, and it took his new players a while to adjust to it. His team won the opener against Missouri, then lost two, tied one, and lost two more. One of the losses was to his old Pitt team—it was the only game the Panthers won that season. There was a win against Northwestern and then two more losses, the last was a 21–0 defeat to Michigan. The

Buckeyes' 2-6-1 season included a last-place finish (1-4-1) in the Big Ten, the only one in school history.

The 1948 season was better—the Buckeyes had a 6-3 record—and they went 7-1-2 and won a Big Ten co-championship in 1949, although one of the tie games was with Michigan.

A 17–14 win over California in the Rose Bowl temporarily pacified the fans, if not Fesler; the day after the win, he told the *Columbus Citizen*'s Lew Byrer that he "is unhappy about the abuse his family has had to take in his experience as Ohio State coach."

Byrer wrote that Fesler "doesn't think that it is all worth it, even in the moments following a Rose Bowl victory" and that "you can expect his resignation at most any time."

Fesler stayed for another year, but he still wasn't happy, and after he lost the Snow Bowl game to Michigan in 1950, the fans weren't happy with him. Fesler resigned fourteen days later saying the pressure of the job was affecting both his health and his family.

Just forty-seven days later, he was named head coach at Minnesota. Or as an old editor might say, he retired.

# 8

# The Wizard

O n a mule-gray December day, the two-and-a-half-story painted white brick house at 120 E. Fifteenth Avenue looked tired and outdated. The century-old duplex, one long pass from the Ohio State University campus, offered no hint that anything of substance has ever happened there, no sign that it had once housed a human hurricane.

The house features two wide porches on the first and second floors, supported by pillars of brick, but it still seems puny compared to the impressive buildings on both sides of it, the Kappa Delta sorority house on the left and the Alpha Phi fraternity house to the right. The most important part—the attic—is the last thing you notice when you view it from the street.

The attic served as Francis Schmidt's home office. If ghosts are merely energy left behind by the dearly departed as some suggest, then this one-room loft must surely lead the Midwest in hauntings. It was in this room that the frenetic Ohio State football coach diagrammed dozens, hundreds, or maybe even thousands of plays—because that's what Schmidt did, in the car, in restaurants, and in his head, while he was strolling around campus, standing on street corners, and crossing the Columbus streets. It explains why Schmidt was an offensive wizard . . . and also why he was a little mad.

The little office is intriguing because of the stories his players have told about it through the decades, of how they would pass the house at midnight or even later, see the light on and know that Schmidt was in there with his mind whirring and his colored pencils scrawling, diagramming more plays. Sometimes he would ask his players to come to his office and study plays for three hours at a sitting. Sometimes he would see them down there on the street passing by, throw open the windows, and yell an invitation that often included an expletive. Almost all of his sentences did.

All of which explains why his football players probably passed his house less and less the longer he was at Ohio State. Most of them liked Schmidt, much the way we like our crazy uncles. But does anyone really want to listen to a football genius/lunatic explain the intricacies of a triple-lateral pass play after having been out on the town with a girlfriend, or maybe even had a few beers with teammates?

"The light was always on in his room; I don't know if he ever slept," former player Nick Wasylik said in 1985. "It seemed like he lived, dreamed, and ate football. He had colored pencils—reds, greens, blues—and he chewed them right down to the stubs when he designed his plays."

Make no mistake about it though. Schmidt was a football genius. From that little room on E. Fifteenth Avenue, the hawk-nosed OSU coach, whom *Columbus Dispatch* sportswriter Tom Reed perfectly described in a 2009 story as "Foghorn Leghorn in a three-piece suit and bow tie," unleashed a tsunami of plays that is the basis of much what is used in football today. In the 2006 Fiesta Bowl, Boise State used three trick plays—the hook and lateral, Statue of Liberty, and wide receiver pass—to stun Oklahoma in one of the most memorable games in college football history. Schmidt ran all three plays at Ohio State during the 1930s.

If Schmidt isn't the most interesting character in the program's history, he is a close second; there are almost as many tales told about him as there are about Woody Hayes. The most familiar one has him taking his Cadillac in for an oil change, and after he explained his request to the attendant, he immediately began—what else?—drawing up a new play. The attendant raised the car on the lift, and while he was down there draining the oil, Schmidt finished his scribbling, opened the car door, stepped out, and dropped five feet to the floor. He was so absorbed in his offensive doodling that he had forgotten where he was.

Players tell of seeing him on campus walking through flower beds and on at least one occasion into the side of a building while he was looking at plays. They talk about how at practice he would have diagrams of plays sticking out of his pockets, under his belt, and in his shirt, anywhere he could stick them. They talk about how no one other than him and the quarterback had a playbook that included the entire play. An end would get his part of the play, a tackle would get his part, a halfback would get his part, etc.; even assistant coaches were only given these curious play sheets, showing only the parts of the plays for the position they were coaching. Schmidt's many plays, which have been estimated at 300 to 400 with the number always growing, were his most valuable possession. He wasn't about to take a chance that someone might steal them. This was top secret stuff.

In an era when football was mostly a run and punt game, Schmidt was well ahead of his time, even if some of the absurdity that accompanied his genius probably kept him from being as successful as he should have been. He coached so much offense that his team had time for little else—no time for annoying things such as conditioning, drills, defense, and so forth. His lack of interest in the game's other aspects, minor as they must have seemed to him, ultimately cost him his job.

Brett Perkins, who wrote the 2009 Schmidt biography *Frantic Francis: How One Coach's Madness Changed Football,* believed that Schmidt suffered from hypomania. The condition is usually associated with bipolar disorder, a mental illness marked by swings between heavy depression and overblown, energetic happiness. That second part, the high, is the hypomania, and some people experience only that part of the illness. According to the American Psychiatric Association's definition, hypomanic behavior includes pressurized speech (rapid speech), inflated self-esteem or grandiosity, decreased need for sleep, and a flight of ideas. Schmidt exhibited all of those traits.

Today, he is remembered by Ohio State fans mostly for starting the tradition of giving out little gold pants pendants to Buckeye players after they had beaten Michigan; this was an extension of the statement he made about the Wolverines when he was hired, that "they put their pants on one leg at a time, just like we do." It's a cute tradition, but it doesn't do justice to the Schmidt legacy. It does explain the mission he accepted when he was hired, however. After five decent seasons, Sam Willaman was out as OSU coach, despite a 7-1 record and a second-place Big Ten finish in 1933. The problem was the loss to Michigan was his second in a row and third in four years, and school administrators and fans considered this unacceptable.

Schmidt wasn't athletic director Lynn St. John's first choice for the job; he first tried to lure two Big Ten head coaches to OSU without success.

After Clark Shaughnessy, in his first year at Chicago, and Purdue's Noble Kizer both rejected his offers and fans at both schools spewed anger at St. John for his breach of conference etiquette, he decided to look to other areas of the country.

Schmidt had no connection to Ohio State or the Big Ten, so it surprised nearly everyone when his name came up in the discussion. Although he had turned the Southwest Conference upside down with his ostentatious offensive displays at Arkansas and Texas Christian, most Ohioans had probably never even heard of him. But St. John had once served on a basketball rules committee with him (Schmidt was also a successful basketball coach) and knew what a dynamo he was, so he thought it might be worth digging a little deeper. The research turned up a couple of concerns: Schmidt's blue language and his sometimes overzealous recruiting. While at TCU, Schmidt frequently refereed high school football games and spent some of his time on the field attempting to convince the players to play football for him with the Horned Frogs. But both traits were byproducts of his high-energy approach, which St. John liked; one of his biggest criticisms of Willaman had been his laid-back style. Attendance at OSU games had also been on the decline during the Depression, so Schmidt's reputation as the national leader of what was called the "open game" style of football was a plus; the OSU athletic director sensed that his wide open offense would put fannies in the seats. Ohio State fans knew little about him, but St. John figured that once the fast-talking, charismatic Schmidt got to Columbus and had a chance to charm the local reporters, enthusiasm for the southerner would pick up.

It did, too. The athletic board had already recommended he be hired when St. John invited Schmidt to Columbus for a final job interview/news conference. After dinner at the Deshler-Wallick Hotel, the six-foot-two, slump-shouldered TCU coach was ushered into a meeting room that held several local newspapermen, faculty members, coaches, and influential alumni. He was given a seat in front of them and asked an assortment of questions, and his folksy manner and distinctive drawl instantly drew listeners in. They probably had never met a man who seemed to exude energy, yet sometimes started sentences with curious phrases such as "Lookee, here . . ." *Dispatch* columnist Ed Penisten wrote that "his reactions were quick" and that he "talks rapidly and to the point." He called his responses "refreshing." Schmidt was funny, charming, and surprisingly informal, and at one point he dropped to his knees, scattered a handful of coins on the carpet and began to show his interviewers various formations and plays. The longer he was down there the more people joined him, and after an hour of his constant shuffling of coins, nearly everyone in the room was convinced that the curious guy in the three-piece suit and bow tie was not only different but also smart.

"This guy is good," OSU assistant coach Ernie Godfrey said.

For a while, at least, there was no doubting it. Schmidt's Buckeyes fumbled eleven times in his debut but still hammered Indiana 33–0 before 47,736 fans, the largest home crowd in three seasons. They finished 7-1 in his inaugural year and amassed a then-school-record 267 points, losing only to Illinois (14–13) and clobbering Michigan 34–0. They finished with a 7-1 mark again in 1935, but this time the loss was a crusher: They blew a 13–0 lead and lost to Notre Dame 18–13 in one of the classic games in college football history, the subject of a later chapter. He also beat Drake 85–7 that year, which helped earn him the nickname "Close the Gates of Mercy" Schmidt; his Buckeyes had beaten Western Reserve, the school where Willaman had landed in a backroom deal with St. John, in a 76–0 rout the year before. While at Tulsa, Schmidt's teams won games by the unheard-of scores of 152–0, 151–0, and 121–0. He didn't have much sympathy for the opposition.

The big scores his teams rolled up during his career were primarily because of the offense, which was especially difficult for under-manned teams to stop.

"I would say that Schmidt was the guy who gave birth to the multiple offense," said Wasylik, who later was a coach himself.

In 1933, major college teams averaged 12 points and ran about 75 percent of their plays between the tackles. Most teams played not to lose, making good punters even more valuable than good passers. In this setting, Schmidt's 1932 TCU team led the nation with a 25.7 point average.

"Francis Schmidt forgot more football than 75 percent of most coaches know," former OSU fullback Jim McDonald said in 1985. "They talk about the shovel pass today, but we did it fifty years ago. Inside end coming around, shovel to him, pass to somebody else and three laterals off it.

The blocking back would go out, fake a block, and they'd pitch to him, and he'd pitch back to the fullback, and the fullback would pitch back to the tailback. We scored two touchdowns in Ann Arbor off that play."

Success against Michigan made Schmidt popular in the early going. Schmidt's teams beat the Wolverines four consecutive years and shut them out each time. And like Woody Hayes, Schmidt thought Michigan had spies watching his practice sessions.

"We'd have a walk-through practice at Michigan Stadium on Friday," end Esco Sarkkinen said. "But you didn't go out there with your jersey number. You'd exchange it with someone else. You'd wear someone else's jersey just in case someone was watching practice. And not only that, we'd put extra people in our formations. Say we were in punt formation or a single wing or double wing, we always had twelve or thirteen people. Two of them didn't mean anything . . ."

Whether that's brilliance or paranoia is open to debate, but it's hard to believe that scouting plays at one of Schmidt's practice session could do much good. He devised so many plays that the quarterbacks had a hard time remembering them all, and in those days it was against the rules to call plays from the sidelines. While Schmidt gave them that wide array of plays to run, the quarterbacks were the ones charged with calling them.

Tippy Dye was one of those quarterbacks and a Schmidt favorite, but he acknowledged years later that there was just no easy way to keep track of all that offense.

"We had certain plays for certain teams, and I'd write them down and put them in my helmet," he said. "During a timeout I'd take them out and check the plays that were supposedly the best for that particular game, and that would make it a little easier for me. We had certain plays that were good against anybody. Maybe we had fifteen or twenty others for a particular team, and we'd put them each on a 3-by-5 card and put them in our helmet."

This, of course, led to another oft-repeated story.

"I got hit once—against Michigan, I think," Dye said, "and my helmet came off and all those cards spilled out on the field."

Even Schmidt sometimes seemed confused by the details of them all. During one practice session, guards Gust Zarnas and Inwood Smith, both destined for All-American status, pulled out and ran into each other in practice. They immediately starting arguing over who had run the play the way it was supposed to be run. Schmidt intervened and called for the manager to bring over the play charts. "I've got it!" he said, throwing the charts on the ground. "You're both wrong."

Life around him could be maddeningly entertaining. His caustic wit left his former players with stories and expressions they would repeat for years. "If brains were shit, you wouldn't even stink," he often said. And then there was a time when a bird overhead relieved himself on one of his players. "It's a damn good thing cows can't fly," he said.

Dr. Jimmy Hull, former OSU basketball all-American who used to serve as master of ceremonies at many Columbus sports affairs, enjoyed relaying stories told to him about Schmidt by halfback Dick Heekin.

"Dick told me that Schmidt was really comical during practice and the entire team would try its best not to laugh too much when he said something—besides his profanity—that was really a groaner.

"Dick recalls one day when Fred Crow, the great end from Pomeroy, missed a pass that Schmidt thought he should have caught. Schmidt reared back, belly out, and roared, 'Crow, you know you couldn't even make the all-bird team.' Heekin also remembers that Schmidt delighted in a snorting jibe to Dr. [Walter] Duffee during any emergency medical crisis [involving] one of his players. On any such occasion, Schmidt would yell, 'Get a doctor, Duffee!'"

Duffee told countless Schmidt stories over the years, and recalled that the only thing remarkable about the coach's historic comment that the Michigan players "put the pants on one leg at a time, just like we do" is that it included no profanity. In a speech at a November 1952 Pants Club meeting that was recorded for posterity, Duffee explained just what he meant.

"I think we have to admit frankly that Francis did use profanity and he used it in almost every conceivable manner," he said. "He used it to give added emphasis. He used it to clarify meaning. He used it to express hatred. He used it as sarcasm. He used it as a term of love and affection. He used it sometimes where it served no purpose whatsoever.

"For example, he said to Gus Zarnas at practice one evening, 'Well, Gus, you missed your man.' And Gus said, 'No, Coach, I got him all right.'

Schmidt said, 'You didn't; you never even goddamned touched him.' Didn't belong there. Didn't add anything. He just put it in there."

Duffee was clearly more amused by this than anything. He said Schmidt never used profanity in front a lady, which if you think about it, is kind of amazing.

"There were two terms that he used always to denote one of the opposition," Duffee continued. "Seldom did he use those terms in association with any of his own players. An opponent was always either a big sonofabitch or a dumb bastard. The only time that he used one of those terms with one of his own men was when he used it as a term of affection."

Attaching the prefix "old" in front of his players' names was another one of Schmidt's habits.

"They were all Old This-or-That," Duffee said. "Old Sark and Old Stan and Old Frank and Old Gus and so on, always Old So-and-So. He never carried a whistle. He always whistled through his teeth to command the attention of the squad. He whistled through his teeth, the team would get around him and he'd say, 'Now, hey, lookie.' Two favorite words, 'hey' and 'lookie.' 'Now, lookie, this is the way we're going to do it. The ball will come back to Old Stan and Old Stan will turn and fake a handoff to Old Frank coming around, and about that time that big sonofabitch comes roaring in here.' And then Francis would chuckle and say 'He thinks he's going to *stop* the play . . .'"

Schmidt's sideline antics were just as colorful. He often called officials "horses asses" and would storm up and down the sidelines shaking his fists at them or holding his nose. On at least one occasion, he was so upset that he grabbed a game program out of a nearby hand, tore out the center spread where the officials' names were printed, and acted as if he were using it as toilet paper.

More than one player recalled standing near Schmidt on the sidelines during games when he would get a phone call from Godfrey with an observation in the press box.

"Goddammit, Ernie, tell me something I don't know," Schmidt would bark, tossing the phone to the ground.

All of this madness gradually began to take its toll on his teams. After those two 7-1 seasons, the Buckeyes went 5-3 in '36, 6-2 in '37, and 4-3-

1 in '38, and lost to Michigan (18–0) for the first time that year. While his teams were exciting, they seemed to lose the big games, often because of fumbles or interceptions, and sometimes because the players weren't in the best of shape. Schmidt's response, naturally, was to draw up more plays, and his playbook reputedly swelled to more than 500.

One of his problems was that he didn't delegate responsibility well; the assistant coaches often stood around and listened to him while he explained plays and had his players run them during practice. His practices sessions often looked like team meetings, with everybody standing in one group, watching and listening.

"Once in a while a lineman wasn't using a proper block or something, and Ernie [Godfrey] would pull him out to teach him," quarterback Jack Graf said. "And he would yell, 'Goddammit, Ernie, put him back in there, and let him learn some football.'"

For that reason, his teams were usually weak on fundamentals, and against a difficult schedule, that would sometimes cost his Buckeyes the game. He also wasn't good at monitoring his players' studies. He didn't want to be bothered. As some of his key players became ineligible and OSU lost games, criticism began to grow.

After a 6–3 loss to Northwestern in 1940, the players got into the act, telling reporters that they had been unable to hold up in the second half due to poor conditioning. Two days later, captain Jim Langhurst called an emergency players-only meeting, and the players vented their frustrations for over an hour. Their lack of stamina was only one of their complaints; they wanted more scrimmaging and block-and-tackle drills and said that the loss to the Wildcats was the result of "too much offensive training and not enough contact and defensive work."

The players' complaints baffled and hurt Schmidt, but what ultimately cost him was losing to Michigan, just as it had Sam Willaman. After beating the Wolverines four years in a row, his teams lost three straight. The 40–0 loss in 1940 was a killer.

"Where we'd get beat once in a while, he didn't have control of the players," Graf said. "The time Michigan beat us 40–0 . . . he didn't have control of the players. They didn't play with a lot of enthusiasm. In fact, we were in there about half hour before game time and [quarterback] Don

Scott wasn't in there and Schmidt said, 'Where's Don?' We all knew he was out selling his tickets. That was disturbing to the whole squad. But [Schmidt] didn't control the attitude of the team very well."

The loss to Michigan left the Buckeyes at 4-4. The high-powered attack that had once been so baffling to the opposition had scored but 99 points in eight games. The school's board of athletic control decided that "a cooling off period" was needed before it decided whether to bring him back for another season, and when the situation dragged on until the middle of December, Schmidt finally recognized the dire nature of his situation and submitted his resignation. It was an ignominious end to what had been an exciting era of OSU football.

Schmidt's life story didn't have a happy ending, either. He applied for head coaching openings at Dartmouth, Marquette, Colorado, Oklahoma, and Baylor and didn't get the jobs. There was talk of the Detroit Lions hiring him and nothing came of it. He finally got the job at Idaho—not exactly a hot bed of college football—at a little over half of his Ohio State salary, and he helped raise a terrible program to respectability. But after his coaching two seasons there, the program was suspended because of World War II. With no football team to coach, he was finally told that his contract wasn't being renewed on February 26, 1944, and his health began to deteriorate shortly after that. He lost weight, lost his strength, and entered a hospital in Spokane, Washington, in September. He died on September 18, 1944, at the age of fifty-eight.

If he had known the storm of offense that he had wrought, he probably would have been much happier at the end. Sid Gillman, one of his former Ohio State players who became one of his assistants, went on to a brilliant coaching career both in college and in the NFL, mostly based on Schmidt's offense. Al Davis was one of Gillman's assistants during his early years with the San Diego Chargers, and he was blown away by Gillman's offensive knowledge. Davis became the head coach of the Oakland Raiders in 1963, and three years later, he hired a young assistant named Bill Walsh, who took what Davis had learned from Gillman and Gillman had learned from Schmidt and expanded upon it further. Walsh's coaching descendents include Mike Shanahan, Mike Holmgren, Sam Wyche, Tony Dungy, Andy Reid . . . well, you get the idea.

"A lot of the plays they're using in the pros right now, we used back then," Graf told me back in 2003.

When you look at the Schmidt coaching tree, it almost goes without saying, doesn't it?

"Francis Schmidt is the greatest coach who ever lived," Gillman told the *San Diego Union* in 1965. "He was years ahead of his time."

And crazy?

Well, yeah. That too.

# 9

# The Greatest Game Ever

The 1935 Ohio State–Notre Dame game was voted the college football's game of the century in 1950 and the greatest game ever in 1969 by two panels of experts. It all seems a little odd now, not so much because it wasn't the greatest—hey, for all we know these guys might really be "experts"—but because it was so long ago and the college football landscape has changed so radically. Today, we see so many games decided on the last play, so many games in which the numbers on the scoreboard flicker like the numbers on a gas pump, that our capacity for shock and awe isn't what it used to be. Sometimes we yawn even at the spectacular.

The game of college football's first century was, uh, 18–13? If you're one of those folks who spends the day invisibly tethered to a Playstation 3 or an XBox 360, a replay of that famous game would probably leave you impatiently drumming your fingers. Notre Dame scored with thirty-two seconds left to finish a second-half comeback after being down 13–0? What's the big deal? It actually *was* a big deal at the time, but this is one of those cases where you almost had to be there to get it. To appreciate why that game was still spoken of with reverence, joy, or anger more than a half-century later, it's important to understand how different things were in those distant days. It's important to have some feel for the history.

Grantland Rice, arguably history's most famous sports journalist, wrote in his autobiography that the 1935 game was the greatest college football game he ever witnessed. Red Barber, a soon-to-be-famous young broadcaster who called the game for Cincinnati radio station WLW and the Mutual network, agreed. When Allison Danzig retired after five decades of work for the *New York Times*, he was presented with a bronze replica of the front page of the *Times* sports section from November 3, 1935, which led with his account of the Ohio State–Notre Dame game.

Many of the accounts of the game from some of the nation's most famous sportswriters leave little doubt that this was a game for the ages, and in the days before television, this was about all the fan had to go on. Even when a game drew a huge crowd as this one did, relatively few people got to see it. A week after this game was over and it was judged a classic, some people got to see highlights of it in newsreels that were shown during intermissions in selected movie theaters, but that was it.

Then there was the residue from it, residue that was still around decades later. Mike Layden, a Notre Dame player that day and brother to then Notre Dame coach Elmer Layden (one of the school's famed Four Horsemen whom Rice christened with his famous lead), eventually became a Big Ten football official and monitored games for twenty-eight years, and every time the public-address announcer uttered Layden's name over the speaker system at Ohio Stadium, the crowd booed.

While playing football at Kent State, future Ohio State assistant and Notre Dame head coach Lou Holtz was coached by Trevor Rees, one of the starters Ohio State coach Frances Schmidt pulled out of the '35 Notre Dame game in the fourth quarter. Holtz tried to talk to him about it, and Rees got mad—"Coach Rees never got mad," Holtz explained later—and started muttering "something about the first-teamers being taken out."

And then there's the curious tale of Fred Crow Jr., an Ohio State player who blocked a PAT kick with his left arm in that game; he was so excited about and looked forward to an OSU–Notre Dame rematch in Ohio Stadium in 1995 that he put special instructions in his last will and testament:

> In the event I should die prior to the playing of the OSU–Notre Dame football game in 1995, I direct my executor to have the funeral director remove my left arm from my body and have it cremated. The ashes of this left arm shall be retained by my said executor until the date of the playing of the game.
>
> George Strode, of *The Columbus Dispatch*, if he is able, or some other prominent person, is to receive said ashes and to distribute them near the goal posts at the southwest corner of the playing field.

Drastic measures weren't necessary—Crow made it to the '95 game and died five weeks later—but the fact that he even considered them says something about the importance of the '35 game to the participants, coach, and fans. Whatever this was, it wasn't just another exciting game. Years later, that much was still clear.

There are many reasons for its status, starting with the fact that the two famous football powers had never met on the field before this. Again, that's probably difficult for today's younger fans to fathom; the two schools met in the Fiesta Bowl in 2005 and had a home-and-home series in the 1990s. And besides, the old, dominant Notre Dame program of Knute Rockne, Elmer Layden, and Ara Parseghian isn't quite the same as the Kansas State–looking program that has been shepherded in recent years by Bob Davies, Tyrone Willingham, Charlie Weis, and Brian Kelly, a nice way of saying that, to younger fans who have never seen it, the once-proud Irish juggernaut of yesteryear doesn't even exist. To the kids of today, OSU's losses in '35 and again at South Bend in '36 (a 7–2 loss that wasn't judged a classic) probably seem about as interesting as a lecture on Calvin Coolidge.

Nevertheless, anyone who takes the time to examine all of the different aspects of the '35 game is bound to come away impressed, even though parts of the legend may not even be true.

For starters, Gene Schoor wrote in *100 Years of Notre Dame Football* in 1987 that when the Irish players took the train from South Bend to Columbus on a Halloween Thursday night, they were greeted by thousands of hostile fans shouting, "Catholics, go home!" Another account said that thousands of fans showed up at the stadium when the Ramblers, as the Irish were then known, went through a light walk-through, and fullback Steve Miller recalled later that "these people were wild and never stopped yelling at us." And still another reported that 15,000 hecklers showed up when Notre Dame arrived at the train station. But the *Ohio State Journal*, Columbus' morning newspaper at the time, described the "thousands" as "five or six downtown fans too eager to wait." And years later, surviving Notre Dame players didn't remember 15,000 hecklers, or even five.

What they remembered was being put up in St. Charles Seminary on the city's east side—St. Charles Preparatory School today—and not seeing much of anybody until they got to the stadium. Their stay there sounded much like Woody Hayes's holing up the Buckeyes in the monastery while his team was in California for the Rose Bowl. There were no distractions, no temptations, and certainly no hecklers. Bor-ing.

"Is sequestered the right word?" Mike Layden asked in 1985. "We were like Carmelites. We couldn't see or hear or talk or anything. That was the point of it. They didn't want us to have any contact with anybody. They didn't want us to be in the downtown hotels, around the crowds."

Religion did provide an intriguing undercurrent to the game, however. Supposedly, after the Irish and the Buckeyes played again in South Bend in 1936, OSU president George Rightmire said he was troubled by the religious overtones that divided his faculty. It was one of the reasons the schools didn't play again until 1995.

Hayes was another reason for that almost-sixty-year gap. Notre Dame athletic director Moose Krause finally got OSU athletic director Ed Weaver to agree to a game in Ohio Stadium on September 17, 1977, only to have Woody cancel it, which forced the Irish to fill the date with a rare no-return road game at Mississippi. The notion that there were mysterious reasons behind the two schools' failure to meet again only added to the mystique.

So here is the setup: In 1935 Ohio State was 4-0 and had just beaten Drake 85–7 with Francis Schmidt's wide-open offense trying all kinds of crazy stunts. The team had a pair of All-Americans in center Gomer Jones and end Merle Wendt. The Buckeyes were favored to win their first mythical national championship. Notre Dame was also 4-0, was coming off an impressive win over a powerful Pittsburgh team, hadn't allowed more than seven points, and had an All-American in end Wayne Millner. The city's hotels were full, the streets were crowded with fans the night before the game, and tickets priced at $3.30 were scalped anywhere from $20 to $50, figures unheard of during the days of the Depression. At today's prices, that $50 ticket would be close to $800. Attendance was 81,018, the most since 90,437 supposedly packed Ohio Stadium for the 1926 Michigan game, which a former OSU ticket director once told me probably didn't happen. (An earlier ticket director had told him that the crowd in '26 was just a guesstimate, that thousands had gotten in free, and they had no way of knowing how many fans were actually in the stadium that day.) Some

23,000 ticket requests and the accompanying checks for the Notre Dame game were returned by the OSU ticket office, and athletic director Lynn St. John said he could have sold more than 200,000. The last time St. John had said something like that, the figure was 60,000 and he championed building a 60,000-seat palace that became Ohio Stadium. Maybe it's a good thing that money was tight during the Depression.

Many of the nation's top sportswriters and broadcasters attended. In his account in the *Dayton Daily News*, Si Burick reported that there were 175 writers in the press box. They included Rice, Danzig, Paul Gallico, Damon Runyon, Wilfrid Smith, and Francis Wallace, along with an expanded troupe of Ohio and Indiana writers. In addition to Barber, Ted Husing was there for CBS and Bill Slater for NBC, although later thoughts that an Iowa sportscaster (who would one day become president of the United States) might have also been there proved to be wrong—Ronald Reagan broadcast an Iowa-Indiana game that day.

Less than three minutes into the contest, Mike Layden dropped back to pass and fired a bullet deep into OSU territory. Ohio State defender Frank Antenucci intercepted and started up field before pitching to teammate Arthur "Frank" Boucher. Boucher zipped the remaining 65 yards to complete a 76-yard touchdown play. Dick Beltz hit the point-after-touchdown kick to make it 7–0. It's a name we will encounter again.

Early in the second quarter, Stan Pincura intercepted another Irish pass to start an OSU drive near midfield. "Jumping" Joe Williams finally scored on a 3-yard run, and although the extra-point kick was missed, the Buckeyes had a 13–0 lead. Through it all, the Irish had been unable to get closer than the OSU 29-yard line against the Buckeyes' defense, so the lead looked relatively secure at halftime.

But this is where the story starts to get interesting. Coach Elmer Layden figured it was time to do something to wake up his team, so he started the second unit at the start of the second half. It didn't pay dividends immediately—neither team scored in the third quarter—but when he reinserted the starters at the start of the fourth quarter, many of them were supposedly fighting mad.

Schmidt, meanwhile, went the opposite way. Sensing certain victory, he pulled out most of his starters at the beginning of the fourth quarter. He thought the fresh legs would help preserve the lead, but the Irish immediately began to take command. This was a huge screw-up on Schmidt's part for one reason: Under the rules of the day, once a player was removed from the game, he couldn't return until the following quarter. In other words, the Buckeyes starters were out, momentum was shifting, and there was nothing Schmidt could do to change it. Today, a mistake like that would probably get a coach fired. Television color commentators would make it sound like the biggest mistake since Burnside threw wave-after-wave of Union soldiers against an impregnable Lee position at Fredericksburg. But alas, there was no TV and there were no post-game press conferences then, and Schmidt's poor strategy became almost a footnote in the day-after-the-game accounts. Even though Notre Dame scored two touchdowns, the second with less than two minutes to play, the Irish missed both PAT kicks and the Buckeyes still led 13–12 and were in position to win.

Two missed PAT kicks? Another clue that this was truly a different era. If Notre Dame had simply made the second one, the game probably wouldn't be counted among the greatest in history.

"There was a minute and a half left when I scored our second touchdown," Mike Layden recalled later. "In today's scheme of things, if we had made the extra point it probably would have ended the game in a tie. Instead, we were still a point behind."

Notre Dame tried an onside kick and the Buckeyes recovered, seemingly sealing the Ramblers' fate. But on Ohio State's first play, Andy Pilney hit backup halfback Dick Beltz from behind, and he fumbled the ball near the sidelines. It went out of bounds, but under the rules of the day, the last player who touched was awarded possession, and that was Notre Dame's Henry Pojman. The Irish suddenly had it on the Buckeyes' 49-yard line and had a chance to win the game. On the first play, Pilney ran for a 30-yard gain, but he tore the cartilage in his left knee and, ironically, never played football again. Bill Shakespeare replaced him and threw a pass on the first play that went right to Beltz, giving him a chance to redeem himself for that lost fumble. He dropped it.

On the next play, at the open end of Ohio Stadium, Fred Carideo took a direct snap from center out of the old Knute Rockne box formation on the Ohio State 19-yard line and pitched back to Shakespeare five yards behind the line. Shakespeare ran left and passed to one Notre Dame end, crisscrossing with the other in the south end zone as a stretcher bearing Pilney, the fallen Irish star, passed in the background. Millner appeared to be well-covered by Pincura, but the OSU safety jumped early and the ball went over his outstretched hands and into Millner's, who grabbed the ball on his fingertips just as Beltz grabbed at his knees. Touchdown. With only thirty-two seconds remaining, Notre Dame had an improbable 18–13 victory.

But even the final score came with a unique story, one that would find its own place in Notre Dame football lore. Coaches seldom called the plays in those days; only a quarterback could speak on his first play in as a sub, and once a player came out he couldn't return for the rest of the quarter. Notre Dame coach Elmer Layden sent in the winning play with fifth-string quarterback Jim McKenna, who wasn't even supposed to be on the trip.

There are varying accounts of how McKenna got there. One had McKenna sneaking aboard the team train to Columbus and his teammates helping to hide him in a berth. Schoor wrote that McKenna borrowed enough money from friends to board the fan special that arrived on the Ohio Stadium railroad siding just two hours before the game; he had no ticket nor the funds to buy one from scalpers, but happened to be standing outside when a student manager walked by carrying equipment. The story is that by falling in beside him and grabbing some of the gear the manager was hefting, McKenna managed to get past guards to the locker room where Coach Layden told him that as long as he was there he might as well suit up and watch the game from the bench. No matter. He was there, and because of the game's restrictive substitution rules, Layden already had used his other four quarterbacks. He saw McKenna sitting there, without shoulder pads on, but what the heck, an emergency is an emergency.

"I was sitting on the bench at that time," fullback Miller said. "By then, they were sending in just about anybody who could go in and call another play."

So it was the guy who should have been back in South Bend listening to the game on the radio who carried in the winning play with Notre Dame at the OSU 19-yard line with forty seconds left.

But that part of the story would only help build the game's legend later; all that was obvious in the immediate aftermath was that in an era when the passing game was about as sophisticated as the horse and buggy, and comebacks of this type were rare, Notre Dame had stormed back with three touchdowns in the fourth quarter to upset Ohio State.

"One of the greatest last ditch rallies in football history toppled the dreaded Scarlet Scourge of Ohio State from its lofty pinnacle today as 81,000 dumbfounded spectators saw Notre Dame score three touchdowns in less than fifteen minutes to gain an almost miraculous 18–13 victory in the jammed Buckeye Stadium," Danzig wrote in the *New York Times*.

"Before this throng, alternately cheering the resistless attack of Notre Dame or praying that time would halt the play while Ohio State still held the advantage, was unfolded a gridiron drama which defies description," Wilfrid Smith wrote in the *Chicago Tribune*.

Henry McLemore, writing for the United Press wire service, called it "the most glorious and heart-stopping rally in the history of football."

In reporters' eyes—and that's the only eyes most fans across the nation had—the game was as good as it gets.

Coach Layden recalled later that Schmidt "raced across the field and shook my hand as if he had won rather than lost. I was rather numb from those last two minutes, but I will never forget his graciousness."

Reporters didn't go to the locker room after the game in those days, although Schmidt was also gracious in defeat in his brief post-game statement that passed for all the quotes that would be heard from him: "It was a great game. Notre Dame made a wonderful finish." In private it was apparently another story. Floyd Stahl was Schmidt's backfield coach at the time, and he later recalled that Schmidt was devastated by his own coaching blunder.

"Francis had forgotten that once you got your top defensive men out you couldn't get them back in during the same quarter," Stahl said. "So we were going in the fourth quarter with a couple substitutes lacking in speed and a sophomore in one of his first games. Smitty felt he was completely responsible. I've never seen a man so disconsolate. And the players, I don't believe I've ever seen a team so low as our team after that defeat."

Crow remembered Schmidt "tearing up" the locker room, and Gust Zarnas recalled that "he took it very bad. So did we."

So did everybody. Backup quarterback Wasylik said that "the tears were hard to hold back, especially in the locker room." The crowd was stunned.

A half-hour later, half the fans still hadn't left the stadium. When a reporter asked Babette Sirak, a fan who had attended over sixty years of games in the old horseshoe, for her lifetime of football memories in the 1990s, she immediately recalled that loss to Notre Dame in 1935.

"Mom and all the children were crying," she said. "I turned and saw Dad and his brother, Si, crying in the back row. We'd never seen our fathers cry. . . . Nobody moved for the longest time.

"In the 16th century, England lost Calais. 'When I die,' Queen Mary said, 'Calais will be imprinted on my heart.' When the old stadium gets changed, that will be the game embedded on its heart."

Beltz was the most stunned of all. He sat alone in the stands for a half hour after the game, bearing all of the weight of the dramatic loss. His wife, Ruth Beltz, later told *Columbus Dispatch* columnist Dick Fenlon about how inconsolable he was afterward, and how even his own friends didn't help much.

"One of my high-school classmates and her boyfriend were at the game and we went to her sister's house afterward before going to dinner," Ruth said. "She opened the door and saw Dick standing there and said, 'You're the one who lost the game!'"

Beltz heard those words, over and over, for years. It was so bad that when the late Paul Hornung wrote a book about Ohio State football after his retirement as *Columbus Dispatch* sports editor, he deliberately left Beltz's name out, hoping to spare him the embarrassment. What he didn't know was that Beltz had long since exorcised those demons himself. Beltz became a high school football coach and spent most of his life relaying his experiences and perspective to the kids who played for him. His advice to players who were blamed for an on-the-field failure, kids who might be tempted to carry their sports tragedies around with them the way he did, must have been invaluable.

"Be unhappy that you didn't win," he said in a 1984 interview. "But remember that this is only four or five seconds in a lifetime. Don't let it bother you. Know what the value of it is and don't let it ruin your life."

Beltz died in 2002 at the age of ninety. But his story reminds us that there are sometimes less obvious reasons why a game of the century might be just that.

"We've never gone back to any of the places Dick coached," Ruth Beltz said, "that somebody hasn't come up to me and said, 'You know, if it hadn't been for your husband, I wouldn't be what I am today.'"

Notre Dame fans tore down the goal posts in the south end zone and marched pieces of it downtown to the lobby of the Deshler-Wallick hotel, where they partied long into the night. The Notre Dame players may have celebrated a bit too hard themselves; the following week they came out flat and were upset by Northwestern.

Around town, there were fans on both sides who got a little carried away, as evidenced by the following accounts in the *Dispatch* police blotter the next day:

John Willis, age 27, was treated in White Cross Hospital for a fractured nose which he received while yelling for Ohio State at Gay and High Streets.

Tome Rieneye, Cleveland, was attended for a fractured nose in the same hospital. He let out a cheer for Notre Dame in the Neil House (hotel).

Richard Cullen, Wilmette, Ill., engaged in an argument with C. V. Marshall, Bluefield, W.Va., in the Deshler as to the outcome of the game, and the latter struck Cullen on the nose, fracturing it.

Those noses would be healed long before the broken hearts of Ohio State fans. A story was long told about how a visitor to Columbus was dining in a downtown hotel years later. He heard an angry voice say "That damn Shakespeare!" and wondered how in the world the Bard of Avon could be held in such low esteem in Ohio's state capital.

# 10
# The Greatest Coach Ever?

The one hundredth anniversary of Paul Brown's birth seemed like a good time to play "what if?" in my newspaper column. It made for a fascinating game, mostly because Brown might have drastically altered the course of Ohio State football history if he had decided to return to his old position in Columbus following World War II.

Brown once called the Ohio State coaching position "the only job I ever wanted," and he made it clear in his autobiography that he probably would have stayed at Ohio State for a long time if World War II hadn't intervened. He had been hired at OSU in 1941 at age thirty-two after creating a powerhouse high school program at Massillon, where he had once starred as quarterback. Shortly after Francis Schmidt resigned, fans launched a statewide movement to hire the young high school coach for the job. They sent hundreds of telegrams and letters to the school president and the governor on his behalf. The state's high school coaches threatened to send their top stars out of state if he wasn't hired.

Brown's eventual hiring was as popular as any in school history, and Brown himself couldn't have been happier about it. This is what the Norwalk, Ohio, native had always wanted to do.

"My first two years as head coach at Ohio State were the happiest, most exciting and rewarding period of my life," he wrote, "better in some respects than the great years in Cleveland because coaching the Buckeyes had been my ultimate dream."

The third year (1943) wasn't so good, in part because the school had aligned with the army's ROTC program during the war, and its rules wouldn't permit students to play football once they turned eighteen. Michigan,

Purdue, Northwestern, and others that associated with the navy's V-12 program were allowed older players and they could accept transfers. The uneven playing field didn't sit well with Brown, and he bristled as his Baby Bucks got beaten up and went 3-6.

The young coach enlisted and left Ohio State for a post at the Great Lakes Naval Training Center after the season, intending to return after the war. Ohio State athletic director Lynn St. John assured him that the job would be his again when he came back. But circumstances changed. The rules were altered to allow older ROTC students to play, and Brown's successor, Carroll Widdoes—a man he had hired as an assistant—coached Brown's players to an unbeaten season in 1944. It's not easy to replace a man after an unbeaten season and Brown knew it.

"I began to wonder about my position at Ohio State because I knew it would be unfair to remove someone whose team had just finished a perfect season who seemed capable of producing future great seasons," Brown wrote. "I called Mr. St. John seeking assurance.

"'You're welcome to return,' he told me. 'But you must know it may be a bit sticky after Wid's unbeaten season and his fine coaching job. Still, we made an agreement and we'll live by it.' I needed more than that. I needed to be pampered a bit and told that I truly would be welcomed."

The sales job came from another direction. *Chicago Tribune* sports editor Arch Ward wanted him to become coach of the Cleveland franchise in the new All-America Football Conference he had started and the team's new owner, Cleveland cab-company owner Mickey McBride, offered him a five-year deal with a $25,000 salary, plus 5 percent ownership in the team. So Brown, who had been hired by Ohio State in 1941 for $6,500, about $1,500 more than his salary at Massillon, was now the highest paid football coach in the country and was off to the team that would be named after him following a local name-the-team contest.

But what if the war hadn't come along, or if the military draft had stopped at age thirty-four instead of thirty-five? Brown was thirty-five when he went into the service in 1944. If there had been no war, or if he hadn't enlisted and had stayed at Ohio State, he might have had a long career there; he was sixty-five in 1974. If he had stayed, Paul Brown Stadium might be in Columbus, not Cincinnati. The Bengals he brought into the

NFL in 1968 might never have existed, and the Browns might not have succeeded without him, or moved from the AAFC to the NFL in 1950.

The effect this would have had on Ohio State football history is just as fascinating. If Brown had coached at Ohio State until 1974, Woody Hayes couldn't have. And with no job to lure him, what if the successful young coach at Miami University had become coach at Michigan, the way Bo Schembechler later did?

We might never have known that unspeakable school "Up North," as Woody Hayes called Michigan, and instead found ourselves smirking over that contemptible school "Down South." The war between Woody vs. Bo might have become one between P. B. and Woody, and the term "Michigan Man" might have taken on a whole new meaning. Woody might have ended up pushing his car across the line to Michigan so he didn't have to buy gas in a despicable place like Ohio. A whole generation of Wolverine fans might be wearing Woody-style, black Michigan baseball caps punctuated with a block "M."

It's hard to believe that one man's career path could make so much difference only until we realize just who this one man was. Brown was a brilliant football coach and innovator. Any discussion of the greatest football coaches in history has to include him, and there is no reason to believe that he wouldn't have had the Ohio State job for as long as he wanted it, and might have won even more games and championships than Hayes did.

Brown's attention to detail is legendary. Fritz Heisler, who played for him at Massillon before joining his staffs at both Ohio State and Cleveland, called him "a perfectionist in every detail" and said "he reminds me of a surgeon; he's impersonal [and] analytical always and icy cold in doing his job." For that reason, *Los Angeles Times* columnist Jim Murray once wrote that he was "a man of glacial contempt" and that "he treated his players like he bought them at auction," which contains a strong element of truth. But in some ways, it was also part of the psychology he used to get the most out of his teams.

He didn't swear and he seldom raised his voice. There was no reason for it. He had a stare that would have scared an axe-murderer. His former Browns players say that when he was watching game films with them and noted a bad mistake, he would sometimes quietly say, "If you can't do it, we'll get someone who can." And he meant it. Finding players who could do it never seemed to be a problem for him, either, because he had an eye for talent as good as any in the sport's history.

His football innovations—the face mask, the messenger guard, the draw play, film study, intelligence tests, and year-round assistants, just to name some of the more prominent ones—would have been enough to get him into the football hall of fame at every level, even if he hadn't had the on-the-field success that he did.

But he did win. In nine years at Massillon High School, his teams went 80-8-2, including 58-1-1 from 1935 to 1940, and won six state titles. When he arrived, the program was in debt and the football team was averaging less than 3,000 fans per home game. When he left for Ohio State in 1940, the Tigers were playing in a 22,000-seat stadium that was filled for every game. The increased revenues generated by the football program enabled the school to build a new swimming pool and observatory, and offer special classes in speech and drama.

He was only at Ohio State for three seasons, but he went 18-8-1 (the winning percentage spoiled by the Baby Bucks' 3-6 mark when the deck was stacked against him) and won one national championship. When he went to Cleveland after the war, his pro teams there went 158-48-8, won four straight titles in the AAFC, won three championships in the NFL ('50, '54, and '55), and played in the league title game for ten consecutive years.

Brown's complex offensive system was more wide open than anything previously seen in pro football. It relied on the forward passing and precision timing, and it took the pros some time to catch up. When his Browns moved to the NFL in 1950, the Philadelphia Eagles were three-point favorites in the league title game, and Cleveland won 35–10. The Eagles defense was unaccustomed to facing anything other than the T-formation running game favored by other NFL teams, and Browns quarterback Otto Graham threw touchdown passes to Dante Lavelli, Mac Speedie, and Dub Jones, and ran for another one.

"We just never played against a team that threw to a spot as well as Cleveland," Eagles defensive back Russ Craft said later. "It was like trying to cover three Don Hutsons. Impossible. Impossible."

Brown called the plays. Quarterbacks didn't like it—they were used to calling their own in those days—but Brown was so smart that it was hard to make a case against him. At one point he even tinkered with the idea of putting a radio transmitter in his quarterback's helmet, another idea that showed he was years ahead of his time.

Former Browns quarterback Frank Ryan once admitted that Brown would "call plays I never even thought about calling, and they always worked. I would come back to the bench and tell my teammates, 'Can you believe that call?' He was always one step ahead of the defense, always thinking ahead."

He started the Cincinnati Bengals in 1968 and coached the expansion team until 1975, so his record there (55-56-1) pales in comparison to the others, but it would be a mistake to think that it was because he had lost his touch. It was just the opposite, in fact. Eleven of the first twenty-five Super Bowls were won by his former players or assistant coaches—a list that includes Chuck Noll, Don Shula, and Bill Walsh.

Former Dallas Cowboys coach Tom Landry once said, "When you played against Paul Brown, it was like playing against par." For years, he was the coaching standard in the NFL.

Whether he or anyone else was the greatest coach ever is obviously open to debate, but there is no denying Brown was at least one of the greats or that he made a strong impression at Ohio State in his brief tenure there. Until Woody Hayes was firmly established in the mid-1950s, there were always cries to bring Brown back, and before Hayes was hired in 1951, a group of students went so far as to send Woody a telegram, urging him to remove himself from consideration. "This is no reflection on your character," the wire read. "We just hold fast to Paul Brown."

When Brown came to Columbus to talk to OSU officials about the job, 1,500 students and a four-piece drum corps showed up to welcome him. The job was never offered, however, and Brown said later that he never seriously considered taking it if it had been. He was established in Cleveland and had the control he needed to be successful. He had moved on.

Gene Fekete, fullback on Brown's Ohio State teams and later an assistant coach at OSU, always said that Brown could have been successful at anything; coaching was just what he did.

"Paul was so well organized in everything he did," Fekete said. "If you would have given him a job selling toothbrushes on the corner of High Street and Broad, he would have made a million dollars."

But what if he had just wanted to spend his life coaching football at Ohio State?

Many things would be different certainly, but it's doubtful the Buckeyes would have won fewer games or fewer national championships. They might have won even more.

# 11

# The Snowiest Game Ever

I t sometimes seems as if just about everyone over the age of seventy has a Snow Bowl story. Even some of those poor attention-starved souls who don't remember that this famous Ohio State–Michigan game was played in 1950, and not 1960 or 1970, can recall amazing things that happened to them that day, even if they weren't born yet.

False memory syndrome may be more common than we think; my unscientific analysis indicates that what we have here is an epidemic of lying. But hey, it's a famous game and it's only natural that people want to be part of it. The "official" count indicates that only 50,535 of the 82,700 people who had tickets to the game showed up, and even that is a lie. The weather was so cold and miserable that day that no ticket takers were stationed at the Ohio Stadium entrances, and anyone brave enough to be there, ticket or no ticket, was allowed in.

So maybe those million or so people who say they were at the game were really there, hiding in the restrooms or huddled under the stands on the concourse or even sitting out there in C deck, disguised as bumps in a snowdrift. Verifiable eyewitnesses claim that there might have been 40,000 in Ohio Stadium at the beginning of the game. They say that probably half of them left at halftime and the number kept dwindling as the snow got worse. Over the years, some people we can be sure were there—players, for example—have said probably no more than 5,000 diehards were still in the stadium at the end of the game. So if you find yourself standing next to a guy at the bar who's talking about how the Snow Bowl game was the coldest he's ever been, a guy who claims the tears froze onto his face after the clock expired on Ohio State's 9–3 loss, it's probably worth considering the odds. Look at him closely. He may be the guy who sold you that '69 Camaro that was supposed to be mechanically perfect, the one that drank oil the way a thirsty kid drinks iced tea on a hot summer day.

November 25, 1950, is one day that doesn't have to defer to the tall tales of wanna-be-there types or even the natural tendencies toward exaggeration of those who were. Conditions were probably as bad as they have ever been for a game of this magnitude, which is why many people including then Ohio State athletic director Richard Larkins and both head coaches, Ohio State's Wes Fesler and Michigan's Bennie Oosterbaan, thought the game should never have been played.

But let's backtrack. Two days before that fateful Saturday, the Midwest enjoyed a balmy Thanksgiving. Although the temperature dropped from the mid-40s to the teens on Friday, there was still only talk about the *possibility* of snow on Saturday, and nothing about how Ohio might soon resemble the white plains of Antarctica. The Michigan traveling party stayed in Toledo the night before the game to avoid the Columbus craziness, and the players walked around downtown Saturday morning while waiting to catch the train. The weather was fine. There was no snow.

It was already snowing in Columbus though, and Larkins had called Michigan athletic director Fritz Crisler to see if he wanted to postpone the game. He didn't . . . and wouldn't. The discussion would resume once the Michigan players arrived at the stadium, but Crisler wanted the game either played or canceled and insisted that it not be postponed. If the game were canceled, the Buckeyes would have won the Big Ten title without playing Michigan, which Crisler knew would be an unacceptable solution. OSU administrators would have taken a public relations beating and, as the *OSU Alumni Monthly* later wrote, "would have never lived this down." Former *Columbus Dispatch* sports editor Paul Hornung was there that day, and he wrote in 1986 that he overheard the discussion between the two athletic directors. He was standing against the east wall of Ohio Stadium, not far from the entrance to the OSU locker room.

"Bundled in a borrowed scarlet football parka, I listened to the entire discussion . . . as to whether the game should be played," Hornung wrote. "Crisler interjected a convincing argument, 'We're here and we're not coming back down here next week,' he said. 'Do you want to refund all that money?'"

Crisler had a point. Despite the deteriorating conditions, thousands of fans were already on their way to Columbus. Larkins repeatedly tried to call Big Ten commissioner Tug Wilson for advice without success, and the clock was against him.

While the teams huddled in their locker rooms, Fesler sent Phil Moseley, one of his team's senior managers, out to hear what Crisler and Larkins were saying on the field in the blizzard.

"They were nose to nose, and referees and officials were there," Moseley said. "The reporter from the *Dispatch* and I were leaning against the wall together, trying to stay inconspicuous if we could. Larkins was on the left and Crisler was to the right, and they were close.

"Crisler wouldn't play the game on Monday. That's what Larkins wanted to do. But [Crisler] wouldn't do it, and Larkins finally gave up, and frankly, even as a young kid, I was disgusted with him. I'm only 5 or 6 feet away from there and Paul Hornung and me, we'd look at each other and say, 'I can't believe they're doing this.'"

Moseley hustled back to the locker room, where Fesler and the players were waiting.

"[Fesler] said, 'Well?' And I said, 'We're . . . going . . . to . . . play . . . the . . . game.' And he said, '*Damn.*' And that was it. We were out on the field within a half-hour. You can't imagine worse conditions for a football game. It was just a tragedy."

At noon, groundskeeper Ralph Guarasci started the tedious process of trying to remove the $3,000 tarp that covered the field. It was such slow going that the P.A. announcer invited the fans to come down from the stands and help, and reports indicated that probably about a hundred did. The new volunteer army helped clear the field of snow and remove the tarp that was now mostly frozen to the field, a job that consumed two hours and twenty minutes. While they were working, Larkins finally gave the word.

"We play," he said.

Well, at least they tried to. The temperature had hit a low of 5 degrees Fahrenheit that morning but was up to 10 by the time the two teams prepared for a scheduled 2 p.m. kickoff that would now be 21 minutes late. Accounts of the maximum wind gusts vary from 28 to 40 mph. In blizzard conditions the visibility was poor either way; there would be more than 9 inches of snow on the ground by evening.

By the time the game started, a couple of chapters of the budding legend had already been written. In some places, that expensive tarp had to be cut up to remove it from the ice and in other places it still couldn't be lifted, and hence became part of the field. From a dry seat in a dry room in 2012, that seems like an untenable solution. Under all that snow, it probably didn't make much difference. The footing was horrible either way.

During the tarp removal, one of the Boy Scouts who had volunteered to help went missing and rumors flew that he had inadvertently been rolled up in the tarp or buried in the snow. The missing scout, later identified as Roy Case, had indeed fallen, but one of his coworkers had noticed and called to the others to stop; Case had managed to roll to the side and avoid a premature burial. Not everyone apparently saw his escape. There was a report in a Columbus newspaper the next day that workers had searched part of the tarp after the game for a Boy Scout thought to be missing. What makes that scary is that in these blizzard conditions with visibility next to nothing, it isn't too hard to imagine that a Boy Scout could be turned into a Swiss roll without anyone noticing.

The game finally kicked off with six-foot banks of snow behind each sideline, the result of all the shoveling. Some volunteers stayed on the sidelines for broom duty, to sweep the goal lines and yard markers as often as possible so the players would have some idea where they were on the field of play. It quickly became clear that running or passing on the icy field was next to impossible, and the game turned into a punting contest with both teams sometimes punting on first, second, or third down to avoid fumbling; the game's forty-five punts were a Big Ten record.

In a game that produced but three first downs—all by Ohio State—all of the scores were set up or accomplished by blocked punts. Early in the first quarter, OSU tackle Bob Momsen blocked a Chuck Ortmann punt and teammate Joe Campanella recovered on the Michigan 8-yard line. The Buckeyes went backward in three plays, one a 15-yard penalty when Vic Janowicz tried a pass into the end zone and it went out of bounds, and in the blinding snow and with the wind at his back, Janowicz lined up to try a 38-yard field goal. Janowicz won the Heisman Trophy that season, and many have written that the kick might have been the most impressive accomplishment of his season, if not his career.

"That was a pretty good kick," Janowicz recalled, years later.

It depends on who you ask, though.

"To this day, I do not think it was good," Michigan's Ortmann said in 1990. "I have nothing against Vic. But I was the one back there playing safety, with the best view. In those days, they didn't have an official standing under the goal post as they do now."

No matter. The officials at least thought they saw it go through, and less than five minutes into the game, conditions were already worsening. Some thought it might be the only score of the game.

It wasn't. Later in the quarter one of Ortmann's punts—he punted twenty-four times—rolled out of bounds at the OSU 4-yard line, and with the Buckeyes backed up, Janowicz was forced to punt from his own end zone. Michigan tackle Al Wahl blocked it, and it rolled out of the end zone for a safety, cutting the Buckeyes' lead to 3–2.

The punting exchange continued until the waning moments of the half, when an Ortmann punt rolled out of bounds at the OSU 9. Two plays gained four yards, and with 3rd down and 6 yards to go at the OSU 13, and 47 seconds remaining in the half, Fesler made a decision that is still debated sixty years later, one that may have lost the game and probably his job—he sent Janowicz back to punt.

Future OSU football coach Earle Bruce was in the stands that day and loves to talk about what happened next.

"I was sitting behind an 80-year-old lady who was unbelievably smart," Bruce said. "After they fired [Wes] Fesler, I would have hired her. The score was 3–2 in favor of Ohio State. There were [47] seconds left in the half. Third-and-[6]. In comes a guy, I think it was Bob Demmel, as he always did. This little old lady starts yelling, 'Don't you punt, Fesler. Don't you dare punt.'

"She was the first person in the stadium who knew. [Janowicz] punted, they blocked it and scored a touchdown. And Fesler never coached another game [for Ohio State]. The old lady was right. She knew if he didnt punt, we'd probably win the game 3–2."

Many people felt that way, including OSU tackle Bob Momsen, whose brother Tony blocked the punt and fell on it in the end zone for Michigan. Harry Allis kicked the extra point.

"If he would have elected to run one more play instead of punting on third down the half might have ended before we would have had to punt," Bob Momsen said in 2000.

"Tony wouldn't have blocked it and scored the touchdown, and we would have probably won the game."

Fesler obviously didn't believe that. He maintained that the Buckeyes couldn't have run out the clock, and forty years later, Janowicz agreed with him.

"We would have had to have punted on fourth down anyway," Janowicz said in 1996. "So it was a 50–50 deal. The bad part was that, at that point, you just couldn't see. So I could only drop back 5 yards."

As Ortmann remembered it, most of the day was like that. He played all sixty minutes, at quarterback and safety.

"Twice, playing safety, I couldn't see Vic in the backfield," he said. "You looked up in the stands at the start and you saw clusters of 5,000 and 10,000 people here and there, and even bonfires. There had been no tarp over the end zones, and there were snow banks in each. I remember one of Vic's punts went into the end zone, hit the bank and bounced back to the 2. That's where they put it."

Conditions actually worsened in the second half, and neither team came close to scoring. Janowicz remembered the Buckeyes getting "thawed out and excited" in the OSU locker room at halftime, but the feeling lasted only as long as it took them to get back on the field and get frozen again. In the second half, he said, "There was nothing left."

The miserable conditions didn't help. The blowing snow got so heavy that players on one sideline couldn't see their counterparts on the other sideline. After each play, the broom patrol had to clear a spot to put the ball for the next play. Scoring became more and more unlikely; the only way to score was on the other team's mistake.

Michigan fullback Don Dufek later said that the centers—Michigan's Carl Kreager and Ohio's Bob Heid—were "really the heroes of the game" because both teams used the single wing, meaning that the snaps were taken in the backfield.

"It wasn't like taking the ball from center," Dufek said. "Vic was a great back and Ortmann was a great passer, but that was negated by the snow. It was very cold. We kept our hands under our armpits in the huddle. Our center [Kreager] didn't wear any gloves. You couldn't get up a head of steam for anything. It was bad news, period."

The blizzard seemed to hit its peak in the fourth quarter, but most of the fans were gone by then. Many of those who remained moved closer to the field, the only way they had a chance to see the players. Some even moved from the seats to the sidelines. Tony Curcillo, who played quarterback in Ohio State's single wing, later recalled catching a pass at the 35-yard line and sliding into the bench. A player was standing there, bundled up in a parka. When Curcillo took a closer look, he realized that the player's girl-friend was huddled beneath the parka with him.

At the game's end, Michigan—the winner—had 27 yards of offense, all on the ground, and no first downs. Ohio State completed 3 of 18 passes for 23 yards, 16 on the ground, and 3 first downs.

Oosterbaan seemed almost apologetic to have beaten the stronger team under these circumstances.

"It wasn't a fair test of football," he said. "Imagine having a team like [Ohio State coach Wes Fesler's] and not being able to use it to any advantage."

When Northwestern beat Illinois in snowy conditions also that day, Michigan found itself with a trip to the Rose Bowl it wasn't expecting. Most of the fans also found themselves with a trip home that wasn't so pleasant. The snow kept coming down after the game ended and the return turned into another ordeal. Some fans couldn't get their snowbound cars out of the parking lots near the stadium. Some fans from Columbus said it took them four hours to get from the stadium to their homes, two or three miles from campus, and some didn't even try.

Jerry Glick was sixteen at the time, and he attended the game in a group of six that included his mother, Thelma Glick, who oversaw the fraternities and sororities at Ohio State. Her car was parked behind University Hall, where her office was, and that was as far as they got after the game.

"We barely made it up that hill," Glick said. "With that much snow, nothing shoveled and most people didn't bring boots, it was hard to get any sort of traction. It was a wet snow, which is the worst, and just getting up that hill was about all you could manage, especially the older people in our group.

"We were hoping that they might get the roads clear, but they didn't. We slept in her office. All we had to eat and drink that night were Coke and peanut butter crackers."

And the Glicks lived in the Columbus suburb of Bexley. For those who had to return to Michigan or other points in Ohio, things were even worse.

*Time* magazine reported that 20,000 cars were stranded along Ohio highways because of the storm. The *Marysville Evening Tribune* reported that 500 fans were stranded in the town, thirteen miles northwest of Columbus, after they found that they could go no farther. After all the motels and tourist cabins were filled, many were lodged in a church basement. One eight-room house in Mt. Sterling, twenty-four miles southwest of the capital, reportedly lodged ninety-two people that night. Circleville, twenty-nine miles south, was as far as many OSU fans got; one news report had 128 fans housed in an emergency shelter in the First Methodist Church.

The trials and tribulations of the fans only added to the circumstances of this unforgettable game, so it isn't surprising that there was already a name for it. What is surprising—at least to most fans today—is that it wasn't called the Snow Bowl. In 1950, the game was tagged as the Blizzard Bowl, a nice piece of alliteration if there ever was one. It was still being called that in the 1970s, but for some reason by the mid-1980s, the Blizzard Bowl had changed identities.

Snow Bowl or Blizzard Bowl, some of the Ohio State players would rather have forgotten about it altogether. One was Janowicz, who punted 21 times for a 32.6-yard average but had two of them blocked to give Michigan both of its scores.

"There is nothing to talk about in regard to 1950," Janowicz told the *Ohio State Lantern* in 1990. "We lost the game. The cold only lasted a day. The defeat has lasted 40 years."

# 12

# The Trailblazer

The moment is seared in my memory, more permanent than any spectacular catch, monster tackle, or game-winning field goal.

In the aftermath of one of those biannual Cleveland Browns–Cincinnati Bengals hate fests, football legend Bill Willis entered the Bengals locker room in a wheelchair, not exactly the vehicle of choice for a man whose speed had made him an All-Pro middle guard and whose courage enabled him to help break the pro football color barrier.

It was 2006. Willis was eighty-four years old, more than fifty years removed from a career with the Browns (1946–1953) that got him elected to Pro Football's Hall of Fame and more than sixty years from the day that Ohio State coach Paul Brown let him know that he was welcome as a black man on an all-white football team.

Bengals president Mike Brown, son of the man who offered Willis his opportunities both at OSU and in Cleveland, asked the former NFL great which player he wanted to see. Willis grinned.

"All of them," he said.

It seemed ironic that a man whose personal Battle of Ohio must have been much tougher than the one that had just been played should be so excited about meeting the young men who had followed him, at least until I had a chance to think about it later. In a way, Willis was surveying his own legacy—and what an impressive legacy it was: rich, talented players, many of them African American, in a plush locker room within a modern stadium, competing in a sport that has become the most popular in America. Every man in the room should have personally thanked him, and some of them did.

Rudi Johnson, fresh off a 145-yard rushing performance, was sitting at a nearby locker, and a team employee pushed Willis in his direction. Willis motioned for his driver to stop, then climbed out of the chair and used a cane to stand face to face with the team's star running back.

Standing wasn't necessary, though it was clear from his struggle that being able to stand and look Johnson in the eye must have been important to him. Age can debilitate the body, but it can't steal a man's pride. If I had been watching this on television instead of in the middle of a crowded locker room, the sight of this proud old warrior summoning the strength to stand might have made me cry.

"I appreciate [what he did]," Johnson said. "He gave all of these people the opportunity to do the things we do now, playing the game we love. Him being the first one, it says a lot. I can't thank him enough, letting him know how much I appreciate it. Everybody should appreciate it."

Marvin Lewis, the Bengals' African American head coach, surely does. Lewis sought Willis out in the crowded locker room and spent close to fifteen minutes talking to him. Later, several players spoke of the letter Lewis read in the team meeting room two days before, which Willis had once written to Paul Brown.

"He wrote Paul Brown a letter thanking him for [first] giving him the opportunity in college," offensive tackle Willie Anderson said. "He thought he'd never play in the NFL. And then (Brown) gave him the opportunity again. It was something."

The case can be made that Willis's number, 99, should have been the first retired at OSU, even ahead of Chic Harley's and those of the school's Heisman Trophy winners. This is the man who broke the color barrier, not once, but twice, a man who also happened to be one of the best players in school history.

Willis was a star athlete at Columbus East High in 1940, but at that point, the thought of playing football for Ohio State barely occurred to him. It was rare for an African American to play football for the Buckeyes, and the door had been completely closed to blacks since 1930.

Howard Gentry, later a successful football coach at Tennessee State, was only a couple of years older than Willis, and he told me back in the early 1990s how he had wanted to play at OSU in the worst way. He had been an Ohio State fan while growing up and was an All-City star at Columbus West for two years, so he tried to make inquiries about playing on Francis Schmidt's teams.

"Some Ohio State alumni who were black took me up there, and the athletic director [Lynn St. John] refused to talk to me," he said. "The head coach [Schmidt] refused to talk to me. Ernie Godfrey, the freshman coach, finally told me that they had all the blacks they could handle at the time and that they weren't very good students. He said I was wasting my time."

The program had had its isolated cases of racial equality, but they were hardly the norm: Frederick D. Patterson became the first black player on the Buckeye football team in 1891 and Julius B. Tyler followed in 1896. Tyler even scored a touchdown.

Patterson, so light-skinned that he doesn't stand out among his white teammates in an 1891 photo, was the son of a prominent Greenfield, Ohio, businessman who owned the C. R. Patterson and Sons carriage manufacturers. Tyler belonged to a successful Columbus family. His brother, Ralph Waldo Tyler, was a prominent journalist who was the *Columbus Dispatch* society editor for thirty years and who was sent by publisher Robert Wolfe to cover the Republican National Convention that nominated William Howard Taft for president in 1908.

But Ohio State didn't field another black football player until 1929, when Bill Bell joined Sam Willaman's squad. Willaman also had another African American player on his team in 1930—Russell Embrey—but he had to leave school because of academic trouble.

No black players had been on the roster since, so it's not hard to see why Willis would have looked elsewhere when he was coming out of East High. But Paul Brown succeeded Schmidt in 1941, just in time to change Willis's mind. Columbus East coach Ralph Webster had played football at Illinois and had set it up for him to go to school there when Brown was named to succeed Schmidt. Webster knew of Brown's reputation for being fair to black athletes on his Massillon High School squads, so Webster told Willis he would be better off under Brown. Willis once told me that Brown was the sole reason he went to Ohio State.

"Paul made a difference," Willis said. "There were only two or three other blacks in the whole league at the time, but I hardly noticed. Paul treated me the same as everyone else, and by the time I left, there were several blacks on the roster."

Willis came to OSU as a sprinter and a lineman, a combination that doesn't seem to make sense. At 6'2", 205 pounds, Willis was considered small for a lineman, but Brown favored quickness over size and Willis was soon rewarded for his preference. Brown once described Willis "as quick as a snake's fang," and he showed that speed even as a sophomore in 1942, when the Buckeyes won the Big Ten and were voted national champions by the Associated Press. Willis starred for two more seasons and was named All-American in 1944 during OSU's undefeated season.

That doesn't mean it was easy, however. Black players weren't allowed to live on campus. As a member of the track team, he once found himself stranded with the only other black team member, Ralph Tyler, because they were forced to accept separate accommodations in Philadelphia when they were there for the Penn Relays. Brown wrote later "As a result, they got separated from their teammates after the meet and suddenly found themselves alone and virtually without money in a strange city, 600 miles from home. Bill called me and I wired money so they could pay for their room and get home. You can be sure I let Ohio State's track coach know I didn't appreciate any of our players being abandoned like that."

His appreciation for Willis as both an athlete and a person was something else. When Brown took over as coach of the Cleveland Browns in the new All-American Football Conference after the war, Willis asked his former coach about the possibility of playing for them. No black players had played pro football since 1930, and Jackie Robinson had still not broken the baseball color barrier, so Willis's acceptance wasn't a guarantee. It didn't surprise Willis when Brown didn't give him a quick answer, and he signed with Montreal of the Canadian Football League. He was about to leave for Canada when Brown called *Dispatch* sports editor Paul Hornung and asked him to bring Willis to the team's camp at Bowling Green.

Willis reluctantly went and soon had a black roommate: Marion Motley, a twenty-seven-year-old former Nevada star who had played for Brown at Great Lakes Naval Station during the war and had been working at a mill. Like Willis, Brown also had an escort bring Motley to camp for appearance's sake—Brown explained later it wasn't "unusual in a player coming to his former coach asking him for a chance to play"—and the two of them, along with Kenny Washington and Woody Strode of the Los Angeles Rams, blazed a racial trail that year in pro football.

Brown knew Willis would be a terrific pro player and he was quickly proven right. Willis often played middle or nose guard in the Brown's five-man defensive line, but Brown began dropping him off the line of scrimmage because his speed and pursuit often got him to the ball carrier before he could be stopped. In technique and theory, it was the beginning of the modern 4–3 defense, and Willis became a forerunner of the middle linebacker.

During their rookie years, Willis and Motley were required to sit out their game against the Miami Seahawks because it was against the law for them to play against white players in Miami. Brown gave both men an extra $500 in their checks and told Willis he would take care of the problem. A bad team took care of it for him. Miami went 3-11 and folded after the season, and its spot was taken by a new team in Baltimore—a little ironic given Bell's experience there back in 1930—called the Colts. Willis's pro football career lasted much longer. He was still with the Browns when they moved to the NFL in 1950 and was named All-Pro in 1950, 1951, and 1952. The Browns were one of the dominant teams in pro football in those days. They won the AAFC title four straight years, moved to the NFL and won again in 1950, and Willis was one of their stars.

Bill Myles, retired as an OSU assistant football coach and associate athletic director, remembered watching Willis play as a kid growing up in Kansas City. Myles came to admire him even more when he experienced some lingering effects of racism while playing for Drake in the 1960s. So when Myles first landed his job at OSU, he appreciated the chance to meet and get to know Willis, who was still living in Columbus. Willis was working for the Ohio Youth Commission then, in the midst of a twenty-year career devoted to giving troubled kids a second chance. Myles later said that Willis ended up being everything a hero is supposed to be.

"What impresses you the most about the man is the dignity with which he's always carried himself," Myles said. "He was a man you weren't going to break. That's what Archie Griffin has got, too. They stand for something that means much more than football.

"He is a man of great pride, a great family man who is devoted to his wife, Odessa, and their children and grandchildren. He became a leader in the community here and has always had great loyalty when it comes to Ohio State and to his friends."

The school retired Willis's number in November of 2007, and he died a few weeks later. His legacy had long since been secured: pro, college, and high school Hall of Famer; racial pioneer; forerunner of the middle linebacker; devoted family man; friend to troubled youth; community leader; and maybe even the best Ohio State player ever.

He was a great man in many ways, yet one thought is never far from any discussion of Willis and his accomplishments: It takes a lot of courage to be a trailblazer.

# 13

# Saint Woody

A fan was lamenting the predictability of Jim Tressel's offense in an e-mail to the *Dispatch* one day when he invoked the name of Tressel's most famous Ohio State predecessor.

"Tressel seems to be a good enough coach," he wrote, "but he's certainly no Woody Hayes."

I winced. Right or wrong, it struck me that the fan's knowledge of the subject might be seriously lacking. Did he really think that Hayes, whose offense had noticeable Cro-Magnon tendencies, knew more about offense than Tressel did? Had he ever heard the expression "three yards and a cloud of dust," or was it just his impression that Woody always unleashed his sophisticated passing attack just after the dust storm cleared? Or more to the point, had this self-appointed expert ever even *seen* a game that Hayes had coached?

While it's possible the correspondent was an old fullback who deplores all this newfangled aerial nonsense, it seemed more plausible that the answer to that last question was probably no. More than thirty years after Hayes conducted business on the Ohio Stadium sidelines, it's safe to say that what most everyone under the age of forty knows about the most successful coach in school history has been gleaned from second- or third-hand info, if even that. Lots of people know of Woody, but most of them didn't know him personally and the bulk of them probably haven't even read much about him. They know that his teams won, know his name and record are emblazoned on a sign inside Ohio Stadium, and know that he's widely revered by Buckeye fans, so they assume he must have been a play-designing, forward-thinking football genius. Because of that, it naturally follows that he almost always made the right calls in every situation and he probably could sketch out a new play on a napkin, a play so intrinsically beautiful he could justifiably be called a football Rembrandt.

And who knows? On occasion, maybe the grizzled old warrior affectionately called the Old Man by many of those around him did just that. But sometimes time has a way of fogging up the windows, and that is almost certainly the case with Woody Hayes. Somewhere between the sideline punch that got him fired and John Cooper's incessant losses against Michigan, the volatile coach morphed into something other than what he was.

Whether Woody Hayes is an Ohio State saint or a football god, he has almost certainly become an icon in the truest sense of the word. He has become an image that has been crafted by hundreds of stories, some true and some not. Even those who knew him have had their memories of him altered by the passage of time. The good old days are always old, but they often aren't as good as we remember them. The mind chooses which memories to keep and which ones to discard, and sometimes shapes and molds them like a wet piece of clay. In the constant molding and remolding of those precious thoughts, some of our once crisp, sharp images can become fuzzy, which can be especially significant when dealing with a figure as complex and fascinating as Hayes.

In some ways, Woody was a saint. He was a generous, kind-hearted soul who genuinely cared about his players and who visited hundreds of hospital patients he didn't know. But he was also a snarling, watch-breaking, cap-ripping, downs-marker-shredding, foot-stomping maniac. He was a selfless, benevolent human being. He was a masochistic brute. He was a Hall of Fame coach with a brilliant record. He was a coaching anachronism, behind the times and too stubborn to change.

Woody Hayes was all of these things, even if the contrasting images make it difficult to imagine. He was a human enigma, although many of today's fans don't know it, not because they don't want to, but because they weren't around to alternately praise him and curse him when he was coaching. To most of them he is an image of Ohio State's football greatness, a guy who would never put up with whatever it is about today's football that they don't like. In that way, he is as close to the perfect coach as a human being can be.

Some fans will don one of his familiar black caps with the scarlet block O and thoughtfully surmise that the Southeastern Conference would never have become dominant over the Big Ten if *Woody* were alive, without realizing that it was probably the beating a team coached by Hayes suffered at the hands of Bear Bryant and Alabama in the 1978 Sugar Bowl that set the perception of the SEC's dominance over the Big Ten in motion. They will affirm that Woody would never have allowed anyone in or near his program to break NCAA rules, without realizing that in 1955 Hayes's own actions in giving some of his needy players cash—the NCAA later discovered that some of his players were also paid for work they didn't perform—resulted in OSU's probation from the Big Ten and a ban from post-season competition for all OSU teams from the NCAA. They will steadfastly maintain that Tressel is the modern-day reincarnation of Woody, without realizing that in some ways the two of them are very much alike and in other ways they are very much different. If this all sounds confusing, don't be distraught: you are getting as clear a picture as possible. It's the image at the center of it that keeps moving.

All of the nice things that Hayes's former players say about him are true. He cared deeply about them and proved it every day. Most of the ridiculous stories, including some where his behavior borders on insanity, are also dead-on. Hayes was a genuinely selfless person. He performed countless acts of charity and tried hard to make sure no one found out about them, in contrast to many of the image-conscious, self-appointed "saints" of today. But he also had a vicious, hair-trigger temper that led to dozens of ugly incidents, including his termination for slugging Clemson linebacker Charlie Bauman on the Ohio State sidelines after Bauman made an interception near the end of the 1978 Gator Bowl. Hayes could be a gentle, grandfatherly figure, but he could also be a snarling, profanity-spewing, fist-pounding beast.

As one who covered his final two seasons, I can attest that there were times he seemed almost schizophrenic. Almost every day during the season, I would visit him in Room 147, his small, windowless office in the old North Facility, and there was no way to know what to expect. Some days he seemed glad to see me. He might even offer me a book or a magazine article that he thought would be beneficial to me; this was the teacher-grandfather Woody.

Other days he would look at me as if I had broken into his office and stolen his playbook, and snort and snarl in ways both scary and intimidating.

"Just what in the *hell* do you want?" he asked more than once, in a tone that indicated that he really meant it.

A psychiatrist could have had a field day examining him, but if one of them tried, Woody almost certainly would have grabbed him by the seat of the pants and pitched him into the street. Depending on which Woody you met, two people could have a completely different image of him. It's why he was both revered and reviled. Either emotion could be easily justified.

Most of his former players sing his praise and they do it in their outdoor voices. If you pick up one of the numerous books that have been written about him in recent years, it's hard not to believe he possessed saint-like qualities. In *I Remember Woody*, a 1997 book by Steve Greenberg and Dale Ratermann, player after player expressed his thoughts on Hayes, and most were effusive in their tributes to him.

"Woody Hayes, to me, was my protector, my father, my mother, minister, all in one," former OSU offensive guard Ken Fritz said. "He just had that kind of power. It's still amazing what that extra power helps me do."

There is no doubting that this affection is real. Hayes undoubtedly changed many of his players' lives, *most* of his players' lives, for the better. The lessons he preached were often those any good parents would offer their own children; unfortunately, children often resist their own parents' teachings. Hayes was a famous football coach, so he had an opportunity to reach some hardheaded young men in ways that their parents couldn't. He was the other voice that confirmed what their parents were saying, and the players mostly believed him.

Hayes was the son of a school superintendent and he saw himself as a teacher first. He recited Emerson. He often compared various aspects of football strategy to tactics used by famous battlefield commanders. He used to take players to educational sites while they were on road trips, and sometimes would even take some of his players into a class on the campus they were visiting and ask the professor if they could attend.

He did this at Illinois in 1968, taking Jim Stillwagon, Rex Kern, and a few others into an auditorium where a molecular biology class was in session. The professor asked if he could help them, and Hayes told him that they were from another Big Ten school and asked if they could sit in and listen.

"Aren't you Woody Hayes?" the professor asked.

The Old Man said he was.

"My name is Woody, too," the professor said.

With that introduction, Hayes and his players sat down in an upper row and began taking notes. The story would be incredible enough if it ended there, but it didn't. At one point, Professor Woody said something that Coach Woody didn't think was right, so the old coach marched to the front of the auditorium and made his case, and Professor Woody had to admit Coach Woody was correct. Hayes spoke to the class for fifteen minutes, and when he finished, the students gave him a standing ovation.

The "word power" classes he taught his players is my most-cited example of why he seemed to me much different from so many of the coaches who came before or since. He thought a good vocabulary was important to success in life, and he wanted to make sure his players had a chance at that success. So he gave them word lists and quizzed them on the definitions, even though the words had little or nothing at all to do with their success in the classroom or on the football field. When people ask about Woody, it is an example I nearly always use. He cared so much about his players that he couldn't stand the thought of one of them being embarrassed in a job interview or even a social situation because of remedial verbal skills. Their success in life was as important to him as their success on the football field. His interest in their long-term well-being was sincere. He didn't do this for show.

The stories of Hayes driving his players to graduate even after they were out of school are almost legendary. Phil Strickland finished his four years of football and was still a quarter term of credits short of graduating. He had money for either classes or books, but not both. Hayes wrote him a check for the books and told him that if he didn't graduate, he owed him the money. If he did, he owed him nothing. Strickland got his degree.

Kevin Rusnak was a couple of years out of school when the phone rang and his father answered it. After a couple of "yes, sirs," he hung up and looked at Kevin. "That was Woody," the elder Rusnak said. "You're going back to finish your degree." Rusnak did.

How many of today's coaches care enough about their former players to keep on them about their degrees years or even decades after they leave school? And maybe a better question: of the minority who do, how many do it primarily to create the right image that might help them in recruiting or at contract time?

Neither was the case with Woody. He wanted players to graduate. It was an obsession with him. Kern once offered up one of the best examples of this to longtime *Columbus Dispatch* sportswriter Paul Hornung.

"Maybe four or five years before he got ill, he asked me if I remembered a certain player I'll call 'Joe' and of course I did," Kern said. "Joe went home for Christmas his freshman year. It was during the uproar over Vietnam and one of his buddies had been killed there. Joe was in a bar and [there] happened to be a lot of antiwar sentiments flying, Joe got hit in the head with a beer bottle and was partially paralyzed. He came back to school for a while, but never played a down for us.

"On my visit to Woody's office, he said 'Joe's had a lot of trouble, but by God, we finally got him graduated, and we got him a job, too.' Here's a guy who never actually played at Ohio State. Woody didn't owe the guy a thing except his commitment to get him graduated from college. And this was probably fourteen or fifteen years later."

Saint Woody? When you hear a story like that, you begin to wonder.

In his book *1968: The Year That Saved Ohio State Football*, David Hyde tells the story of reserve player Bill Pollitt, who returned to Ohio State as a grad assistant but wanted to go to law school. Unfortunately, Pollitt's grades weren't good enough to get him in. After several law schools rejected him, Capital University seemed to be his last chance. Woody wrote a letter of recommendation for him, but the interview didn't go well. When Pollitt told Hayes about it, the Old Man went crazy, banging on tables and throwing things around the room. Finally, he settled down.

"Goddamnit, do you want to go to law school?" Woody asked.

Pollitt said he did.

"Will you make it?"

Again, Pollitt said yes.

"You'd better. Because if you screw up, you'll not only screw it up for you, you'll screw it up for every player who comes after you. My word won't mean shit."

Three days later, Pollitt received his surprising acceptance letter. Today, Judge H. William Pollitt Jr. presides in the Franklin County Municipal Court.

"He changed my life," Pollitt said.

Saint Woody? Well sometimes, he *was*.

But what about that other Woody, the guy who seemed to live up to the "10 percent rule" that was explained to new assistant coach Bill Mallory in 1966 by Lyal Clark, the retiring coach whose job he was taking.

"Let me tell you about the man you're about to work for," Clark said. "Ninety percent of the time, he's as fine a person as you'll ever meet, the kind of man who will do anything for his players and to make you a better coach. But there's that other 10 percent of the time. When that kicks in, get your ass out of the way."

It was no joke. Hayes was an accomplished boxer as a kid and kept it up through college at Denison, building his reputation with a string of knockouts during intramural bouts there. That physicality was part of who he was, and when combined with that hair-trigger temper, it made for a painful experience for many players and assistant coaches throughout the years. Maybe the most valuable piece of advice handed down from veteran players to newbies consisted of two simple rules: don't do anything to tick him off, but if you do, remember that he's left-handed. New players sometimes learned the hard way that it didn't pay to stand down range from his left fist. More than one player over the years took a powerful punch to the gut for a mistake they made or, even worse, for one they didn't. Being in the wrong place at the wrong time when something happened to make Woody angry could be just as painful.

Unlike Tressel, when Hayes got mad the expletives began to flow. "Shoot-shoot-shoot" turned into "goddamnit" or "goddamnit to hell" and worse. He knew he was a poor loser and he didn't see that as a character flaw. One time when he heard that a northern Ohio quarterback he wanted as a Buckeye was going to attend Michigan, he picked up a film projector and tossed it across the meeting room. More routinely, he would throw books, chairs, desks—whatever was near enough to grab.

"When we lose a game, nobody's madder at me than me," Hayes once said. "When I look into the mirror in the morning, I want to take a swing at me."

Sometimes, he did it. He would get so mad he'd bite the palm of his hand or punch himself in the face. Some of his tantrums were calculated;

it's true, for example, that he sometimes had his equipment men cut the bill of his caps so he could easily rip one up during practice. But many weren't. A reserve lineman who was kneeling next to Hayes during the 1968 spring game recalled seeing Hayes take off his wire-rimmed glasses and hold them in his hand. When he looked over later, an angry Hayes had crushed the glasses and his hand was cut and bleeding.

I often saw him loudly berate his assistants in front of his players during practice for a mistake that one of their players made, and I'll never forget the day in Ohio Stadium when some of the players who were on the sidelines sat down in some of the wooden field seats that had been left there from the previous game.

Tom Pastorius, my able *Columbus Citizen-Journal* counterpart, was standing there with me behind the chairs, and he looked at me and smiled. "I don't think the Old Man's gonna like this," he said.

And sure enough, there was an interception or a fumble on the field and Woody started ranting. After a few seconds, he looked over and saw those players sitting there—I'm guessing he had noticed them before and was waiting for the right time to explode—and came charging over, screaming like a man whose pants were on fire. Players were scrambling to get away, and Hayes began firing the chairs in every direction, screaming the whole time. I never saw those chairs there again during the stadium practice sessions, but it wouldn't have mattered. No one would have dared to sit in them, including reporters.

Jack Tatum wrote in *They Call Me Assassin* about how Phil Strickland once stood up to adjust his shoulder pads during one of Hayes's halftime talks, and the tone of the Old Man's voice didn't change "as he lashed out with four or five jabs to Phil's head. Then Woody went on talking as if nothing had happened, but Phil had been knocked over backward from the punches to his head."

Saint Woody? Uh, definitely not *that* Woody, although that is a Woody that many modern fans who have come to think of him as the coaching standard don't know much about.

But we still haven't answered the real question: was Woody Hayes really a great football coach, or did much of his success flow from an Ohio State football factory that had been churning out championships for more than thirty years before he arrived? His career record notwithstanding, it is an intriguing question.

Woody wasn't a particularly good tactician; that was confirmed time and again. When a longtime OSU equipment man went on with what he thought was an off-the-record rant with a (Cleveland) *Plain Dealer* reporter about how Woody and Michigan coach Bo Schembechler were so conservative and hardheaded that the coach who won the upcoming game would likely be the one who screwed up the least, he was only saying what he believed to be true. He loved Woody, but he thought his conservative nature and hardheadedness could be a curse, especially in big games.

Hayes's teams sometimes lost because of his stubbornness, which goes against the "great coach" definition. His teams sometimes lost because he got a lead, threw out the game plan, and all but shut down his offense. His teams sometimes lost because he wouldn't listen to the sage advice his assistants were trying to give him.

In 1973, his team was undefeated and ranked No. 1 in the nation when it jumped to a 10–0 lead in Ann Arbor against No. 4 Michigan. Then, in the second half, he acted as if his already ultraconservative game plan posed a serious danger to his lead and tightened the screws even further. Freshman fullback Pete Johnson, who had run roughshod over the Wolverines in the first half, sat out most of the third quarter and carried only once after halftime. Quarterback Cornelius Greene didn't attempt a pass and carried the ball less than usual. The wingback counter, a play that had been used with tremendous success all year, wasn't called once. Instead, he ran Archie Griffin into the line on play after play after play, and the Michigan defense jammed the line with eight men and disregarded any chance of a pass. It couldn't stop Griffin—he gained 163 yards in 30 carries—but the Buckeyes didn't score, either. With the score tied 10–10, 1:01 left, and the chance for a national title fading, Woody replaced Greene with senior Greg Hare and had him attempt the first OSU pass of the day, which Tom Drake intercepted and returned to the OSU 33. Only a missed 44-yard field goal by Greg Lantry kept the Buckeyes from losing. Afterward, some of the OSU players complained about his tactics privately. One said he "choked." One said that Hayes had called but three different plays the entire second half.

"It wounds his pride to pass," one OSU player said. "It's like admitting weakness."

Everyone has bad games, of course. But in Woody's case, there were similar games, similar incidents that would seem to run counter to the great-coach arguments. Most of those stories end with assistant coaches growing more and more exasperated with their failed attempts to reason with him. In his 1974 book *Buckeye: A Study of Coach Woody Hayes and the Ohio State Football Machine*, Robert Vare penned a memorable image of assistant coach Ralph Staub trying to send in different plays during that '73 Michigan game, and Hayes constantly rejecting them. Woody "kept pulling his cap down harder and harder and saying, 'Fuck that fucking play!' 'Fuck that fucking play!' 'Fuck that fucking play.'" No one who knew Woody would have a hard time believing it. It was vintage Hayes.

Woody had a tendency to take the best athletes of every recruiting class for the offense, because that's the side he coached. This proved to be a problem in the 1960s when the program was stalled. The defensive coaches complained, but it did little good until defensive coordinator Lou McCullough finally made inroads with the group known as the super sophs in 1968. Hayes agreed to have a draft of players that alternated between offense and defense, and not until the fourth pick, when McCullough picked Tatum and an angry Woody let him stay there, did it become clear that the Old Man was going to go along with the change. Tatum had been recruited as a running back and had played fullback on the freshman team. But Tatum was OK with the move, not only because he liked defense, but he knew Woody wasn't going to let him run the ball the way he wanted.

Fullbacks were Woody's bread and butter. They were his babies. But they had to stick to the plan. Hayes's fullbacks talk of taking the handoff, seeing the hole clogged, and bouncing outside to gain five or six yards and then getting the scolding of their lives from Hayes. John Brockington had this happen to him in his first scrimmage. He took the handoff, saw the hole was jammed, and juked outside for a nice 7-yard gain. He did it again on the next play for a gain of six. As he kneeled down to slip on a shoe he had lost, he looked up and saw the Old Man glowering at him.

"If you ever run the football like that again, you'll never play a down at Ohio State!" a red-faced Hayes bellowed.

Why? Because that's not the way his teams were supposed to play. Punch them in the face. That was Hayes's offensive philosophy. Punch them in the face again. And again. And *again*. See if they can take it. Show them who's boss. It wasn't a thing of beauty and it wasn't supposed to be. As long as he was in charge, a "twinkle toes" would never be his fullback.

George Chaump recalled sitting through two *days* of meetings about the same off-tackle play—Robust 26 or Robust 27, depending on which direction it went—shortly after he joined Hayes's staff in 1968. Chaump's John Harris High School had just completed three undefeated seasons in Harrisburg, Pennsylvania, using a wide-open offense—the kind of offense he used later to win a Division II national championship as the head coach at Marshall—and he was stunned by what he was seeing.

Years later, I sat with Chaump in a bar on the road somewhere and listened as he poured out his frustrations over the uninspired offense the Old Man was running with a young quarterback named Art Schlichter. Chaump had obviously lobbied repeatedly for changes, and Hayes wouldn't hear of it. The Buckeyes would throw the ball more, but there would be none of that fancy stuff. A sophisticated passing attack was the last thing the Old Man wanted. Deep down, all Woody really wanted to do on offense was punch them in the face. Passing was too prissy.

But by the time Chaump arrived he was much more open to offensive changes than he had been, and he could surprise on occasion. In 1968, he stunned Purdue with a no-huddle offense he got from watching Marv Moorehead's powerhouse Upper Arlington High School teams that played a short distance from his Cardiff Road home. Purdue's tackles were huge for that era—275 pounds—and the Buckeyes were smaller and faster. Hayes might not be an offensive wizard, but he knew a good idea when he saw one.

After a bad run in the 1960s that could have gotten him fired, he begrudgingly made some adjustments in the offense. He adopted the "I" formation with that class of super sophomores in 1968, and continued to inch forward offensively through the 1970s, even if he didn't like it. But he would have been insulted if anyone had ever implied that he was cutting edge. If he saw the spread offenses many coaches are using today, he would probably start throwing things. In his mind, it might even be proof of the decline of Western civilization.

There's more to coaching than X's and O's, though. Leadership, preparation, motivation techniques, and salesmanship can all be important factors in coaching success, and Woody excelled in all of those areas. He tried
to work harder than everybody else and may have done it. He liked to say
that what he didn't know, he made up for with hard work, and he generally succeeded at that. Salesmanship can be particularly important in college coaching, where a coach must first be a good recruiter and then must
win over the players he recruits to his system, his methods, and so forth.
More than one good player came to Ohio State because Woody did a great
recruiting job with the player's mother.

He seems to have been a natural leader. His older sister, Mary North,
recalled that even as a kid growing up in Newcomerstown, Ohio, "the boys
around the neighborhood used to follow him around and do exactly what
he said. He was the toughest kid on the block."

And his motivation techniques were extraordinary. In 1970, after
Michigan's stunning upset in the '69 game, the Buckeyes walked into the
locker room on Monday of Michigan week and in place of music were the
voices of Michigan's radio team doing play by play from that nightmarish
game. The announcers' enjoyment of the moment wasn't lost on the players, and neither was Woody's message.

He turned the act of hating Michigan into a lifestyle. Some of the stories are simply legends—it's doubtful Woody actually ran out of gas and
pushed his car over the Ohio-Michigan state line to avoid buying gas in
Michigan—but he did seem capable of delivering an emotional, anti-
Michigan diatribe on cue.

Those who think Hayes and Tressel are one and the same probably
missed the speech Woody delivered to his players during Michigan week
1968. A talented class of sophomores dominated that team, and Woody
wanted to make sure the young players understood the intensity of his feelings toward the Wolverines: "I despise those arrogant sons of bitches! I
despise them all. I don't hate them. I'm not a hater. You can't be a hater in
life. But I despise them. It's OK to despise. . . . Those arrogant sons of bitches
tried to break Hoppy's leg."

"Hoppy," Howard "Hopalong" Cassady, played from 1952 to 1955, and
Hayes was still bitter about a cheap shot he thought that Michigan end

Ron Kramer had made on him. In Woody's world, there was no statute of limitations on perceived Wolverine injustices in the OSU-Michigan game.

I was on a local radio show several years ago with former players Pete Johnson and Ray Griffin during Michigan week, and Griffin gave the Wolverines credit for something on the air. During a news break, Johnson got so upset with Griffin over his comments that I thought he was going to go over the table after him. It was no act. Pete *hated* Michigan. Even after all these years, the Old Man's message was as strong as ever. As a coaching psychologist, he was as good as they come.

If a college coach is a good tactician but a poor recruiter or motivator, chances are he won't win. Hayes was a so-so tactician, yet he had more success on the field than any coach in school history. He coached the Buckeyes to 238 victories and won 13 Big Ten titles in 28 seasons. Two of his teams, in 1954 and 1968, went undefeated and were awarded national championships.

Longtime OSU alumni magazine editor Jack Fullen, who was a Hayes supporter early in his OSU career and also one of Woody's most vehement critics later, gave Vare a quote for his 1973 book that summed up the complexities of the man as well as any:

Woody Hayes the man is such a strange contradiction of qualities, you can't really catalogue him. He does take a sincere interest in the welfare of his kids, but he'll also bully them and smack them around if they don't produce on the field. Next to losing, the thing he hates most is being crossed. He can be really vindictive and violent. But he is also one of the most literate and articulate men in coaching. When he wants to, he could charm a bird off a tree. He's a complex institution, all right—a real Jekyll and Hyde. I'll tell you one thing, though. If I wanted to win football games, I'd go out and hire Woody Hayes as coach. I don't think there's ever been a better one.

Okay, so maybe Woody *was* a great coach, but was he a saint?

They may be debating that one in heaven even now, and celestial debaters should keep one thing in mind: Hayes is left-handed.

# 14

# The Rivalry

The adjectives attached to the Ohio State–Michigan rivalry have been looking a little dog-eared lately. Some describe it as the greatest rivalry in sports, and after No. 2 Michigan finally defeated the No. 6 Buckeyes 42–27 in 2021, a good case can still be made that it belongs in the top five. But with Ohio State having beaten Michigan in eight straight games before that (five with Jim Harbaugh at the Wolverines' helm) and in fourteen of the last sixteen, it is clear that the rivalry can definitely use some work. If it's not exactly on its death bed, it at least has a high fever.

"The Game" has seemed more like *a* game in recent years, more like OSU-Toledo or Michigan–Western Michigan. As nicknames go, "The Big One" suddenly seems three sizes too large, like an XXL sweatshirt draped over a dieter who has lost a hundred pounds. Imagine the suddenly svelte winner of television's *The Biggest Loser* wearing a sweater that looks more like a tarp. At the moment, that sloppy-looking creature is the "greatest rivalry in sports." Could this be a case of mistaken identity?

Surprisingly, this isn't a rare condition. Like all rivalries that have tilted too far one way or another for an extended period, this one has previously seemed as if it were headed for extinction. Long ago and far away, in a game of leather helmets and bloated pigskins, Michigan-Minnesota was one of college football's biggest rivalries. The Little Brown Jug wasn't a Triple Crown harness race, but the traditional prize for the winner of a Triple Crown–style football game that often determined the Big Ten football champion. Today, after decades of dominance by Michigan, Minnesota-Michigan doesn't amount to much. If you're going to throw out the record book for that one, you might as well toss the game in the trash with it. Unless the schools' presidents are looking for a cute container for their latest batch of moonshine, that prestigious Brown Jug would fit nicely on a shelf with their bowling trophies.

Nothing is forever, although it takes more than a decade of dominance to douse a rivalry as intense and storied as this one. Before Tressel arrived in 2001, Michigan won five of the previous six matchups. Under John Cooper, Tressel's predecessor, the Buckeyes went 2-10-1 against Michigan. Back in 1993, after the Wolverines beat OSU 28–0 to go 5-0-1 in the series over six years, UM guard Joe Marinaro talked about how speeches by former coach Bo Schembechler and teary-eyed former player Corwin Brown had given the players some perspective and said, "Basically, I think we feel like we have to uphold the tradition of Michigan always beating Ohio State."

No kidding. He said that. He said *always*. But then he had no way of knowing that while runs such as that one occasionally happen in rivalries, they seldom last forever. In the early 1970s, OSU was 3-0-1 against Michigan. Back in the early '60s, OSU won four in a row. From 1945 to 1951, Michigan was 6-0-1 against the Buckeyes. Ohio State won four in a row in the 1930s. Michigan won six in a row in the 1920s. Hey, it happens to the best of them.

In fact, the only reason the rivalry isn't nearly deadlocked after over one hundred years of competition—Michigan owns a 58-44-6 advantage in the series—is because this wasn't a rivalry for the schools' first fifteen meetings. It wasn't even one of the highlight games on the Wolverines' schedule. From 1897 to 1918, Michigan owned a 13-0-2 advantage against an OSU team that for all but the last of those years wasn't in the Wolverines' league, literally or figuratively.

In 1910, the lead story in the *Columbus Dispatch* after the Ohio State–Michigan game in Columbus started with a taxi driver heading north on High Street just as the crowds were coming the other way.

"What was the score?" he asked a boy in the crowd.

"Three to three, Ohio State," the happy boy replied.

That's the way it was in those days. Michigan was the Midwest's preeminent college football program, one of the founding members of the powerful Western Conference. Ohio State was one of the Wolverines' schedule fillers. Remove those years from the series record, and the series stands at

45-44-4 in Michigan's favor. For all of the runs that have occurred both ways over the years, it can't get much closer than that.

There are plenty of reasons why this grew into a terrific rivalry, going all the way back to an ancient war that the two states almost fought over the territorial ownership of the strip of land where the city of Toledo sits. As the old joke goes, you can decide for yourself which side won. But it was definitely elevated during the so-called ten-year war between Woody Hayes and Bo Schembechler from 1968 to 1978 when both programs were among the best in the nation. And there is no denying that Woody probably did more to lift the rivalry into its own class than anyone, before or since.

Hayes recognized early on that a coach's success at Ohio State was tied to success in this game, and he focused on it year-round, sometimes even to the exclusion of whichever opponent was on that week's schedule. Years later, many of Hayes's players still harbor an intense hatred toward Michigan. It was difficult to spend time around Woody and not come to feel that way.

When Howard "Hopalong" Cassady traveled from his Florida home to have his number retired at halftime of the OSU-Michigan game in 2000, the 1955 Heisman Trophy winner made it clear that the ceremony was secondary.

"The main reason I'm up here is to see Michigan get their ass beat," a grinning Cassady said. "And it just so happens they're going to retire my number at the same time."

He said that when Ohio State had lost five of the previous seven to the Wolverines, he was suffering. It really bothered him that hating Michigan wasn't what it used to be.

"We practiced all year for them," Cassady said. "We were always ready for them. From day one, that was always on your mind. The seniors, they talked about it all the time. If you're a sophomore or a junior, you'd better be hurting somebody. Anybody standing, you knocked down."

That was the essence of Ohio State–Michigan as long as Woody was involved, or at least as long ago as Cassady can remember. Hayes spent all year trying to devise ways to get under the Wolverines' skin.

"We go to Michigan [in 1955] and we're in the locker room, and Woody's got us all set," Cassady said. "And they had that tunnel, and our locker room was above theirs. And we know through the years, that you come running down the tunnel, cheering and really fired up, and just as you get to their locker room, they storm out. So Woody says, 'Hey, start yelling and screaming and run out and when they get ready to run out, stop and come back in.'

"So we ran out the door, went part of the way down there, and then here comes Michigan, zoom, up in front of us and out onto the field. And we stop and go back in the locker room and sit down. We're sitting down there laughing our asses off and they're out on the field waiting. And we're not talking two minutes here. We're talking like ten minutes. The umpires have to come up the tunnel and come into the locker room and say, 'Hey, you guys gotta get out there.' So then we come storming out and we're laughing our ass off at them and they're really ticked. Yeah, they had a bad day all the way around."

Hayes's former players all have stories like that. For Woody, hating Michigan was a way of life, which is the only reason the story about him pushing his car across the Ohio border just so he wouldn't have to buy gas in the state of Michigan has any semblance of believability. In the real world, there might have been only one guy who hated Michigan enough to put himself through that kind of inconvenience, and it's because of him that many otherwise sensible people are still walking the Columbus streets practically spitting the word "Michigan" at anybody who dares mention the rivalry to them. True or not, it's that kind of junk that turned this into a monster rivalry and has managed to keep it one, despite the dominance of one team or the other from 1988 through 2010.

Gary Moeller, an OSU captain in 1962 who was later a Michigan assistant and head coach from 1990 through 1994, once said that back during his playing days this great rivalry lived mostly in the mind of one man.

"When I played, the Michigan game was a big game," Moeller said. "But I can remember coming [to Ann Arbor] as a junior and there were about 60,000 people in the stands. We still got a pair of gold pants every time we beat Michigan. We had a special banquet in Columbus where they would present you with a pair of gold pants every time you beat Michigan. We didn't have the kind of knock-down, drag-out fights against Michigan at that time.

"I can remember Woody talking about several things about Michigan when I was a player. He would get hyper about a lot of things. He said

[Michigan athletic director] Fritz Crisler put the johns in the locker room and made them so loud that you couldn't concentrate on the game. [Woody] wouldn't let anybody flush the johns when I played. The manager had to go around when everybody went out to warm up and flush the johns because they were too noisy. He used to tell stories like that and it meant something to you, but for me, it really all started in '69 and then the battle we had in '70, and then it continued in the early '70s."

There was a time in the maize-and-blue tinted days of the 1990s when Moeller said Ohio State–Michigan wasn't as big a rivalry as Michigan State–Michigan, a comment that seemed to hearken back to the days when Woody delighted in giving the other side an occasional mental jab. Moeller's successor, Lloyd Carr, even added to the insult by saying that the Michigan State rivalry was more intense than Ohio State–Michigan.

While that theory is understandable on some levels, it's interesting that no one on the Michigan side has tried to sell that junk in recent years. Those remarks proved a good ploy back when the Wolverines were winning this game almost every year, a nice way to apply more pressure to the OSU players and punch the OSU fans in the gut at the same time. But if Rich Rodriguez had tried one of those lines on the news media during his three-year term as Michigan coach—he was 0-3 against the Buckeyes before he was fired in 2011—he might not have gotten out of the building before the fans gave him a tar-and-feather sweatsuit. To some, a stupid remark like that would have "proved" he didn't understand the rivalry—a refrain heard through the John Cooper years—and indisputable evidence to justify his dismissal.

Hoke made it clear from his first day on the job that *he* wasn't about to go there, using his introductory press conference as Michigan's coach to emphasize, "It is the most important game on that schedule," and banging his fist on the podium between each word.

But it is amazing how things changed after Tressel was hired in 2001 and the Buckeyes started dominating in the series. Back in the 1990s, Columbus needed a psychiatrist's couch the size of Wyoming for all the Ohio State fans who could have used one. The OSU players behaved like Rhodes Scholars who had somehow flunked a high school math test, would be given but one more chance to pass it, and were confused and anxious about their failures. Football detectives were out in full force, searching for a formula that would somehow bring a victory over Michigan. A reading on the old angst-o-meter might have been higher in Ohio's state capital than at any other place, at any other time, in the history of the world.

In those days, if you ran into a guy wearing an Ohio State t-shirt in the grocery store, he probably had bloodshot eyes and a nervous tic. Today, the same guy is as laid-back as an actor in a Cheech and Chong movie. Michigan now seems about as threatening to these folks as a bunch of giggling schoolgirls, even if the Wolverines finally won in 2011. Everyone on the OSU side considered that an exception, a result attributable more to a season of turmoil that produced an atypical 6-6 team than any change in the rivalry, and believed the Buckeyes' recent dominance would resume with Urban Meyer as OSU coach.

If it does, those little gold pants that Ohio State players receive for winning the Michigan game may become worthless trinkets. They used to be as rare as gold doubloons. During the Tressel years, they seem like loose change. In 2010, fifth-year seniors had five pairs.

Back in the 1990s, there were lots of stories about how Ohio State fans took the game much more seriously than Michigan fans, and that still seems true. But the image some UM fans tried to peddle—that they're more sophisticated, that winning just isn't as important at Michigan as it is at OSU, etc.—got exposed when Carr came under intense fire for losing to Ohio State for the fourth year in a row in 2007 and was fired. Rich Rodriguez was hired away from West Virginia, and it became clear that having a Michigan man was no longer as important in Ann Arbor as winning.

That image took another hit when Michigan lineman Justin Boren, the son of a distinguished former UM linebacker, criticized the new coaching staff's methods and transferred to Ohio State. When Boren played his first game in Michigan Stadium as a Buckeye in 2009, those laid-back Michiganders were lying in wait for him.

He faced a storm of expletives and some trash-talking from his former teammates on the other side of the line. A lady in the stands behind the south end zone held an anti-Boren sign that was a takeoff on the popular Jason Bourne movies:

*Matt Damon's Latest Film Trilogy:*
*The Boren Quitter*
*The Boren Traitor*
*The Boren Loser*

As Boren left the field and headed up the ramp toward the locker room after OSU's 21–10 win, a Michigan fan was leaning on a rail waiting for him. The fan's face was as red as brake lights. He snorted and steamed and unleashed a firestorm of obscenities at the former Wolverines player with an intensity that was almost frightening.

"I don't know [how to explain it]," Boren said. "It's an intense rivalry. I grew up a Michigan fan in a Michigan family. I knew about the rivalry. I guess some people take it pretty serious."

Take, not took. Rodriguez was fired after a three-year run that included 42–7, 21–10, and 37–7 losses to the Buckeyes, and that last one may have sealed his fate. It was clear from the lack of enthusiasm in Ohio Stadium that day that this wasn't your father's Ohio State–Michigan game, nor even a third cousin to the one that rose to unprecedented heights in 2006, when the game matched the No. 1 and 2 teams in the nation and some fans even demanded a rematch in the national championship game. If Woody and Bo had come back for the 2010 game, they might not have even recognized this abomination.

While standing on the sidelines near the end of the game, a local radio reporter who unabashedly admits his love for the Buckeyes looked at me with a long face and uttered a phrase I never thought I would hear after a win over Michigan: "This is no fun."

Rodriguez certainly wasn't all to blame. The rivalry's illness could probably be attributed to a combination of things: Rodriguez's struggles as a non-Michigan man, Tressel's successes (he was also 6-1 against Carr's teams), former OSU Heisman Trophy winner Troy Smith's natural talents as a Michigan killer, and maybe even the law of averages.

When Tressel was asked afterward if Ohio State and the Big Ten needed Michigan to return to its spot among the nation's elite programs, he did a deft verbal dance around the edges of the topic. He seemed like a guy who didn't want to see his coaching counterpart fired, in part because he's a peer and he feels some empathy for him, and in part because Rodriguez's successor might present a more formidable challenge.

"Michigan is among the elite programs and will be, and their record will reflect that in the course of time," Tressel said. "But you know we all have our ups and downs and periods and so forth. [The Big Ten is] highly competitive, [and] it's going to become more competitive because we're adding Nebraska. The world changed when we added Penn State, the world changes even more when we add Nebraska. The world got tougher when Dino [former OSU defensive coordinator Mark Dantonio] went over to Michigan State. It constantly changes. But Michigan will be back. You don't have to worry about that."

Hoke's hiring in 2011 gave Michigan hope. Tressel's forced resignation on Memorial Day 2011—for not reporting his knowledge of NCAA violations by his players—added to it. But after Hoke's Wolverines beat Ohio State in his first season, Michigan lost the next three, and Harbaugh replaced him. Harbaugh's five straight losses to OSU put another dent in the rivalry, but the Big Ten itself had already delivered what seems like an even bigger blow. When it created a conference championship game in 2011, it put a higher-stakes game on the schedule behind an OSU–Michigan game that usually determined the champion in the final game of the regular season. Bringing the rivalry all the way back from that shot may take more than parity.

# 15

# The Cogs

One day in the late 1970s, a feeble old man stopped by the old North Facility, the football practice complex that was later expanded into the larger Woody Hayes Athletic Center. If he had come to hand out $20 bills he couldn't have been greeted with any bigger smiles. Everyone who saw him treated him like royalty, treated him with a deference that seemed a little too strange to me at the time. But the old guy *was* royalty, Ohio State football royalty. Ernie Godfrey had probably done more for the OSU program than just about anyone, dead or alive.

When I learned he was a former OSU assistant coach, I vaguely remember wondering why that was such a big deal. There were probably enough former OSU assistant coaches out there to start their own university. If Gary Tranquill or Joe Bugel came back, would they be treated this way? Even when I learned that the Columbus chapter of the National Football Foundation was named for Godfrey, it probably didn't register with me.

This old guy used to be an assistant, huh? So?

The problem with youth is that you don't know what you don't know. Those who knew Godfrey knew where he had been and what he had done, knew what he had meant to the program. If Godfrey had pushed for it, he might have been the Buckeyes' head coach at some point—other major schools tried to hire him over the years—but he didn't and he wasn't. Yet in many ways, he had a much bigger impact on the program than he might have had as the head man.

Godfrey was one of the cogs that had made Ohio State football what it was then and what it is now. Every successful program has cogs like him, a small army of people in the background who have built and sustained it. Godfrey is probably the king in this category at OSU.

He was an Ohio State assistant for thirty-three years, under seven head coaches. After playing end and center at OSU from 1912 to 1914, first for John Richards and then for Jack Wilce, he served as a successful head coach at Wittenberg College in nearby Springfield, Ohio, for eleven years. He joined the OSU staff when Sam Willaman, one of his former teammates, took over for Wilce in 1929, and he was still there on Woody Hayes's staff in 1962. In that span, he worked for Willaman, Francis Schmidt, Paul Brown, Carroll Widdoes, Paul Bixler, Wes Fesler, and Hayes; when he retired, he had played or coached for every OSU coach since 1912. The fact so many new coaches kept him on when it came time to hire their own staff says something about what a valuable resource Godfrey was for the program.

There aren't enough words to describe all the jobs, great and small, that an assistant coach tackles in thirty-three years. Probably the best you can do is to say that he was on the scene day after day, year after year, decade after decade, coaching, recruiting (for many years, he was reputedly the best on the staff), philosophizing, lecturing, and counseling—in effect, doing all of the little tasks most of us never see.

It's not surprising that when old-time Buckeyes tell stories about their football days, Godfrey's name repeatedly comes up. In his book *You Win With People!*, Hayes wrote of how he had retained four coaches from Wes Fesler's staff:

> The oldest was Coach Ernie Godfrey who had been at Ohio State for many years and who is the greatest kicking coach in college or professional football. He was 58 when I came to Columbus and he retired from the staff in 1963 at the age of 70. Ernie worked as a defensive coach for three years, but in 1954 we made him freshman coach, and although he was a man 61 years old, he did an exceptional job with our freshmen. One year the Asian flu hit and since the freshm[e]n had not been inoculated, many of them came down with the flu. We couldn't take them to the infirmary because it was full, so we kept them in their respective dormitories. It was Coach

Godfrey who continually carried orange juice and toast to these young men to help them recover. Those men never forgot Ernie's thoughtfulness. To use an overworked phrase, he is a "true legend" at The Ohio State University.

In the book, Hayes mentions Godfrey's ability to coach kickers several times and with good reason: Jimmy Hague's field goal won the 1950 Rose Bowl, Don Sutherin's kick won the 1958 Rose Bowl, and John Stungis's famous "fifth quarter" field goal beat Illinois ten minutes after the game was thought to have ended in 1943.

But Godfrey was also memorialized in other places for his kicking insight. He helped to refine the kicking talents of an Ohio State freshman named Lou Groza in 1942; Groza kicked five field goals in the three games the freshman squad played, including a 48-yarder against Pittsburgh and a 25-yarder that nipped Michigan 15–14. But Groza was drafted into the service in the spring of 1943 and served in the South Pacific during World War II. When Groza got out, Paul Brown signed him to play for Cleveland. And when the Browns beat Los Angeles and won the 1950 NFL title 30–28 on a 23-yard field goal by Groza with 16 seconds remaining—his 16th field goal of the season—it was Ernie Godfrey whom Brown credited afterward.

"I would say . . ." Brown said, "that Ernie had a lot to do with Cleveland winning the championship."

Maybe Brown was overstating the case; Groza did play in the NFL for twenty-one years during a Hall of Fame career. Or maybe Brown was still grateful for the two field goals "The Toe" had kicked to beat the New York Giants in the Eastern Conference title game 8–3. Either way, it shows how much he valued Godfrey, a feeling shared by all of the coaches privileged to have had Godfrey on their staff.

He was a respected line coach when Francis Schmidt arrived at OSU, and there seems little doubt that Schmidt's "open game" could not have been as successful had Godfrey not been able to quickly absorb the intricacies of the linemen's assignments in the new offense and impart that to his players.

What's interesting about the Schmidt-Godfrey relationship is that they were almost complete opposites. Schmidt's profanity is legendary; Godfrey was deeply religious and never swore. Despite Godfrey's relatively quiet nature, his quotes are still remembered by some friends and teammates, in part because he was so excitable and sometimes erupted in unintentional malapropisms. Years later, his former players still smile about Godfrey expressions such as "scatter up in bunches" or "pair up in threes."

It's funny stuff, but the value of his wisdom wasn't loss on his bosses.

"Ernie Godfrey used to repeat many times: 'The greatest thing about a football team is graduation,'" Hayes wrote. "He would go on to say that time after time with three years on the varsity team a man started to become complacent and should graduate and move on, for that was the purpose for which he came to college. Also, he pointed out, this gave the younger players the incentive to move up."

Godfrey worked on the same staffs with other cogs, notably Esco Sarkkinen and Harry Strobel. "Sark" was on the OSU coaching staff from 1946 to 1977 after playing end there from 1937 to 1939 and earning all-American honors his senior year.

Strobel is remembered today mostly because he was one of the final four candidates for the head coach vacancy after Fesler was fired in 1950—the others being Paul Brown, Chuck Mather of Massillon High School, and Hayes, then at Miami University. Strobel had joined Fesler's staff in 1949, after coaching Bellevue to the Class B state basketball title in 1945 and Barberton to the mythical 1947 state football title with a star lineman named Glenn "Bo" Schembechler.

"Harry had been considered seriously for the head coaching position in 1951, and it was a rather awkward situation for both of us," Hayes wrote. "[But] Harry became an extremely efficient guard and center coach. Most important, he understood me better than any coach on our staff. When I'd be uptight about something, he'd come up and put his hand on my arm and say, 'C'mon, Coach, now it really isn't that important, is it?' and we'd go on from there. He could quiet me down and understand my moods and tensions better than anyone else."

Strobel coached guards and centers for Hayes until diabetes forced him into retirement after the 1967 season. He then served as the school's assistant director of intramurals while in retirement until he died of a heart attack on November 28, 1971. He was sixty-three.

He wasn't forgotten though. When OSU great Jim Parker was chosen for the Pro Football Hall of Fame in 1973, he asked Hayes to formally introduce him during the induction ceremonies in Canton, Ohio. Woody agreed to do it but told Parker, "Jim, I know I'm second choice. If Coach Harry were alive, I know you'd want him to do the honors." Parker nodded. "You're right, Coach. If it wasn't for Harry Strobel, nobody would have ever heard of Jim Parker."

Sarkkinen is more familiar to most current fans than Strobel, if only because he continued on the OSU staff through 1977 and remained a familiar face—and voice—in the Columbus area almost until he died at the age of seventy-nine on February 28, 1998. Sark was a news media favorite during Michigan week and whenever a reporter needed a good source for information on OSU football traditions and Woody Hayes.

Because he was with Hayes through all but the last year of his OSU coaching career—Sark retired in 1977, a year before Woody's infamous punch in the Gator Bowl—he came to be regarded as the consummate Hayes assistant. But like Francis Schmidt and Ernie Godfrey, Sark and Woody were as unlike as two guys could be. Sark was always upbeat and positive and never blew up at his players in front of their teammates.

In William L. Harper's 2000 book, *An Ohio State Man: Coach Esco Sarkkinen Remembers OSU Football*, he quoted several of his former players on that topic and their descriptions of his style are unanimous.

"Sark had one quality that everyone who played under him appreciated," former player Tom Marendt told Harper. "Whenever you goofed up, he never corrected or criticized you in front of the other players. He would take you off to the side for privacy. Coach was not a wimp. He could be very demanding and wouldn't hesitate to get in your face—but never within earshot of your fellow team members. This considerate kind of one-on-one coaching was rare and all of us appreciated it."

Like Godfrey, Sark also had opportunities to become a head coach elsewhere and never did, preferring life as OSU assistant to the limelight somewhere else. He was as good a scout as there was—we'll never know how many of the Buckeyes' biggest victories over the years would have been losses without Sark's detailed scouting reports—and his willingness to do that work also says much about his willingness to subvert his own desires and ambitions for the good of the team. For most of his time as an OSU coach, he seldom saw the Buckeyes play; he would coach the players during the week and then scout the following week's opponent on Saturdays.

One of the players Sark coached at defensive end in the spring of 1971 became an Ohio State cog in his own right. Fred Pagac moved to tight end and played briefly for the Chicago Bears and the Tampa Bay Buccaneers. After his pro career ended, he returned to OSU as a coach in 1978. He coached linebackers until 1995, then became defensive coordinator and eventually assistant head coach under John Cooper. He left in 2000 when Cooper was fired, and he was an unsuccessful candidate for the head coaching position that went to Jim Tressel.

Only Godfrey, Strobel, and Sarkkinen served on the OSU staff longer than Pagac, who was hired by the Oakland Raiders as linebackers coach in 2001. After three seasons in Oakland and two in Kansas City, he moved to the Minnesota Vikings and became the team's defensive coordinator in the 2010–11 season. His input at OSU didn't end when he left though. His son, Fred Pagac Jr., also played at OSU and was a graduate assistant coach on Tressel's staff.

Not all cogs got that way because of longevity; these are just the easiest ones to identify. Aside from the four already mentioned, seven other assistants—Grant Ward, Clarence MacDonald, Lyal Clark, Gene Fekete, Bill Conley, Tim Spencer and Jim Heacock—spent ten or more years on the OSU staff. Luke Fickell, an OSU assistant for nine years before serving a year as head coach after Tressel resigned, was named co-defensive coordinator after Urban Meyer was hired to succeed him. And although assistant coaches are involved with the team's day-to-day operation as much as anyone, you don't have to coach to be a vital element to the program.

For years, no one was more familiar to OSU football fans than Tony Aquila, the legendary Ohio Stadium groundskeeper. Born in Italy, Aquila worked as a ditchdigger and stonecutter in several European countries before he came to America in 1901. He bounced from city to city before landing in Columbus in 1906, which proved to be perfect timing. Jimmie Kelly, the groundskeeper at University Field, was retiring, and the school offered Tony $40 a month to maintain the athletic grounds. Aquila's first job was to dig ditches and install drainage tiles beneath the playing surface, so his experience probably had something to do with his hiring.

It wasn't long before he was a familiar figure on campus. University Field grew into Ohio Field and Tony was there. Ohio Field gave way to Ohio Stadium and Tony was there. He named his first son Chic Harley Aquila while Harley was playing at OSU and named another son Navy Aquila to honor OSU player Harold "Hap" Courtney, who was killed during World War I while serving in the navy. He named a third son Robert Watts Aquila, because he was born when "Fighting Bob" Watts was OSU's biggest star.

Students, faculty, and fans loved to hear some of Tony's time-worn tales, always relayed through a thick Italian accent, like the time he told Harley to take a truckload of garbage that had been removed from the field somewhere to burn it.

"The truck, she was old and wouldn't start," Tony said. "Chic, I say, dump the stuff and then drive away before you start the fire. That crazy Chic forgot. He set the fire to the truck because she wouldn't start and I say, 'Aw heck, it'sa old truck anyhow.'"

He failed the citizenship test twice because he had trouble memorizing the names of the presidents, historical dates, and the states and their capitals, but finally passed it in 1931.

"I got it right, now," he said at the Columbus Federal Building afterward. "The Revolutionary War was from 1775 to 1883."

His job grew to include practice fields, the Fairgrounds Coliseum (where the basketball team played), and even the Scarlet and Gray golf course, but he devoted most of his time to football. When his wife, Pasquilina, died in 1944, he moved into Ohio Stadium.

He was supposed to retire at age seventy, the state's manadory retirement age for university employees, but the OSU trustees extended his employment another year so he could go out with retiring athletic director Lynn St. John in 1947. Over 500 people turned out for a testimonial to him on February 27, 1947, at the Neil House, across the street from the state capitol.

"Ima proud," he said, before launching into some of the tales he had become known for, including all of his problems passing the citizenship test.

"Dey ask me da capital of Utah, I say Salt Lake City," he said. "Dey ask me da capital of Wisconsin, I say Madison. Dat was pretty good . . . but den de ask me da capital of Ohio and I say 'Cleveland.' Datsa no good."

Aquila's successors as groundskeepers weren't as colorful as Tony—not many are—but Ralph Guarasci and Mike Dolan both were important cogs to the OSU football program, even though their jobs continued to expand until that was just a small part of it. And no could have more closely associated with the program than Dr. Bob Murphy, the OSU team physician from 1952 to 1993. "Dr. Bob," as he was known to nearly everyone, was a familiar face at the old North Facility and in the OSU locker room, and his opinion was respected by everyone, including Woody Hayes. His name also comes up frequently when old players are reminiscing about the past, including stories about the day when Woody finally gave in and wore a jacket on a bitterly cold afternoon instead of trying to prove a point in his trademark white short-sleeved shirts.

Hayes had disappeared that game day in 1969 when the Buckeyes exited the locker room. All-American defensive tackle Jim Stillwagon remembered thinking how weird that was.

"We were down in one big area and everybody was getting ready to roll, and Woody was late and he was never late," Stillwagon said. "He was always punctual, and he would go [off] on you if you weren't punctual."

When Woody finally showed, the players were stunned.

"He comes out wearing a red coat, and it was like those old E. F. Hutton commercials. Silence," Stillwagon said. "Well, he knows what we're thinking, 'The old man's got a coat on,' so he yells, 'OK, let's get this out of the way. I talked to Dr. Bob and he said for me to be a better coach today, I should wear a coat. And that's all about that, and I don't want to hear anything more about it.'"

No one but Dr. Bob probably could have told Hayes to do that without receiving a punch in the gut or a few choice expletives to the face.

Not even Sark.

# 16

# The Hero

When Florida quarterback Tim Tebow won the Heisman Trophy in December 2007, much of Ohio emitted a collective gasp. It wasn't so much because Tebow had helped administer a 41–14 shot to the Buckeyes in the BCS National Championship Game the previous January, but because he was only a sophomore. It meant he might have two more chances to win another Heisman, and even casual Ohio State fans understood the threat: it jeopardized Archie Griffin's status as the only two-time Heisman winner. Some fans regarded this with the same concern and urgency as a physical threat to their family.

Tebow didn't win it again, of course, but the stress didn't stop. Oklahoma sophomore quarterback Sam Bradford won in 2008, only his threat fizzled when his junior season was cut short by injury in 2009 and he decided to enter the 2010 NFL draft. But the 2009 winner, Alabama running back Mark Ingram, was also a sophomore, so the Ohio State fans who cared deeply about this again faced a threatening scenario. But like Tebow and Bradford, Ingram didn't win it as a junior in 2010; he underwent minor knee surgery the week before the Tide's season opener against San Diego State. Although he returned in the third game, he never made a serious bid to repeat. Auburn junior quarterback Cam Newton won it. Then at the end of the season both Ingram and Newton decided to enter the NFL draft early, removing any immediate assault on Griffin's status. All of those people who had been holding their breath for over three years—at least the ones who hadn't died from the lack of oxygen—could finally breathe normally again.

The angst some fans feel over this has always seemed silly to me. Having another two-time winner won't diminish Griffin's accomplishment. He will always be the first, which isn't all that bad if you think if about it. Yet some fans still fret over the possibility that Archie will lose his exclusive status. For thirty-seven years, one succinct phrase—"the only two-time Heisman Trophy winner"—has been attached to Griffin like a shirt with a severe case of static cling.

I've often wondered what it must be like to have even a complimentary phrase hung onto you like that, what it must be like to return a box of wrong-sized nails at the Home Depot and have the clerk look at your credit card and utter those fateful words: "Say, aren't you college football's only two-time Heisman Trophy winner?"

But then anyone who knows Archie—most fans refer to him by first name only, just like Woody—realizes this wouldn't bother him. He is always grateful for the recognition and appreciative of who he is, even if his unique status usually seems more important to much of the Buckeye Nation than it is to him.

Yet to some OSU fans, the thought of having another player win two Heismans must be frightening. In their minds, having the only two-time Heisman Trophy winner is an important part of the Ohio State legacy, one of those things that sets the program apart. When Tebow won his Heisman, I considered calling Griffin for his reaction, but it seemed both a waste of time and potentially insulting to him. The only two-time Heisman Trophy winner (oops, there it is again) is a humble guy, one who wouldn't give two seconds of thought to what it means to have a sophomore win the trophy for the first time. Besides, whenever somebody wins a second one, and it's bound to happen sooner or later, Griffin will be the first to congratulate him. It won't be a formality, either. His good wishes to the second two-time winner will be sincere.

One thing definitely won't change if and when it happens: Archie Griffin's status as Ohio State's biggest football hero. Having two Heismans doubtless has something to do with that, although anyone who has ever met him knows there's a lot more to it than a couple of huge chunks of bronze modeled after a 1934 star player of the now-defunct New York University football team. Woody Hayes's famous quote about Griffin, that "he's a better person than he is a football player, and he's the best football player I've ever seen" bears repeating, because it still says a lot about who he is. Thirty-seven years after his collegiate playing career ended, Griffin is still defined by his humility. Because of his numerous acts of public service and his friendly, self-effacing manner, he is probably even more popular with Ohio State football fans today than he was when he played.

When one of my sons was in the second grade, he came home one day excited about the fact that Archie had spoken at his school. I asked what he had talked about, thinking the boy would tell me about his Heisman trophies, and he surprised me with his answer.

"The three Ds," the seven-year-old said. "Desire, dedication, and determination."

My jaw must have hit the floor. I later asked his teacher what occasion had brought Archie there and she said there wasn't one. The school had asked him if he would speak to the students and said he had readily agreed.

Do an Internet search on recent news stories about him and the results are littered with reports about his numerous appearances at charity events. He read Dr. Seuss's *Green Eggs and Ham* at a "Breakfast for Books" events. He participated in an auction for the Children's Tumor Foundation and Neurofibromatosis research. He helped entice a new airline to Columbus, to help improve the city's air service. He and Jim Tressel campaigned for the passage of a much-needed Columbus public school levy. (Needless to say, it passed.) He hosted a charity golf classic in Florida to benefit the Boys and Girls Clubs of Sarasota County.

He always seems to be doing something to help, and many people have noticed. In March 2010, Ohio State opened a luxurious, new $118 million student union, which included a grand ballroom named after Griffin. A couple who asked that their names not be used donated $1 million to have the room named in his honor, and also pledged $1 million to create an endowment fund for the Ohio State Alumni Association, which Griffin leads. The donors asked the university not to use their names because they wanted to ensure that the focus remained on Griffin, even though it could be argued that if anyone doesn't need the focus, it is him.

His name is everywhere—with that of Illinois star Red Grange on the Big Ten football MVP trophy, on the media suite at the Woody Hayes Athletic Complex, on an award given to OSU's offensive player of the year, on the football field at Eastmoor Academy where he played high school football, and so on. And whenever he attends a charity function or lends his hand for a good cause, news photographers insist that he be in their pictures. It's a good way to make sure they are published.

Ohio State and Ohio Wesleyan officials unveiled a plaque on the site of the first Ohio State football game on the Ohio Wesleyan campus in Delaware in May 2008, and Griffin spoke that day. At his introduction, a crowd of about a thousand cheered him wildly, far eclipsing the cheers for Tressel, OSU athletic director Gene Smith, and other dignitaries. A mob of autograph seekers and well-wishers swamped him after the ceremony ended, and I remember thinking he had made an excellent choice when he elected not to go into coaching or even pursue the OSU athletic director's job that he coveted for many years after his nine-year pro football career with the Cincinnati Bengals ended.

Heroes can quickly lose their luster when they go into coaching; the guy everyone cheered as a player quickly becomes the dope who should have gone for it on fourth down. Remember three-time All-American/football idol Wes Fesler? OSU fans couldn't wait to run "Coach" Fesler out of town. Even athletic directors can find themselves living on the wrong side of public opinion when they advocate raising ticket prices or defend an embattled coach the masses want to see fired.

Griffin traveled that road for a while. He became a special assistant to OSU athletic director Jim Jones in 1985 and received a promotion to assistant athletic director in charge of fund-raising, marketing, and promotions in 1987. When Jones retired in 1994, Griffin made a bid for the top position and didn't get it, but became associate athletic director, second in command under Andy Geiger.

He seemed like a natural for the job when Geiger retired, but before that happened, the OSU Alumni Association named Griffin president and CEO in 2003. It proved to be the perfect fit for him. He served on the search committee to find Geiger's replacement—he took himself out of the running as soon as Geiger announced he was quitting—and happily went about his business, making speeches, giving advice, and being the gracious hero he has always been.

His incredible career as an Ohio State running back seems almost secondary now, although obviously it isn't. His story has been told and retold many times, how he was born at the Ohio State University Hospital and grew up as an OSU fan in Columbus, but initially thought he would go to either the U.S. Naval Academy or Northwestern. He was on the small side, and at 5 foot 10, 185 pounds, he didn't think OSU was interested. Then Woody Hayes called one day and that sealed it.

The NCAA made freshmen eligible for the first time in 1972, the first clue that fate was on his side. Archie got in for one play in the opener against Iowa, fumbled and feared he might not get another chance, at least for a while. He might have been right if running backs coach Rudy Hubbard hadn't lobbied hard to get Woody to use him. He practiced with the scout team all week and didn't think he would play against North Carolina. The Tar Heels were ahead 7–0 midway through the first quarter when he heard his name called, and when the game ended he had carried 27 times for a school record 239 yards. The Buckeyes won 29–14 and Archie Griffin was an unlikely hero. That adjective would never be paired with the word "hero" when used to describe him again.

"I have never been for or against the freshman rule," Hayes said, afterward. "But Archie tends to make me change my mind."

Griffin always said that he didn't remember much about that day, comparing it to "an out of body experience." But there was plenty to remember from that point forward: His incredible career included 31 consecutive games of 100 yards rushing, a then NCAA record 5,177 rushing yards, and yes, those two Heisman trophies. Almost forgotten today is that he finished fifth in the Heisman voting as a sophomore, with teammates John Hicks second and Randy Gradishar sixth. If the vote hadn't been split among the three Buckeyes—that is, if any one had received all those votes—they would have finished ahead of the winner, Penn State's John Cappelletti.

Amazingly, the team's success eclipsed Archie's personal success during those years. The Buckeyes went 40-5 during his career and came within one game of finishing No. 1 during each of his final three seasons, a 10–10 tie with Michigan as a sophomore, an 18–17 loss to USC in the Rose Bowl as a junior, and a 23–10 loss to UCLA in the Rose Bowl as a senior. In the latter case, the Buckeyes had beaten the Bruins during the regular season.

"That's the one regret that I have, that we didn't win the national championship," he said.

But that has had no effect on his status as the program's biggest hero, and it shouldn't.

In February 2008, the *Columbus Dispatch* asked its young readers to share stories about their black role models in honor of Black History Month, and one from twelve-year-old Kent Ford said much more about Archie than any national championship could:

"My role model is Archie Griffin. I have met Archie several times, and each time he has encouraged me to be a better person. He also helped give me more self-confidence in sports with his saying, 'It's not the size of the dog in the fight, it's the size of the fight in the dog.' This inspired me because I am short, but like sports. Thank you, Archie Griffin."

The silly kid didn't even mention that he is the *only* two-time winner of the Heisman.

# 17

# Brother Earle

An encounter with Earle Bruce on the morning of the 1979 Ohio State–Michigan game is an indelible memory. The first-year Ohio State coach was standing in the lobby of the team's Ann Arbor hotel, much the way a nuclear power plant stands there generating electricity. The hair on my arms stood up. You could feel the energy from ten feet away.

I spoke to him a few minutes and saw something in his eyes I had never seen before. I felt the heat emanating from his body, and I quickly departed for my own safety. It occurred to me this might be one of those rare cases of spontaneous human combustion—Bruce was so revved up, he seemed likely to explode.

Today, I realize this is just the way he is; thirty-three years later, his body is still intact. But I also know that what I saw in his eyes was the essence of one of sport's fiercest rivalries, animus gleaned directly from Woody Hayes. After that, it never seemed a coincidence that Bruce's team won more than he lost against Michigan—his teams were 5-4—or that Jim Tressel, Bruce's former assistant, also had the Wolverines' number. The coaching blood-lines from Woody to Earle to Tressel to Urban Meyer are undeniable, even if the naked eye can't detect even one emotional outburst, ripped baseball cap, or broken sideline marker.

If Hayes taught Bruce anything, if Bruce taught Tressel and Meyer anything, it was this: "[Ohio State–Michigan] is the game," Bruce said. "Anybody who has been associated with Ohio State football would have to know the importance of this football game. And it is the game, it is the big game, and sometimes people say it is the only game. I don't believe that because you've got to play 10 or 11 others, but it is doggoned important.

It lets you walk the main streets of Columbus, Ohio. If you lose, you go to the alleys, buddy."

Bruce has walked those alleys, but he has also been feted by the College Football Hall of Fame. A guy who was once maligned by fans for a string of six consecutive 9-3 records—think about *that* for a moment—has become one of the program's most beloved figures. There is irony in the fact that when Bruce was fired in 1987 after nine years as Ohio State's head coach and Hayes's successor, school officials saw him as dull and lacking in pizzazz. Since then, he has become an outspoken commentator for Columbus' radio station WTVN, a colorful storyteller, and a prime source for countless news stories about OSU football, past and present.

When he was inducted into the college hall in 2002, it was hard not to wonder about all of the critics who were sure he had undergone a frontal lobotomy before he started coaching. For any coach with the words "Ohio State" on his resume, that group always numbers in the tens of thousands.

"My first loss in [Ohio] Stadium, we got beat by UCLA 17–0," Bruce said. "I come walking off the field with two policemen, and there was this guy running along the east side of the stadium, yelling all kinds of things. It was like he was out of his mind, and he was yelling at me. And one of the policeman looked at me and said, 'I believe if he had a gun, he'd shoot you.'"

Bruce laughs about that now. Wherever that lunatic is today, he isn't in the Hall of Fame. Bruce is. Vindication is too strong a word to describe what has happened to him since his coaching days ended. He didn't need the Hall of Fame or a microphone to validate his abilities, especially when history has already done it.

By the time Bruce was fired by then OSU president Edward Jennings in 1987 after nine years as coach, he had endured his share of heat, especially during that last unlucky season when an injury-weakened team was headed for a 6-4-1 record.

Bruce didn't cut a sleek, dashing figure. He also wasn't glib enough or flashy enough to be wildly popular. So the OSU administration set out to find the anti-Bruce to right the program's perceived ills, to get a guy willing to go in a new direction, a guy unburdened with those stodgy OSU ties.

It's intriguing to see how things appear across the vast expanse of time. A lot of the things administrators liked about John Cooper in 1987, they didn't like about him later. Thirteen years later, administrators went looking for the anti-Cooper, who had been perceived to be the anti-Bruce. In Tressel, Ohio State came up with a guy who learned much of his football under Bruce, a guy whose football leanings were much more like Bruce's than most fans and reporters knew at the time. When it hired Meyer to replace Tressel, it found a coach who has called Bruce "second only to my father," one who started his college coaching career as a graduate assistant on Bruce's OSU staff in 1986.

Bruce was with Meyer when he suffered his meltdown at the Southeastern Conference championship game against Alabama in 2009.

"I was with him the night he broke down at dinner," Bruce said. "I said, 'What the hell is wrong with you? You're not thinking right. You're playing for the championship, and you're not even here.' That's not like him. He got stressed out."

When Meyer assembled his new staff, he hired Bruce's grandson, Zach Smith, as his receivers coach. Smith had been a graduate assistant coach on Meyer's staff at Florida and Meyer has known him all his life.

"A lot of people grow up watching players in the NFL and say, 'I want to be like Jerry Rice or Eddie George,'" Smith said. "I grew up saying I wanted to be like Earle Bruce."

Bruce, the dull conservative that the administration couldn't wait to replace, did have his moments, and some of them were as colorful as any in the program's long history. He came within one 83-yard, fourth quarter drive by USC in the 1980 Rose Bowl from an unbeaten season and a national championship in his first year as Ohio State's head coach. The Buckeyes led 16–10 when the Trojans started that drive with 5:21 to go; running back Charles White accounted for 65 of the 83 yards with runs of 32 and 33 yards and finished with 247 yards rushing for the game.

The critics started then—losing even once is unacceptable to some fans—so after Bruce fell into the habit of going 9-3, it was only natural that he would become a bigger and bigger idiot. It never fazed him, though.

"That's part of the game," Bruce said. "It is part of the game. I coached for 44 years. I found out real quick that some people are with you one week, against you the next week and with you the next.

"I coached at Massillon [Washington High School] for two years and I was 20-0. It's a good thing, too. They said if you lose a game, we're going to dump a load of garbage on your front yard. They always did that. First time you lose, they bring up a load of garbage. That's their way of telling us we don't like to lose. That catches your attention."

Six straight 9-3 seasons caught the fans' attention, but the string had to end in 1986 because the regular-season schedule included an extra game. The Buckeyes lost that one, a Kickoff Classic opener against No. 5 Alabama at the Meadowlands. They also lost at No. 17 Washington, and then won nine straight before losing at No. 6 Michigan to finish the regular seasons at, uh, 9-3.

The Buckeyes and Bruce were in a rut, and Earle decided to do something about it against No. 8 Texas A&M in the Cotton Bowl. An overweight Bruce had been stung by a *Columbus Dispatch* column by Mike Harden that described him as looking like "some character lined up for seconds at a fried-dough booth at the Ohio State Fair," and decided to change his image by donning a fedora and replacing his OSU golf shirt with a spiffy new suit. In a span of a few seconds, a frog became a prince and the school had another story for its football annals.

"I decided I was going to dress up, and the only person who really knew about it was my wife," Bruce said. "I had the manager take [the suit] into the dressing room. I came out in my regular gear, then went back in before we came out for the ballgame. And I went back into the coaches' room all by myself and changed clothes. And by that time, some of the coaches had already gone to the press box.

"So I came out and walked up and down in front of the team before the game, giving them my little pregame speech, and no one even looked at me like I [wore anything different]. I thought someone might say, 'Hey coach, what's going on?' Or, 'What the hell's this?' or, 'What are you doin'?' But no one said a word."

The OSU players admitted later that they had noticed but didn't want to make a big deal about it. Besides, they were preoccupied with a subtle makeover of their own, new red shoes from Nike. If the Buckeyes couldn't make a football statement against the heavily favored Aggies, they could at least make a fashion statement.

"I was kind of dejected, to tell you the truth," Bruce said. "The team goes out of the locker room, and I normally lead them out. I'm the first one out.

But I was so dejected that I sort of got in the middle of the pack and drifted to the rear. When I get out there, I thought 'Boy, this is terrible. Here I am all dressed up, and nobody even recognizes you.' . . . So I walked out on the field to yell something to the team, and [assistant coach] Tom Lichtenberg was up in the press box, and he said on the phone to the guys down on the field, 'Get that guy who's got the suit and the hat on off the field, will ya? What the heck's he doin'? He shouldn't even be out here. Get him off the field.' And they said 'Wait a minute, Tom. That's coach Bruce.'"

As it turned out, the game itself was every bit as memorable. After a devastating 26–24 loss to Michigan sealed when Matt Frantz narrowly missed a 45-yard field goal with 1:01 remaining, OSU's 28–12 win over the Aggies seemed more than a cosmetic altering of the Buckeyes' rut of six consecutive 9-3 seasons; it seemed like the precursor to a bright future. Chris Spielman, with an amazing 29 tackles against Michigan, had turned in another strong performance against A&M that included two pass interceptions. Nate Harris had six receptions for 105 yards and Cris Carter made four catches for 61 yards, a couple of which were spectacular. But by the following July, Carter was declared ineligible by the NCAA for accepting money from a sports agent and Harris was out of school, never to return. It was the beginning of a difficult season that would result in Bruce's termination before the Michigan game.

The Buckeyes had their troubles, including an embarrassing 31–10 home field loss to Indiana. But three straight losses, the third on a 28-yard, 4th-and-23, game-winning touchdown pass from Iowa quarterback Chuck Hartlieb to tight end Marv Cook with six seconds left, apparently gave OSU president Jennings the excuse he needed to fire the coach. For the first time since 1966, the Buckeyes had lost four games in the Big Ten.

Two days after Iowa's 29–27 win was in the books and a few hours after Bruce told reporters "I am staying" at his weekly news conference, OSU athletic director Rick Bay read a seventeen-line statement from Jennings announcing that Bruce had been fired with one year remaining on his contract. Bay, who had supported his coach despite mounting criticism, promptly resigned in protest of the move and called it "a dark day for Ohio State."

As it turned out, it was the beginning of Bruce's days as a much-beloved Ohio State icon. Firing a coach with the best record among Big Ten coaches

(80-26-1) since 1979 and one whose program had never had a hint of scandal was widely criticized as the classic example of all that was wrong with college sports. Students staged rallies in support of him, and even many of his critics switched sides and blasted Jennings and the administration for the move. Meanwhile, Bruce still had one game to coach against Michigan, a game suddenly awash in emotion.

The Ohio State players wore headbands emblazoned with "Earle" across the front, then overcame a 13–7 halftime deficit for a 23–20 victory at Michigan Stadium. In his final game as coach, a fist-waving Bruce was carried off the field by his jubilant players. He was wearing that trademark dark suit and fedora.

His popularity kept rising after that, even after Bruce filed a $7.4 million lawsuit against Jennings and the university for breach of contract and for making false statements about him. (The university settled out of court a week later, paying him $471,000 that amounted to eighteen months' salary, a retirement buyout, and outside income he would have received.)

It probably helped that new coach John Cooper didn't turn out to be the panacea for all of the program's ills and also had trouble beating Michigan, but Bruce somehow suddenly seemed more lovable and entertaining as the former OSU coach than he was when he had the job.

There was his rip-roaring senior tackle speech in 1996 that was so good that the Michigan players said that it fired *them* up.

"Mike DeBord, the Michigan offensive coordinator who coached for me at Colorado State, called me up and said, 'Coach, we listened to that [on TV] and that fired us up,'" Bruce said later. "I hated that. I wanted to punch him out, to tell you the truth."

There was all of that remarkable candor on the radio that he felt he could never display publicly as a coach.

"If Illinois scores at all," he said, one morning before the Illini played OSU in Ohio Stadium, "it will be late in the football game against the second or third team."

And then there was a two-year stint as head coach of the Arena Football League's Columbus Destroyers, when everybody got a chance to remember what it was like to have an intense, emotional coach pumping up his players with that loud, deep, booming voice, even during practice.

"Hey! No off sides! No more! Discipline . . . that's football!"

And. . .

"Nobody ends up on their back! Nobody *ever* ends up on their back!"

And. . .

"We don't want any glitches! We don't want any glitches!"

While it seemed familiar to some reporters, it invoked a huge grin and a head shake from Destroyers' assistant coach and former OSU offensive tackle and All-Pro Jim Lachey:

"Flashback City. . . Still stubborn and ornery as hell."

And popular as hell. For Bruce's first game as Destroyers' head coach, twenty-three grown men from the Blueberry Hill Sports Bar on Columbus' west side showed up in t-shirts and black fedoras. The t-shirts bore a cartoon drawing of Bruce in that dark suit and fedora he wore at the Cotton Bowl. They called themselves "Bruce's bunch" and professed to be huge Earle fans.

As amazing as that seems, Bruce knows that it is all part of coaching, especially at a win-everything, win-all-the-time place such as Ohio State. He remembers the airplanes with the "Good-bye Woody" banners that flew over the stadium. He knows it is always easier to profess love for a coach who's no longer coaching.

"When [Woody] was coaching, people always complained that three yards and a cloud of dust was the most boring thing in the world," Bruce said. "When Woody had a bad year, he was a terrible coach."

He laughed.

"I was here," he said. "I know. Woody became a successful coach thirty years after he was gone."

And Earle?

The former coach's popularity is probably at an all-time high.

# 18

# The Season

For the longest time, whenever an Ohio State football fan hit the reverse button, his memory stopped on 1968. That's where nirvana was. It was the Buckeyes' last national championship season and had become the standard for success.

For many, winning it all had gone from a goal to a dream to an obsession. Why hadn't a program they regarded as preeminent in college football been able to win the sport's biggest prize? Why had there been so many close calls without that final title-clinching victory? How could lower-profile football schools such as Brigham Young and Clemson have won national titles more recently than Ohio State, one of the nation's foremost football factories?

If you thought about this too much, it would drive you crazy, and many fans thought about it way too much. The longer the championship drought continued, the more maddening it became. The more maddening it became, the more it elevated that glorious 1968 season. Long before the Buckeyes finally ended the drought at thirty-four years in 2002, the 1968 season had become the most celebrated in the school's 120-year history with an organized football team. Whenever fans started talking Ohio State football success, 1968 was never far behind.

It indeed might be the greatest season in school history, although the gap between titles doubtless added to the infatuation. This isn't intended as a slight to the '68 team; the notion of a long drought adding to its stature was first advanced by one of its own. As the 12-0 Buckeyes prepared to take on Michigan in 2002, Larry Zelina spoke honestly about what a win and a subsequent Ohio State victory in the BCS national championship game would mean.

"It's been a good run for us," said Zelina, starting wingback on the '68 team. "Because we were the last, we have gotten a lot of attention over the years that we probably wouldn't have gotten if [the Buckeyes] had won another one in there somewhere. I really appreciate what you guys [in the news media] have done for us over the years. You've been good to us."

That conversation has stayed with me both because it was probably the last time I spoke with Zelina, a good guy who died of a heart attack in 2005, and because what he said made so much sense. There are many reasons for Ohio State fans to be infatuated with that 1968 campaign; it was a magical year with a loaded roster that included some of the most popular players in school history. But as Zelina said, the long national championship drought that followed almost surely was a factor. If one or more of those three Archie Griffin teams that finished one game from the national title in the early 1970s had won, maybe it would have taken on the mystic qualities that attached themselves to the '68 squad. If the 1979 team that lost the No. 1 ranking with a one-point loss in the 1980 Rose Bowl had won, maybe there wouldn't have been quite so many nostalgic trips back to the late 1960s.

There have been three books written about the 1968 season—one coauthored by Zelina in 1998—and hundreds of newspaper stories. The team's players have been popular on the rubber chicken circuit in Ohio and elsewhere; they are, after all, still regarded as some of the Buckeyes' biggest heroes. If you wanted to get some bodies into your new Columbus or Cleveland liver-and-onions restaurant, all you would have to do was run an ad announcing that Rex Kern or Jim Stillwagon would be there signing autographs for the opening. OSU fans, including the most devout liver haters, would storm the doors. They might even choke down a few bites if that were the price of a signature. Autographs of players from the '68 team are among the most prized by Buckeye fans.

More than any other, 1968 is *the* season in Ohio State football annals. Today's fans could probably name more of its players than any OSU team, with the possible exception of the 2002 title team and the current one. It's not all because of 1968 either; some of it is because the super sophomores of that year had an incredible three-year run. Many fans still lament that they weren't able to finish No. 1 all three years. It's the tip of the iceberg hiding all that frustration.

Memories of the loss to Michigan in 1969 when the Buckeyes were unbeaten, ranked No. 1, and seemingly headed for their second straight national title, are still as fresh—and as disgusting—as a bag of wet, smelly, bug-infested Wolverines. Any college football historian asked to rank the school's most devastating football losses would almost certainly put that 24–12 loss on top of the list.

"We had all these records," Stillwagon said. "All these things had been said about us. We had had such a great season, but that one game, it made a whole season seem like it was horseshit."

That devastating loss in 1969 is part of those '68 memories, as is the revenge the Buckeyes got by beating Michigan in 1970. They're hard to separate. The image of that group comprises a remarkable three-year period when those incredible sophomores won like crazy (27-2), grew into seniors, and finally graduated.

Many doubtless would still have beaten a mental path back there, no matter how many national titles had been won in the meantime. But there is no denying that as the years of almost-titles piled up, the angst in OSU fans grew. The one beacon in all that emotional fog was 1968, when there was no "almost" about it, when they were the best in the nation and everybody knew it.

Ironically, the Buckeyes sank to perhaps their lowest point during Woody Hayes's OSU tenure the year before. They had just struggled through a rare losing season when Kern, Stillwagon, Jack Tatum, and company arrived as freshmen. The team hadn't won a Big Ten title for five years. Five games into the '67 season, OSU was 2-3 overall and 1-2 in the conference. After a 17–13 loss to Illinois, the fans began calling for Hayes's firing. His staff, aware that the freshmen team had been regularly embarrassing the varsity in practice, suddenly realized the irony of the situation.

"We thought, 'My God, would we turn over something if we were fired,'" then assistant coach Earle Bruce recalled years later. "'Somebody's going to walk in here and be a national champion.'"

They might have, too. Even after winning the last four games of the '67 season to finish 6-3 overall and 5-2 in the league, the fourth place finish, coupled with the sixth-place standing in 1966, gave Woody his worst back-to-back finishes in his seventeen years as OSU's coach. The Buckeyes hadn't won a conference title in six years and hadn't been to the Rose Bowl in ten, a trend that had been accelerated by the Faculty Council's vote against sending the '61 Big Ten title team to Pasadena. That had also been the beginning of the slump, which is probably why Hayes and his staff survived. The administration knew it was partially to blame for the problem.

Stubborn as he could be, Woody realized he had to win and to do that he might have to change some things. After the '67 season ended, defensive coordinator Lou McCullough finally convinced him that he would have to spread his talent more evenly between offense and defense. Woody coached offense and he tended to hoard the best recruits for himself, a system that no longer seemed to be working. He reluctantly agreed to a draft of the wildly talented, soon-to-be-sophomore class, alternating between offense and defense. It was a radical departure from the past and it resulted in one pick that stung him deeply: Tatum, whom Woody coveted as a running back, ended up as a rover on defense.

Woody had always been against playing sophomores; his oft-repeated expression was that "you're bound to lose one game for every sophomore you start." He also knew that this group was different, and he probably never uttered those words again. Sixteen of the twenty-two starters on the '68 squad were sophomores, and they blended in with a small group of talented juniors (Jim Otis, Ted Provost) and seniors (Rufus Mayes, Dave Foley) to form a young but formidable team that still ranks among the best in college football history.

The familiar tales that have been told hundreds of times over the years started in the opener—a 35–14 win over Southern Methodist University. The Mustangs' Chuck Hixon completed 37 of 69 passes for 417 yards that day, but it was Kern who set the tone for an era. He remembered a conversation he had with Hayes during training camp, one where he was told that sometimes he would see things on the field that the coaches didn't and would have to go with his "gut reaction."

OSU was leading 20–7 just before halftime, and the Buckeyes had a 4th-and-10 near midfield. Hayes sent in the punter, and Kern—in the first game of his college career—waved him off, quickly huddled up his teammates, and called a play. It would be good to have a photo of Woody's reaction. Kern later admitted that he didn't go near Woody when the teams went to the locker room at halftime.

"In my perspective, and my teammates', we were one play from making something happen and blowing that team out," Kern recalled later. "We didn't need to kick. So I called a robust delay pass, and doggone it if they didn't cover the thing well. Nobody was open, I'm 5 to 7 yards deep, and the corner is blitzing me. I try to avoid him, but he hits me. I do a 360-degree pirouette, land on my feet, run for my life, and pick up the first down. The crowd just went nuts. That kind of set the tone for the class for the next three years."

Kern was injured early the next week against Oregon and senior Bill Long, the starter at quarterback in '67, struggled. In went sophomore Ron Maciejowski, who threw a 55-yard touchdown pass to sophomore Bruce Jankowski to ignite a 21–6 win.

If No. 1 Purdue hadn't been next on the schedule, that might have unleashed a flood of optimism. But the Boilermakers had Heisman Trophy candidate Leroy Keyes and quarterback Mike Phipps and had pounded the Buckeyes 41–6 in Ohio Stadium the season before.

This would be the game that gave everyone a peek at the success that lay ahead. After a scoreless first half, cornerback Provost intercepted a Phipps pass in the flat and returned it 35 yards for a 6–0 lead in the third quarter. Later in the quarter, Stillwagon, the nose guard, dropped to cover the tight end across the middle and intercepted another Phipps pass at the Purdue 28-yard line. Two plays after replacing an injured Kern, Long ran 14 yards for a touchdown. The Buckeyes, 13-point underdogs, emerged as 13–0 winners.

Tatum went into that game as an unknown and emerged as a star; he broke up five passes and shadowed Keyes, holding him to 19 yards rushing and 46 yards receiving. The Buckeyes' ball control strategy also helped; OSU out-gained Purdue 411 yards to 186. That gave birth to a memorable story *Sports Illustrated* printed about Hayes the following week, after the *SI* reporter wandered into an OSU locker room and saw a comment on the chalkboard he thought had been written by Woody: "Keep cool baby and run those fat tackles to death."

As scout team member Jim Conroy recalled later, it had actually been put there by scout team captain Horatius Greene after he gave a funny pregame speech to the backups in the *scout* team locker room.

"Horatio saw the article just before practice on Thursday while in the training room at the athletic facility and flipped," Conroy said, "thinking that Woody would find out who wrote the damn thing and throw the 'dumb bastard'—a Hayes staple, usually used in the plural—off the team. Horatio immediately sought out each of the [All You Others] and, with panic in his eyes and the threat of unleashing a wrath learned only on the streets of his hometown in New Jersey, swore us all to secrecy.

"In the usual prepractice team meeting that day, Coach Hayes went through his normal routine. He quoted some Emerson, screamed about how the bastards from 'up North' tried to break Hoppy's leg in the '54 game—unfortunately, none but the diehards among us knew who this 'Hoppy' guy was—and otherwise gave his usual insights into the world and a little, very little, about the upcoming opponent, Northwestern.

"Just when Horatio and his fellow AYO conspirators felt we had dodged a bullet, sure enough the Old Man made reference to the *Sports Illustrated* article, particularly the headline. All the AYOs cringed and waited for the interrogation to begin and wondered whether our bond of loyalty would survive coach's cross-examination. But Woody, with kind of a 'cat swallowing the canary' grin on his face, said something to the effect that 'although I don't remember writing anything on the blackboard about Purdue's fat tackles, I guess I must have, and anyway it was accurate, their tackles were fat and if Purdue doesn't like it then to hell with them.'"

There was no way to know exactly where this season was going, but this was the first real sign that it was going somewhere special. Were the Buckeyes really this good? Hayes was smug. Maybe they were.

The Buckeyes beat Northwestern 45–21 and then had a scare at Illinois, their first road game. They led the unbeaten Illini 24–0 at halftime before the home team rallied for three touchdowns and three two-point conversions to tie the score. In the closing minutes, Maciejowski and Zelina hooked up on a 44-yard pass play to the Illinois 2-yard line and Otis scored the TD for a 31–24 win.

It was one of three wins by seven points or fewer that season; the next week there was another, 25–20, over Michigan State. They won 43–8 at Wisconsin and at Iowa 33–27, sending them against Michigan in the horseshoe in a battle of unbeatens. Although the game was tied 14–14 at halftime,

The first Ohio State football game was played on a meadow just south of Delaware Run on the Ohio Wesleyan campus in Delaware, Ohio, on May 3, 1890. The site doesn't look much different today than it did then. *Courtesy of Lucy S. Wolfe*

John Sigrist is buried in a cemetery in Congress, Ohio, where his family lived. He shares a marker with his parents and two sisters. There is no mention of Ohio State or the football injury that killed him. *Courtesy of Lucy S. Wolfe*

Ohio Field was located west of High Street, south of Woodruff Avenue. This photo was taken on November 4, 1916, during the Buckeyes' homecoming game with Wisconsin, which OSU won 14–13. *Courtesy of Ohio State University photo archives*

OSU's 1916 team was undefeated in seven games and won the school's first Western Conference (which would eventually become the Big Ten) title. Back row (from left): William E. Cramer, Leon Friedman, A. T. Leonard, Harry Lapp, Bill Daugherty (manager), Earl Johnson, Clarence McDonald, Kelly Van Dyne, and B. E. Sullivan. Middle row: L. W. St. John (athletic director), Roy Kirk, Fred Norton, Howard Yerges, Chic Harley, Dick Boesel, Paul "Frosty" Hurm, Charles Daughters, Virgil Dreyer, Gordie Rhodes, and John W. Wilce (coach). Front row: Dwight Peabody, Howard G. Courtney, Harold J. Courtney, Irwin Turner, Frank "Swede" Sorenson (captain), Fritz Holtcamp, Charlie Seddon, Robert Karch, and Charles "Shifty" Bolen. *Courtesy of Ohio State University photo archives*

Chic Harley was the school's first great football star, a three-time All-American (1916–1917, 1919) who helped create the explosion of interest in Ohio State football and the need for Ohio Stadium. When the stadium opened in 1922, it was called the "house that Harley built." *Courtesy of* Columbus Dispatch

Chic Harley did it all—running, passing, kicking, and punting. He is shown here punting on **Ohio Field.** *Courtesy of* Columbus Dispatch

The public was asked to donate $1 million for the construction of Ohio Stadium, and the fund-raising campaign began in 1920 with a parade of more than 3,000 Ohio State students dressed in athletic garb down High Street to the Statehouse. Broad Street is in the background. The parade drew an estimated 100,000 spectators. *Courtesy of* Columbus Dispatch

OSU students play a pickup baseball game near the construction site of Ohio Stadium in May 1922. The first game was played against Ohio Wesleyan on October 7, just five months later. *Courtesy of* Columbus Dispatch

When Ohio Stadium expanded in 2000, a wall was built outside the original stadium walls in order to add more seats to C Deck. The rotunda at the north end is the only section or the original stadium visible from the outside. *Courtesy of Lucy S. Wolfe*

While Jack Wilce was coaching the Buckeyes from 1913 to 1928, he earned his medical degree. He practiced medicine when he quit after the 1928 season and served as the director of student health services at OSU from 1934 to 1958. *Courtesy of* Columbus Dispatch

Francis Schmidt was hailed as an offensive genius when he succeeded Sam Willaman as Ohio State's coach in 1934. His popularity soared when his teams beat Michigan four years in a row with scores of 38–0, 34–0, 21–0, and 21–0, but the Buckeyes lost to the Wolverines the next three seasons and he was fired. *Courtesy of* Columbus Dispatch

Francis Schmidt and his 1936 coaching staff, from left: Cookie Cunningham, Ernie Godfrey, Schmidt, Fritz Mackey, Ted Hieronymous, Howard "Red" Blair, and Floyd Stahl. Godfrey played at OSU from 1912 to 1914 and served on the football staff from 1929 to 1962. Stahl later became the school's head basketball coach and was an assistant athletic director. *Courtesy of* Columbus Dispatch

Francis Schmidt and his wife, Evelyn, lived in this house on 15th Avenue, a short walk east of campus. The attic served as the coach's office, a place where he drew many of his famous plays at all hours of the day and night. He often called down to his players from here, when he saw them pass by on the street. *Courtesy of Lucy S. Wolfe*

Paul Brown was hired out of Massillon High School in 1941 to succeed Francis Schmidt and won a national championship in 1942. He might have coached the rest of his career at Ohio State if World War II hadn't interrupted; he went into the service in 1944 and, when he returned, began a successful football career with the Cleveland Browns and Cincinnati Bengals that earned him a spot in the Pro Football Hall of Fame. *Courtesy of* Columbus Dispatch

The football is loose, and Michigan players and Ohio State players (in white helmets) go for it during the famous 1950 Snow Bowl game. The temperature was 10 degrees at kickoff and accounts place the wind gusts at 28 to 40 mph. All of the scores in Michigan's 9–3 victory were set up or accomplished by blocked punts. *Courtesy of* Columbus Dispatch

Wes Fesler was a three-time All-American end at Ohio State from 1928 to 1930 and became head coach in 1947. He coached the Buckeyes for four seasons but resigned after the Snow Bowl loss to Michigan in 1950. Just forty-seven days later, he was hired as head coach at Minnesota. *Courtesy of* Columbus Dispatch

ABOVE: Fans were asked to help remove the tarp from the field prior to the 1950 Snow Bowl game. The tarp was frozen to the field, and the ordeal took more than two hours to complete. *Courtesy of* Columbus Dispatch

LEFT: Bill Willis broke the football color barrier twice, both in college and in the pros. His number has been retired at OSU, and he is a member of the Pro Football Hall of Fame. *Courtesy of Ohio State University photo archives*

Bill Willis was a combination sprinter and lineman when he came to OSU. Willis weighed only 205 pounds, but Coach Paul Brown preferred speed over size and Willis rewarded him for it. Willis was named All-American in 1944. *Courtesy of Ohio State University photo archives*

Paul Brown once described Bill Willis (99) "as quick as a snake's fang," which an unidentified Iowa Seahawks ball-carrier (35) may have discovered himself in this 1943 photo. *Courtesy of Ohio State University photo archives*

Woody Hayes was a candidate for the OSU job but was still coach at Miami when the *Columbus Dispatch* published this photo on February 12, 1951. The caption that day read, "Hayes is making a study of game movies, a part of football coaching which he has developed to a fine art." *Courtesy of* Columbus Dispatch

Woody Hayes looks over a letter in 1956, his sixth year as Ohio State coach. *Courtesy of Arthur Greenspan*, Columbus Dispatch

Howard "Hopalong" Cassady was the school's third Heisman Trophy winner in 1955 and was inducted into the College Football Hall of Fame in 1979. He played pro football for nine seasons, seven of them for the Detroit Lions. He also played baseball at Ohio State and served as a coach for the International League's Columbus Clippers for many years. *Courtesy of Fred Shannon,* Columbus Dispatch

Woody Hayes and his staff met nearly every day in Ohio Stadium, although this scene in May 1956 was held in preparation for a football clinic and spring practice sessions. Back row (from left): Gene Fekete, Harry Strobel, and Clive Rush. Front row: Esco Sarkkinen, Ernie Godfrey, Lyal Clark, and Bill Hess. Hayes is seated at right, addressing the group. *Courtesy of* Columbus Dispatch

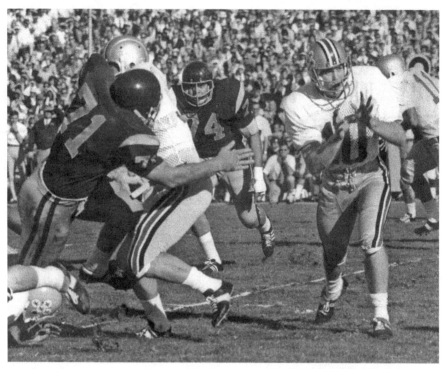

Rex Kern quarterbacked the 1968–1970 Buckeye teams that went 27-2, including an unbeaten season in 1968 that resulted in the national championship. He is shown here pitching out against Southern California in the 1969 Rose Bowl, which OSU won 27–16. *Courtesy of* Columbus Dispatch

Archie Griffin rushed for a then-NCAA-record 5,589 yards on 924 carries with the Buckeyes from 1972 to 1975. He won the Heisman Trophy in 1974 and 1975, becoming the only two-time winner. He rushed for at least 100 yards in thirty-four games, including an NCAA-record thirty-one consecutive games. Today, he is president and CEO of the Ohio State Alumni Association. *Courtesy of Ken Chamberlain,* Columbus Dispatch

Art Schlichter is Ohio State's career passing leader with 7,547 yards from 1978 to 1981, and was the fourth pick in the 1982 NFL draft. A gambling addiction cut short his NFL career, and he has been in and out of prison for various crimes related to it. *Courtesy of* Columbus Dispatch

Eddie George had 1,927 rushing yards in 1995 and won the Heisman Trophy. His 3,768 yards are second only to Archie Griffin (5,589) on the school's career rushing yards list. Here he is shown leaping over the line for a touchdown against Indiana in 1995. *Courtesy of Eric Albrecht*, Columbus Dispatch

Maurice Clarett burst onto the scene as a promising freshman in 2002 and helped lead the Buckeyes to the BCS national championship. He left school for the NFL after his freshman year even though there was a rule against it, sat out two seasons, and didn't make it in the NFL after he was eventually drafted. He served three and a half years in prison after being convicted of a robbery charge. *Courtesy of Mike Munden*, Columbus Dispatch

Bill Willis waves to the crowd after having his number (99) retired during a halftime presentation at the OSU-Wisconsin game on November 3, 2007. He died a few weeks later. *Courtesy of Neal C. Lauron*, Columbus Dispatch

the Buckeyes scored 36 points in the second half and won, 50–14. Otis rushed 34 times for 142 yards, Kern added 96 and Zelina 92 as the Buckeyes racked up a season-high 421. The defense forced five fumbles.

Another legend was born that day. When Otis scored the Buckeyes' final touchdown, Hayes supposedly elected to go for two and told reporters he did it "because I couldn't go for three," the ultimate show of his hatred for Michigan.

It's a great story, but it isn't true. Otis, who broke Hop Cassady's school record with his sixteenth touchdown of the season on the play before, ran off the field screaming, "Let's go for two." On the sidelines, Woody heard him and started screaming, "One, one, one!" and even held up one finger to make sure the players on the field got the message.

The players on the field weren't listening: they had their own problems. John Muhlbach was the snapper on extra points and he was hurt and out of the game. Jim Roman was the backup long-snapper but he was also the kicker. Maciejowski, who had kicked at Wisconsin, was on the sidelines. Long looked at Roman and said, "You can't snap it *and* kick it." Roman grinned. "Aw hell, let's go for it." And that's what they did, all the while assistant coach Bruce was screaming, "Don't go for two, don't go for two" from the sidelines, knowing that the Michigan players would never forget this.

Long tried a pass and it fell incomplete. The score remained at 50 and a legend was born. When Hayes was asked about it later, he said something about Muhlbach being injured and a mix-up on the field and changed the subject, nothing about wishing he could go for three. In some ways, the story of a kicker and a third-string quarterback deciding to go for two is even better.

While the win sent No. 2 Ohio State to the Rose Bowl for the first time in eleven years to face No. 1, defending national champion University of Southern California, there was more drama before the Buckeyes left for California. On the first day of bowl practice in French Field House, Woody had the heat jacked up to 90 degrees to get the players "acclimated to the weather" in L.A. He had them running and hitting and sweating in the sauna-like atmosphere, and he called to quarterbacks coach George Chaump to bring his players over and have them take a run at the blocking sled.

This is what is known as a bad idea. Kern was first, and when he rammed into the pads, he slumped to the ground.

"Oh, shit!" Hayes screamed. "Shit, shit, shit!"

Kern had dislocated his left shoulder and didn't work out again until the team arrived in California. It could have been disastrous—it could have been a coaching moment to put alongside Wes Fesler's decision to punt just before halftime during the 1950 Snow Bowl game—but amazingly, on game day, Kern was never better.

O. J. Simpson had an 80-yard touchdown and the Buckeyes fell behind 10–0 in the second quarter; Simpson would carry the ball 28 times for 171 yards and catch eight passes for 85. But the Buckeyes stormed back to tie the game at halftime. Otis capped a 69-yard drive with a 1-yard touchdown plunge, and Roman kicked a 16-yard field goal with three seconds left.

USC fumbled twice inside its 25-yard line in the third quarter, and Kern made them pay with touchdown passes of 4 yards to Leo Hayden and 16 yards to Ray Gillian, who caught 4 passes for 69 yards. Kern completed 9 of 15 passes for 101 yards and rushed for 35, and the Buckeyes won 27–16.

The players were chanting "Rose Bowl, Rose Bowl, Rose Bowl" in the locker room afterward when some of the players saw the door open and O. J. slip inside. The chanting stopped, the boisterous atmosphere suddenly replaced by hushed silence.

"You're the best fucking ball team in the country and don't let anybody tell you you aren't," Simpson said. "Congratulations!"

A few minutes later, the head of the Helms Foundation entered holding a silver trophy awarded to the game's most valuable player. He handed it to Kern, who held it up in the air and credited his teammates for making it happen.

"The greatest team in the country!" he shouted.

It may have even been the greatest in Ohio State history; if not, it is probably at least the most popular. The national championship started a love affair with moon-eyed fans that was still going strong more than forty years later, even after the Buckeyes' 2002 title win over Miami.

More has been written about the 1968 team than any team in any sport in school history and all of the attention is justified; this team was not only good, but captivating, the source of some of the program's best stories.

That doesn't change the fact that Zelina was right. It was *the* season, at least in part because the football-mad school went so many seasons without another national championship.

# 19

# The Survivor

The day a certain courageous Columbus sports columnist told one of his editors that he was going to write a column suggesting that John Cooper belonged in the College Football Hall of Fame, the editor erupted in laughter.

"Boy, you'll get some e-mail on that one," he said.

He was right, of course. That is what we in the journalism business call a hot-button issue, and that courageous columnist—all right, "reckless" might have been a better word to describe me—received a stream of angry rants from tortured souls I thought had long since either died, given up following football, or moved to New Zealand.

Oh, no. This was 2007, and seven years after he had lost his OSU job after thirteen seasons, these pitiless folks still wanted Cooper's hide.

*Hall of Fame? That man doesn't deserve to be in the Hall of Anything.*

Somehow, over the course of time the dumb columnist had forgotten: Cooper was evil reincarnate. He couldn't beat Michigan.

Cooper made the hall a year later, as he should have. He coached an impressive 193 victories in a twenty-four-year career, won nine conference championships, and coached in fourteen bowl games. He won 111 of those games in his thirteen years at Ohio State and landed shares of three Big Ten titles, a Rose Bowl win over Arizona State after the 1996 season, wins over Notre Dame in 1995 and 1996, and second-place finishes in the major polls in 1996 and 1998. But as has been chronicled more thoroughly than the life of Lincoln, he was 2-10-1 against Michigan, and everyone knows that no OSU coach before Cooper ever lost that consistently to the Wolverines and kept his job so long. Maybe that was even part of all that lingering animosity. Many people may have been miffed because Cooper was somehow able to cheat the system, that he made lots of money for doing a job that would have gotten him fired long ago.

Say this for Cooper. The man is a survivor. Only a survivor makes it thirteen years as Ohio State football coach. He was criticized and condemned, ridiculed and rebuked, scorned and scolded, berated and blamed. He was called an idiot and a fool, a moron and a dullard, a dimwit and a dolt, a dunce and a dummy. He was even asked, in descriptive ways that would never be approved by Amy Vanderbilt, to take his sorry, uh, act, to another state.

It takes a special guy to coach football at Ohio State. Yes, the OSU coach makes more money than your average brain surgeon, but he might have to deal with more daily stress. Brain surgery is life and death; a lot of Ohio State fans view their favorite football team in the same terms. Some fans probably would be more accepting of a surgical mistake than a loss to Michigan. Hey, priorities are priorities.

When Cooper made the Hall of Fame, my first thoughts were of days spent standing in front of Ohio Stadium's South Stands, waiting for the Buckeyes to come off the field at the conclusion of just about any OSU game as we media wretches prepared for the postgame interview session. The stuff some of the fans used to scream at Cooper as he passed by was brutal. Some of it would even make a grown man blush.

*"You should be fired, Cooper! Fired!"*

*"You suck, Cooper!"*

*"Resign. . . . Resign!"*

There are more, but many of them couldn't be printed in *Penthouse* magazine, let alone a respectable book or a family newspaper.

I used to tell friends about this, and the frequent refrain was "So what? I could listen to a few insults for a million dollars a year." But these were more than insults. There were murderous looks on some of those faces. This wasn't mere disappointment in losing games. What some of these screamers felt obviously approached hatred.

Why hate a friendly, accommodating guy who wanted to give the fans everything they wanted, even if he sometimes failed?

The record against Michigan was paramount, but there were other things. That unexpected loss to Michigan State in 1998 when the team seemed headed for a national championship was one. A subpar record in bowl games was another. An ill-advised hot tub commercial when he first took the job, his Tennessee background . . .

*For God's sake, the guy isn't even from Ohio. Did you ever hear him talk?*

Truth be told, that Tennessee background caused a lot of the anguish when he was hired in 1988 and continued to cause it until the day he stepped down. He was replacing Earle Bruce, a native Ohioan who had coached with Woody Hayes, who had replaced three-time OSU All-American Wes Fesler, who had replaced Ohio native Paul Bixler, who had . . . well, you get the idea.

Despite his successful head coaching career at Tulsa and Arizona State, Cooper was still an outsider. He grew up in Tennessee and played college football at Iowa State, and in the minds of his detractors, he clearly didn't understand the Ohio State–Michigan tradition.

The hot tub commercial got him in trouble because: a) he got a pile of money to leave Arizona State for OSU, and b) his team went 4-6-1 that first year, OSU's worst season since 1959. Fans don't like losing. They like it even less when they see their rich new coach repeatedly enjoying an energizing dip in a hot tub on television. He was immediately cast as a carpetbagger who was scooping up all the cash he could get his hands on when he should have been coaching.

School officials had to be stunned by these developments; in hiring Cooper, they had landed a coach who was a hot commodity in hiring circles, was seen as more colorful and media-friendly than Bruce, was an outstanding recruiter, wasn't wedded to the school's conservatism on offense, and whose ASU team had beaten Michigan in the '87 Rose Bowl.

All of that seemed to say that he was the perfect guy for the job, and he might have been if only he had been able to scare up a few more wins against Michigan. But when his teams lost to the Wolverines during his first four seasons at OSU, tied in 1992, and then lost again in 1993, all of the things about Cooper that seemed refreshing in the beginning became the reasons that he lost.

Closing practice wasn't Cooper's style. Michigan paranoia wasn't Cooper's style. Snapping at reporters wasn't Cooper's style. But when Cooper acted like Cooper, skeptics were sure that that was why OSU didn't beat Michigan. Woody used to beat Michigan regularly, and Woody's ways were different.

They said Cooper didn't know enough about the program's great tradition, so OSU officials tried to help him by turning a small family gathering called senior tackle into the biggest circus this side of Disney World. That didn't work, so Cooper closed senior tackle to the public and generated a storm of protest from those who said none of the previous coaches ever shut out the public. As usual, Cooper was caught in the middle, but because his teams had so much trouble beating Michigan, he was probably never afforded a chance to put his own twist on the school's tradition the way Jim Tressel did.

From 1993 to 1999, he fielded some of the most talented teams in school history and probably would have satisfied even his harshest critics were it not for a handful of ill-timed losses. A 28–0 loss to Michigan in 1993 when OSU was 9-0-1 and ranked No. 5 was a killer. So was a 13–9 loss to Michigan in 1996 when OSU was unbeaten and ranked No. 2 that may have cost him a national championship; the Buckeyes beat No. 4 Arizona State in the Rose Bowl and finished No. 2 nationally. That 28–24 loss to unranked Michigan State in Ohio Stadium in 1998 when the Buckeyes were unbeaten, ranked No. 1, and again looking like national champs is still stuck in the craw of some OSU fans, years later.

But that '96 loss to Michigan shows how different things might have been, were it not for a handful of plays he had no control over. The Buckeyes were up 9–0 at halftime and had 211 yards total offense to Michigan's 70. But on one play, Pepe Pearson made a great run down the sidelines only to be knocked out at the 4-yard line—if one of the OSU wide receivers had successfully executed a block on a defensive back who came from the other side of the field to make the play, the Buckeyes would have scored a touchdown there instead of a field goal. Then in the second half, All-American cornerback Shawn Springs lost his footing—the third overall pick in the 1997 NFL draft and a future All-Pro *slipped*—on a Brian Griese pass to Tai Streets in the second half and it turned into a 69-yard touchdown. The one thought that most OSU fans probably came away with from that game? That stupid Cooper lost to Michigan again.

But "it's the nature of the beast," as Cooper often said, and it must be noted that that game wasn't supposed to be decided by a play or two or even three. Ohio State was the clear favorite that day, just as it was on that fateful day in 1998 when it suffered that loss to Michigan State, which seemed almost shocking. That loss to the Spartans was probably the beginning of the end for Cooper, even though the Buckeyes rebounded with wins over Iowa and Michigan and then whipped No. 8 Texas A&M in the Sugar Bowl to finish No. 2 again.

Disaster was around the next corner. The team was 6-6 in 1999 and stumbled down the stretch in 2000 with a run of disciplinary, academic, and legal problems. After it was announced that the program was last in Big Ten graduation rates (28 percent), the 8-3 Buckeyes went to Tampa for the Outback Bowl and experienced a week that would make *The Jerry Springer Show* seem like reruns of *Ozzie and Harriet*. Wide receiver Reggie Germany was dropped from the team for failing to attend classes. Linebacker Matt Wilhelm questioned co-captain Ken-Yon Rambo's leadership. Offensive lineman Tyson Walter sued fellow lineman LeCharles Bentley for $50,000 for punching his lights out during one of the previous year's practices.

When you have a runaway freight train, you're not surprised when it has a cataclysmic crash, and that's what happened in the game. The heavily penalized, discipline-free Buckeyes were hammered 24–7 by South Carolina. The star of the game? Ryan Brewer, a former Ohio Mr. Football from Troy whom the Buckeyes didn't recruit because he was too small.

It was an embarrassing finish to an embarrassing month and Cooper was quickly fired, supposedly because of poor graduation rates and the other off-the-field problems. It wasn't because of losing, of course; it seldom is. But if Cooper had been able to beat Michigan a little more often, including the previous November, if he had beaten the Gamecocks in the Outback Bowl and hadn't accumulated a 3-8 record in all bowl games, it's doubtful those other problems would have loomed quite so large. If Cooper's Buckeyes had gone 12-0 or 11-1 in 2000 instead of 8-4, poor graduation rates probably would have been something for the OSU athletic council to debate when it wasn't raising ticket prices. As it was, it was the justification for his firing.

"The decision had been building, and the concerns had been there, for some time," OSU president William E. Kirwan said at the time. "I think Andy [Geiger] and I were looking to see what direction things would begin to move. I think it was Andy's assessment after the [Outback Bowl] that the events of the last three or four weeks had convinced him . . . that the situation was getting worse."

For a while Cooper was determined to get another job and those extra seven wins to reach the 200 mark. But after he talked to his younger brother, Frank, about it, he began to realize that 200 was only a number.

"He made a comment to me that was loud and clear, 'Big . . . deal,'" Cooper said in 2008. "He said, 'On your tombstone, all they'll have is, 'Here lies John Cooper—200 victories.' That put a stop to that. I decided to spend a little more time with my wife, my children, and my grandbabies."

Ironically, Cooper didn't move back to Tennessee or Arizona. He took a part-time consultant's job with the Cincinnati Bengals, did a little TV work, and settled in to a family-oriented retirement . . . in Columbus, the place where some at least had always treated him as an outsider.

He still regularly attends Ohio State games and sometimes seems an even more integral part of the OSU family than he did when he was coaching.

"Coach Cooper has been a tremendous part of our program," Tressel said. "He was one of the first ones when our staff got here to reach a hand out and say, 'What is it we can do to help? We're making Columbus our home. We're Buckeyes forever.' What a warm feeling that was for us."

Cooper's love for both the school and the city makes it seem all the more ironic that some fans are so unforgiving they still would like to tie him up and toss him in an empty boxcar on a freight train out of town.

Will that hostile crowd of Cooper bashers ever forgive him for going 2-10-1 against Michigan and not plucking a couple of ripe national titles? Probably not.

But here's the good news: the crowd seems to be getting smaller.

# 20

# Satans

Every generation of Ohio State players and fans has its own archenemies. In Chic Harley's day, it was Bob Fletcher, the brother of an injured Illinois place-kicker who spoiled the Buckeye All-American's near-perfect three-year run with the only field goal of his college career. In the pre–World War II era, it was Michigan's All-American Tom Harmon, who boldly scrawled his John Hancock all over a 40–0 rout of the Buckeyes in 1940. In the 1980s, it was Michigan quarterback Jim Harbaugh, who guaranteed an unlikely victory in 1986 . . . and delivered.

Harbaugh added a new element to the role that has been a characteristic of almost every anti-OSU villain since: the mouth. Since then most of the players whom the fans see as Satans have engaged in enough trash-talking to raise the intensity of hatred to new levels. The mouth can't be fatal—well, sometimes it seems *suicidal*—but it can sound like fingernails on a blackboard to those on the other side.

Buckeye fans in the 1940s respected Harmon, even though they hated what he did to them. Many OSU fans in the 1990s detested Charles Woodson. Most doubtless respected him, too, but they couldn't get over what he did, how he did it, and what he said about it afterward. To them, he was a poor winner and won the 1997 Heisman Trophy at their expense.

Woodson could do it all. He was a terrific cornerback, an excellent pass receiver, an amazing punt returner, and a talented blabbermouth.

Before the 1997 Ohio State–Michigan game, the Wolverine cornerback kept quiet. During the game, he prattled on like an auctioneer, jabbering at Buckeyes receiving star David Boston, who had been doing some talking of his own before the game.

Boston at times seemed more preoccupied with Woodson than winning, which from an OSU perspective made it seem that much worse.

"I was talking to [Boston] all day," Woodson said after the game. "For a guy like David Boston, who's not that great a receiver—he wasn't fast, he couldn't get through my jams—for him to come out this week and call me out and say he has played against better cornerbacks in practice, well . . . he hasn't. . . . And I just let him know that. I was in his chest all game."

Woodson may or may not have been the best college football player in the country that season—he sure got my Heisman vote—but during the Wolverines' 20–14 victory, he was definitely the best player in the game. He returned a punt 78 yards for a touchdown. He set up another touchdown with a 37-yard pass play. He intercepted a Stan Jackson pass in the end zone. He took Boston, who really was a heck of a receiver, out of the game except for one play. OSU quarterback Joe Germaine went 5 of 17 for 84 yards and was sacked five times; Stanley Jackson was 4 of 9 for 49 yards and two interceptions. That wasn't all Woodson, obviously, but he had earned his right to talk, as grating as it was for Buckeye fans to hear it.

"We rattled [Jackson] a little bit," Woodson said. "I just heard today that he called me out in the newspaper by saying I was good, but I wasn't that good. I don't know how he can say that when they don't trust him to play a full game."

Maybe you can see how this Woodson character earned a permanent place near the top of the OSU enemies list. He entered that game with an outside chance to win the Heisman and turned it into a personal highlight film that helped him become the favorite. He's also a bad memory for Buckeye fans for another reason: he's a native of Fremont, Ohio.

That is a common theme among many of the villains who played for Michigan: they left Ohio to play Up North. Desmond Howard, the 1991 Heisman Trophy winner, played high school ball at Cleveland St. Joseph's. Normally, that would be enough for an OSU fan to strike up a mild dislike for him, and that's probably all it would be if he hadn't run a punt back 93 yards for a touchdown against the Buckeyes in 1991 and struck the Heisman pose in the end zone. Howard accumulated 223 all-purpose yards that day, including pass receptions of 50 and 42 yards, in a 31–3 Michigan win that was OSU's worst loss in the series since 1946. But the pose created most of the animosity toward him. It was like a physical manifestation of trash talking, like spitting in his opponent's face.

If ability didn't factor into the equation, Marcus Ray might be near the top on the modern hate list because he a) was from Columbus, b) was on Michigan teams that beat OSU three out of four times, and c) probably talked about it as much as any player in Michigan history. When you combine the traitor factor with the big mouth factor, the hate factor goes through the ceiling. Ray played high school ball at Eastmoor, Archie Griffin's former school. And Ray was good—he was second-team all-American as a junior—he just wasn't as good as some of these other guys. Besides, talk doesn't hurt OSU fans as much as losing.

After the '97 game when Woodson wrapped up the Heisman, Ray wore a scarlet pullover with an Ohio State logo and the '97 Rose Bowl insignia to postgame interviews. He tried to claim that the "red was just for the roses" and that there was nothing more to it, which got a laugh from reporters who heard it. They knew that this was Ray's personal Heisman pose.

"I'm sure Coach [Lloyd] Carr will get on me for wearing it," Ray said, "but I'll just get up in the morning and do whatever punishment it takes because I'm so happy."

He said the pullover was a "gift" from former Ohio State defensive back Anthony Gwinn, who played in OSU's victory over Arizona State in the 1997 Rose Bowl.

"He gave this to me as a gift, as if to say, 'If you don't ever get one, you can have this one,'" Ray said. "It says, 'Ohio State, Rose Bowl 1997,' so I guess that means we beat Ohio State in 1997 to get to the Rose Bowl. At least that's the way I'm interpreting it."

In 2006, when Ray was back in Columbus and working for Columbus Public Schools (he lives in the Detroit area today), he told the *Columbus Dispatch* that "I love living here, but I hate Buckeye fans. It's just that I'm not a Buckeye fan. Every time I look up, everything they do is the greatest in the world. 'This is the greatest linebacker. He's the greatest.' It's all a hype machine. I can barely watch TV."

In 2008 when his brother, Youngstown State linebacker Roshon Simons, was about to open the season against Ohio State, Ray made a prediction in the hometown *Dispatch*:

"Friday, I'll let him breathe. Saturday, he should have about 15 tackles."

In its own way, it was an impressive performance. Ten years after his college career had ended, Ray was still doing a good job of getting on the Buckeyes' nerves.

Harbaugh did it with both his mouth and his talent. He rallied the Wolverines for a late touchdown and that 26–24 win he guaranteed in 1986, although OSU's Matt Frantz missed a 45-yard field goal with 1:01 left in the game that would have rendered it all meaningless. It has been so long ago now that he started to slide down the Buckeyes' enemies list. That started to change when Rich Rodriguez was fired in January 2011 and Harbaugh, then a successful coach at Stanford, looked like he might become the next Michigan coach. Some OSU fans were even fretting over the possibility. They knew that Harbaugh was not only a good coach, but he understood the rivalry as well as anyone out there; they were afraid that if he got the job, the Buckeyes' dominance in the series would finally end.

Harbaugh accepted the head coaching job with the San Francisco 49ers instead, and he went back to being just another jerk on the OSU enemies list. And honestly, he hasn't pricked the Buckeye Nation in recent years the way some of the other guys have. When asked about Ohio State in recent years, he has even said good things about the program on occasion.

"As a kid [growing up in Michigan] I put those guys up on a pedestal," Harbaugh once said, ticking off the names of Archie Griffin, Cornelius Greene, and Art Schlichter. "Those were the guys I picked to look up to."

He might have meant every word, but . . . skepticism of one's archenemies runs deep. As an ambitious coach who knows how quickly things can turn in any job, Harbaugh *might* have been merely trying to keep his options open. He is sharp enough to know Gary Moeller was an Ohio State cocaptain before he became head coach at Michigan. Hey, if it could happen at Michigan, it could happen at Ohio State. Not.

Some players make the enemies list based strictly on performance. Stanford quarterback Jim Plunkett (1971) and USC running backs Anthony Davis (1974) and Charles White (1980) all used big days to help snatch national titles from the Buckeyes in the Rose Bowl, but they somehow still don't seem quite as irritating as Michigan's Buckeye killers, of whom Harmon, Rick Leach, and Tshimanga Biakabutuka stand out.

Just the mention of Leach still makes some OSU fans retch. The Wolverines quarterback lost to the Buckeyes as a freshman in 1975 and then beat them three straight years, including Woody Hayes's last as coach. All three came with the Big Ten championship and a Rose Bowl berth on the line, which made Leach's sleight-of-hand performances as a triple-option artist all the more galling.

Leach didn't do anything off the field to make OSU fans hate him though. In 2003 he even admitted that he had become good friends with former Buckeye linebacker Tom Cousineau and had been rooting for Ohio State in its game against Purdue the week before its game with Michigan. He didn't want a loss to spoil what promised to be a huge game. While that may not be quite the same as simply rooting for the Buckeyes for their sake, it still says something about Leach's lack of animosity for his former rivals. Some of Woody's former players would rather spend the day locked in a dark closet than root for Michigan.

Harmon and Biakabutuka each had huge one-game performances against OSU. Harmon played a major role in wins over the Buckeyes in 1938, '39, and '40, but the 40–0 win over OSU in '40 is what old No. 98 is remembered for in Ohio: he scored three touchdowns, passed for two, kicked four extra points, rushed for 139 yards, passed for 151, averaged 50 yards on three punts, and returned three punts for 81 yards. In those days of two-way play, he also played an outstanding defensive game. A few weeks later, he won the Heisman Trophy.

Impressive as it was, those Buckeyes were 4-3 when Harmon nailed them. When Biakabutuka ran wild on the Buckeyes in 1995, they were unbeaten and ranked No. 2 in the nation. Michigan Stadium was supposed to be a place where the Buckeyes simply gassed up on the way to Pasadena. Biakabutuka turned it into a house of horrors. He ran and ran and *ran*, gaining more yards than any opposing runner in OSU football history— 313—and flattening the Buckeyes' national championship dreams as a freight train would a penny. It was a one-game monument to a Heisman candidacy that had been shoved into the background by a mediocre Michigan team and a string of injuries.

OSU's Eddie George entered that game as a leading candidate for the Heisman and he eventually won it. But his 104 yards on 21 carries, a solid five yards per carry, paled in comparison to Biakabutuka's remarkable performance: 105 yards on his first five carries, 195 yards at halftime, and 313 yards on 37 carries for the game, an 8.5-yard average.

If Biakabutuka didn't steal any of George's votes for the Heisman, he must have at least given undecided voters a few more factors to consider. The performance gave Biakabutuka a school-record 1,724 yards rushing for the season, still below George's OSU record of 1,826, but close enough for serious analysis.

"I don't even think about that," Biakabutuka said afterward. "I still think he's the best running back."

It's hard for most of us to work up a good hate for anyone that gracious; there is no such problem with former Michigan wide receiver Walter Smith. Smith may even rate higher than Biakabutuka on the fans' hate list, not because of talent or production but because of the sheer gall of what he said.

In 1994, the injured senior wideout went to the Wolverines' Ohio State week news conference and bluntly told reporters—well, we'll let him do the honors. . .

"We want to get [OSU coach John] Cooper fired. That's what I want to do," Smith said. "We want to keep on beatin' 'em and beatin' 'em until he's no longer there."

At that point, Cooper hadn't beaten Michigan in six tries as coach, and what Smith said *was* plausible. What made it all the bizarre—and irritating to OSU fans—was that Smith had suffered a knee injury in the final scrimmage of preseason practice and had been in for only one play all season, a ceremonial appearance against Minnesota in which he caught a 2-yard pass in his final game in Michigan Stadium.

But twice after he made the remark, Smith was asked if that really was what he meant to say, and each time, he had replied, "Yeah." The second time, he added, "It's better than getting coach Mo fired."

That was pretty much Smith's last hurrah. The Buckeyes beat Michigan 22–6 in Ohio Stadium that year, and Smith spent the game on the sideline trying to hide under a ball cap and a hooded sweatshirt. Ironically, one of OSU's future villains was a red-shirt freshman that year and he didn't want Smith anywhere near him.

"I was standing as far away from Walter as I could," Ray said, two years later. "I know how that crowd can be. It was rowdy. When I was running into the locker room at halftime, somebody was standing above the entrance yelling, 'Where's Walter Smith? Where's Walter Smith?' Then he saw me and said, 'Marcus Ray, you made a mistake; you should have stayed home 'cause we're gonna beat your ass.' I just thought, 'Hurry up and get me out of here.'"

Because of OSU's recent dominance against the Wolverines, Harbaugh has been the only Michigan man to seriously raise the ire of Buckeye Nation in recent years.

In 2020, he interrupted OSU coach Ryan Day during a conference call among Big Ten coaches and accused the Buckeyes of breaking rules regarding on-field instruction. A miffed Day snapped back with "How about I worry about my team and you worry about yours?" and he told his team later that day that the Wolverines had better hope for a mercy rule this season because his team was "going to hang one hundred on them."

The 2020 game was canceled because of the pandemic, and Michigan gave Harbaugh his first win as a coach over OSU a year later. When he was asked after the game whether the Buckeyes' trash talk had motivated the Wolverines in their 42–27 win, he took a jab at Day, the third-year head coach who moved up when Urban Meyer quit after the 2018 season.

"There's definitely stuff people said that spurred us on," Harbaugh said. "Sometimes people that are standing on third base think they hit a triple, but they didn't."

# 21

# The Forgotten

The football poster offered on the Internet auction site eBay bore the name "Scarlet and Gray Immortals," the perfect setup for a writer preparing to do a chapter called "The Forgotten" in a book about Ohio State football.

Pumphrey's, a Columbus men's clothing store that also wears the "forgotten" label, issued the poster in 1946, and it featured photos of eighteen players surrounded by the words "All-Americans." As soon as I saw the age of the poster, my face must have brightened. This was akin to planting a tree in the backyard and striking oil.

Of the eighteen players featured, Chic Harley, Les Horvath, and Bill Willis are football immortals in the truest sense of the word. Their numbers have been retired, and at least some Ohio State fans will never forget them. Don Scott has his name on the university airport, which is a form of immortality, although it might be fun to do a survey and see how many OSU fans identify him as a football player. Scott was a good enough player to become a two-time All-American; he got his name on an air strip because he was killed during World War II. Wes Fesler's brush with immortality is likewise unrelated to his feats of athleticism, considerable though they were. Fesler is known today not so much for what he did before the poster was printed—he was a three-time All-American end from 1928 to 1930—but instead is known for being the losing coach in the Snow Bowl, and resigning afterward. Immortality is forever. It isn't always positive.

There are other names on that poster that might be familiar to modern fans, but how familiar they are probably depends on the age of the person doing the identifications. After he starred for OSU in 1937–39, Esco

Sarkkinen was a longtime Ohio State assistant coach and a familiar face around Columbus and around the state. Gaylord "Pete" Stinchcomb played in the same backfield on those first great OSU teams with Harley and was the star after Harley was gone. A ninety-something fan once told me he thought Stinchcomb was better than Harley. I listened, nodded, and respectfully declined the temptation to question the old gent's sanity. But for anyone to even consider the possibility of that says a lot about Stinchcomb's ability.

All-American center Gomer Jones later served as an assistant coach at OSU, John Carroll, and Oklahoma, was briefly head coach at OU, and then was athletic director there for seven years. Because of that, Sooner fans may know him better than Buckeyes fans do; it's also a good bet that some Ohio State and Oklahoma fans have vaguely heard of him because he is in the College Football Hall of Fame.

Of the others, two-time All-American lineman Warren Amling is the most recent of Pumphrey's "immortals," having finished seventh in the Heisman Trophy balloting in 1944 and served as team captain in 1946. He worked as a veterinarian in London, Ohio, twenty-eight miles west of Columbus, so there are doubtless plenty of people in that area who at least know of him. Jack Dugger was a star on both the football and basketball teams in the 1940s and played a little pro football after he got out of school. Because his pro career ended in 1949, he didn't get a chance to prolong his fame by exchanging quips with Terry Bradshaw or Boomer Esiason on one of those NFL television network yuk-fests, the way many of today's best athletes ultimately avoid the "forgotten" label.

So much for the vaguely familiar names. The other "immortals" on the poster were Leo Raskowski, Edwin Hess, Lindell Houston, Gust Zarnas, Regis Monahan, Inwood Smith, Merle Wendt, and Bill Hackett. They were all accomplished players during their eras; it's probably safe to say that not 2 percent of today's Ohio State fans would have the slightest idea who they are. That doesn't mean they don't deserve better. They do, obviously. It does mean that "immortality" doesn't always have much shelf life as it relates to college athletic stars. Most players' fame is good for two generations, three tops. This has been proven time and time again.

Maybe the best example occurred in 2000 when the Touchdown Club of Columbus selected an eighty-man all-century Ohio State football team.

Why the erudite members of the TC settled on eighty has never been revealed, but the naming of the team created an instant news story when Lew Hinchman, one of only six three-time All-Americans in school history, didn't make the team. No one ever explained why he was left off the list; I guess it's possible the TCC staff had one of those surviving Pumphrey's posters in its possession and figured if Hinchman wasn't good enough to be considered an "immortal" in 1946, he surely didn't merit one of those eighty coveted spots fifty-four years later.

While it's difficult to know why those pants-and-shirt-selling football geniuses at Pumphrey's didn't include him—maybe they just couldn't scare up a photo of him to slap on the poster—he definitely belonged there. Hinchman earned All-America honors as a quarterback and halfback in 1930, '31, and '32; was team captain and MVP in '32; and also lettered in basketball, baseball, and golf. He was such a prominent guy in his hometown of Dayton that he served as the commentator on the University of Dayton basketball TV broadcasts for several years, even though he wasn't a UD grad.

Given the TCC's snub, Hinchman is probably the poster boy of "forgotten." Would it really have made a difference if the all-century team list had eighty-one players instead of eighty? And then again, maybe Hinchman wasn't even on their original list of candidates. Four two-time All-Americans also failed to make the eighty-man squad, including Hess and Raskowski. The other two were Joseph Gailus, who was Hinchman's teammate in '31 and '32 and also played in '33, and offensive lineman Rob Murphy, who flunked out of school before his senior season in 1999.

"Forgotten" covers a great deal of territory. Because most modern fans ignore most of the players they never saw play no matter how good they were—the increasingly common "if it didn't happen in my lifetime, it didn't happen" mentality—this isn't an exclusive grouping. To truly be "forgotten" a player should have had a career truly worth remembering, which is a convenient way to avoid listing every OSU starter from 1890 to 1950 and turning this chapter into the second coming of *War and Peace*.

But not every good long-ago player was lucky enough to be immortalized by Pumphrey's or the Columbus Touchdown Club, and they no longer have living witnesses to give them their due. All of the players before 1900 are in this category; because the program was still in its infancy and relatively undistinguished, there's not much reason to remember many of them for their football prowess, anyway.

Edward French gets an occasional mention in a book or a historical piece because his brother was Thomas French, who most modern fans don't know either. Edward French was an end, captain of the 1894 team, and an accomplished player during an era when most Buckeye players really weren't. He is listed here because a) if he hadn't played his brother might not have taken such a strong interest in OSU athletics, and b) if his brother hadn't gotten interested, today's fans might be sitting in fold-up chairs on the sidelines watching Buckeye football games played in a glorified cow pasture. Okay, that's an exaggeration, but you get the idea. Without Edward French, there might not be an Ohio Stadium, at least not as we know it.

Several of the players on the 1899 team that went 9-0-1 and won the state championship—its schedule consisted of only Ohio teams—merit a mention, including captain Del Sayers, a tackle on a team that gave up only five points all season; fullback James Kittle, who scored seven touchdowns; halfback B. F. Yost; guard Homer Wharton; and quarterback Paul Hardy. While whooping the likes of Otterbein, Wittenberg, and Muskingum doesn't exactly rank with a Rose Bowl win over USC or a national championship win over the Miami Hurricanes, it's important to put what those faceless names did in context. In the Buckeyes' previous nine years of football, their best season was a 5-3 campaign in 1892 and one of the teams they beat that year was the Dayton YMCA.

The players from the early years of the twentieth century are no more familiar to modern fans, but two do stand out as deserving of a brief remembrance. Fred Cornell may or may not have been a good football player, but he did have talent. He wrote the words to *Carmen Ohio* on a train ride home from an 86–0 loss to Michigan in 1902, a result that indicates that his football skills probably weren't extraordinary. Even so, in composing the words to the school's alma mater he made a more lasting contribution to Ohio State than most of its All-Americans.

Josephus H. Tilton is the other. Tilton not only played on that 1899 team, but he was also captain of the 1900 team that followed up with an 8-1-1 record. The tie was a 0–0 game at Michigan, the first time OSU ever emerged from a game against the Wolverines without losing. It's not as impressive as it looks though. The game was played in a blinding snowstorm.

To be truthful, the Buckeyes didn't cause so much as a blip outside of the state's borders in those days, either as a team or as players. End Boyd Cherry was the first OSU player whose talent was recognized on the national level and that didn't happen until 1914, the school's second year in the Western Conference. Cherry was honored by the now forgotten International News Service, forerunner to the now-defunct and nearly forgotten United Press International, as a second-team All-American that year, the first time a Buckeye player was accorded that honor. Sportswriter Walter Camp, a former player and the sport's leading authority of the day, made him an honorable mention selection. Cherry must have been good. After OSU had gone 0-for-24 years without a player receiving any kind of national acclaim, Cherry doubtless had to be much better than some of his counterparts at other schools just to get the attention of the guys doing the picking.

That changed when Chic Harley arrived on the OSU varsity in 1916 and the Buckeyes began winning, although his teammates are still mostly anonymous names to today's fans. Outside of Stinchcomb, none were even considered "immortals" in 1946. Harold "Hap" Courtney and his brother Howard were former teammates of Harley's at Columbus East High; Hap was killed during World War I in the midst of his college football career. Charles "Shifty" Bolen, Iolas Huffman, and quarterback Howard Yerges all deserve more thought than the fleeting mention they are receiving here. In their day, they were Ohio football heroes and fans paid to see them play in alumni games for several years after they were gone.

Harold "Cookie" Cunningham was one of the OSU players who bridged the gap between Harley's teams and the ones that began to receive more notice in the 1930s. The 6-foot-4 Cunningham was an All-American end in 1924 and also starred on the OSU basketball team. He parlayed both into pro football and basketball careers, or at least as much as one could have in those days. Cunningham played football for the Cleveland Bulldogs, Chicago Bears, and Staten Island Stapletons, which says much more about the NFL in those days than it does about him.

Hoge Workman, the first OSU quarterback to earn All-America honors (1923), was also a multisport star. He played briefly in the NFL—for the

Cleveland Bulldogs, Cleveland Indians, and New York Giants—and also played in eight games with the Boston Red Sox as a relief pitcher in 1924. His brother, Noel, also played at Ohio State, and the Workmans probably aren't totally forgotten in their hometown of Huntington, West Virginia, where five of them starred for Huntington High.

But of all the "forgotten" OSU players, Bill Bell may be the only one who can give Hinchman a run for his money. While Bell doesn't have Hinchman's on-the-field track record, he did have talent; he was a three-year letterman and an honorable mention All-American at guard. Some of the holes Fesler ran through when he lined up at fullback were created by Bill Bell.

There is more to Bell's story than that though. When he joined Sam Willaman's squad in 1929 he was the first African American football player at the school since 1896. Willaman welcomed Bell to the roster, but he wasn't welcomed everywhere. He wasn't allowed to travel to Baltimore for a game with Navy in 1930 because northern schools weren't permitted to use blacks against southern schools. It was an occasion that helped school officials justify discouraging other African Americans from coming out for the team. After Bell used up his eligibility, another black player didn't make it onto the Buckeyes' roster until Bill Willis arrived in 1942.

In part because of his courage in again breaking the color barrier, both at OSU and in professional football, Willis is a football immortal. It hardly seems fair that Bell has a starring role in a chapter titled "The Forgotten."

# 22

# The Beloved

In a crowded Atlanta hotel lobby a few days prior to Super Bowl XXXIV, a twenty-something guy wearing an Ohio State hat stood out. He identified himself as "just a fan." I asked him who he was rooting for.

"Tennessee," he said.

Why?

"Because of Eddie."

Eddie. Like Woody. Or Archie. Or Hop. No last name required.

"I want to see Eddie win the Super Bowl," he said.

Most Ohio State fans would doubtless understand. To many of them, maybe to most of them, that Tennessee–St. Louis Super Bowl was going to be Eddie George's game.

"I have a lot of friends back [in Ohio]," Eddie said at the time.

He still does. Friends, fans, acquaintances, and customers at his restaurants. People who remember once getting his autograph at OSU's picture day, or the way he smiled at them at the team hotel in Pasadena, California, or the day he offered them a pleasant "hello" in the frozen food aisle of a Columbus supermarket.

It doesn't matter, really. Eddie may be the biggest hero Ohio State football has had since Archie Griffin, the two-time Heisman Trophy winner, lugged the ball around the 'Shoe in the early '70s, and his popularity hasn't faded in the seventeen years he has been gone.

His '95 Heisman is an obvious reason. His success during a nine-year NFL career was another. The Columbus restaurant he has owned near the OSU campus—Eddie George's Grille 27—since he retired from the NFL is yet another. A better one: nearly everybody in and around Columbus knows Eddie George as a model citizen, as a genuine smile-a-minute, say-hello-to-everybody, feet-on-the-ground kind of guy.

Hop is another former player who has that status, a guy whose last name isn't really necessary at any kind of Ohio State function. It's been fifty-seven years since Howard (Hopalong) Cassady ran his way into Buckeye hearts and even a number of young fans who never saw him play can identify that name. It helps that they don't know anybody else called Hop—it's not as easy to achieve first name recognition with a name like "Bill" or "John"—but Hop was a visible presence in Columbus long after he was out of school.

New York Yankees owner George Steinbrenner earned his master's degree at Ohio State and served as a grad assistant to Woody Hayes, and he hired Hop as a coach in his team's farm system. The Yankees had their Triple-A team in Columbus from 1979 to 2006, and Hop spent fourteen years working with the Clippers. That included a twelve-year run as the team's first base coach, which ended with his retirement in 2003. During that time, Hop could often be seen in the Columbus dugout after the lights had been turned out in the stadium, signing autographs for adoring fans. He wouldn't leave until they did.

Just like Eddie, Hop kept adding to his popularity. He has lived in Tampa, Florida, for years, but his face is as familiar to as many Ohioans now as it was when he won the 1955 Heisman Trophy. He has thousands of true fans who have never seen him play.

Chic Harley is probably the only other player OSU fans could identify by first name only, although those days have long since passed with the generations. A number retirement, two books, a video, and a planned garden in his honor have helped push him back before the public eye, though he can never regain his once lofty status. Most now know him only as an unfamiliar face in a black-and-white team photo, or a last name and number on the Ohio Stadium façade. Many of those who see it probably don't even know his first name is Chic. Once upon a time, that was all he was: Chic. Alas, it was a long time ago.

First-name fame doesn't mean a player isn't one of the Ohio State beloved, though. The school has had seven Heisman Trophy winners and only two could be instantly identified on an Ohio street by only his first name.

Say "Vic was a real player" in a Columbus or Cleveland sports bar and the first question is likely to be "Vic who?" It might be Victor Martinez or Vic Power. "Les" might be Les Wexner. "Troy" could be anybody.

There is no doubt that Vic Janowicz and Les Horvath, the first two Ohio State Heisman winners, are still revered by Buckeye fans of their eras. I still run into old-timers who claim that Janowicz was the best player they ever saw and they have a point. In 1950, the year the Elyria, Ohio, native won the Heisman, he was a single-wing tailback and defensive back. In the first five minutes against Iowa that season, Janowicz ran 11 yards for one touchdown, returned a punt 61 yards for another, passed 12 yards for a third, kicked all three extra points, kicked off after each score, and caused a fumble with a tackle. In all, he ran for two touchdowns, passed for four, and kicked 10 extra points in Ohio State's 83–21 win. The 10 extra points remain a school record.

Horvath, the 1944 Heisman winner over Army legend Glenn Davis, was also a two-way star, playing quarterback when the Buckeyes operated out of the T-formation and halfback when coach Carroll Widdoes had them in the single wing. He played safety on defense. Some old-timers still have a fuzzy recollection of Horvath's speech to his younger teammates before the winning drive in the '44 Michigan game.

Horvath was a twenty-four-year-old dental student who had missed the '43 season because of an army regulation, and his team was composed mostly of freshmen. With the Buckeyes trailing 14–12 and with eight minutes to play, Horvath huddled up his troops at the 50 and told them what was about to happen:

"We are not going to pass. We are not going to fumble. We are not going to give up the ball. We are going right in with a series of first downs. Now, everyone block as he has never blocked before."

The drive played out just as he had said it would, and the Buckeyes won 18–14 with Horvath playing all sixty minutes. Those who were around in those days still speak of him with awe.

The status of 2006 Heisman winner Troy Smith is a little more fuzzy. Smith may have been the best quarterback in school history; his legacy also suffered when he bombed badly in the 2006 BCS national title game against Florida, a month after he won his Heisman.

A good case can be made that it wasn't his fault—the offensive line's play *was* offensive that night—and yet the persistent image after OSU's embarrassing 41–14 loss was of a guy who got fat and happy after being named college football's top player. Rumors swirled that his teammates were angry with him and that he didn't care. True or false, his image took another beating after a company overpaid him to market his autographs and then had him sign 8-by-10 photos for $69.95, mini-footballs, mini-helmets, magazines, etc., for $99.95 and football jerseys for $139.95 in an attempt to get its investment back. One of the Cleveland-area stores that had him in to sign actually included a line on its website—"We apologize for the high prices"—that spoke to the merchant's embarrassment with what he was charging.

Smith, an exciting player and a huge Buckeye hero before the Florida game, suddenly had become a self-centered mercenary in the eyes of many of those who were once his biggest fans. He was simply fulfilling his obligations to the company that paid him a big fee, but so soon after his performance against Florida, the public was ready to turn on him. Only time will tell whether he ever receives the love displayed for the school's other Heisman winners. His play before the Florida game had been captivating.

As impressive as a Heisman is, other former players probably rank higher than even some of the winners on the OSU popularity scale. When the *Columbus Dispatch* ran a poll in 2007 seeking to identify a fourth OSU coach or player for an imaginary Mount Rushmore of OSU football—Chic, Woody, and Archie were already penciled in as the first three—former linebacker Chris Spielman came in third, behind Jim Tressel and Hop, and ahead of Eddie.

Only 466 votes were cast on the Internet so it wasn't necessarily an accurate representation of the entire OSU community; still, it spoke to Spielman's enormous popularity. There are other factors in his recognition besides his talent as a football player: Having his own Columbus radio show for a while and being an ESPN football analyst has kept him in the public eye, and he briefly coached the Columbus team in the Arena Football League. His late wife, Stefanie, probably also bolstered his standing with her courageous public fight against breast cancer, and both Spielmans worked tirelessly to raise money for cancer research. When he was honored for his selection to the College Football Hall of Fame at halftime of the OSU-Navy football game in the fall of 2010, Stefanie, in a wheelchair, and their four children were at his side. It was a memorable scene and an emotional moment. She died two and a half months later. He has continued to make appearances on behalf of the Stefanie Spielman Fund for Breast Cancer Research, which they established in 1999, and wrote a book that included intimate details of the end-of-life experience to benefit the fund. More than $10 million has been raised since the fund's creation.

Spielman's football talent merits inclusion on any list of elite Ohio State players. He was a two-time All-American and four-time All-Pro with the Detroit Lions who was a defensive demon on the field. But like Archie and Eddie, he is also known as much for who he is off the field as who he was on it. He took a year off from the NFL when his wife was first diagnosed with breast cancer, which speaks to his high character.

There are a handful of others who also seem to hold a special place in the hearts of OSU fans over and above the heroes who are produced by the program every year: quarterback Rex Kern, middle guard Bill Willis, offensive tackles John Hicks and Korey Stringer and guard Jim Parker. As the quarterback, Kern was obviously the most visible hero of those memorable 1968–70 teams and Willis's contributions as a player and a racial pioneer required his own chapter. Hicks finished second in the Heisman voting in 1973, and Parker should have finished at least that high in 1956—he was the best player in college football that season and might have won in a landslide if he hadn't been a lineman. Both were immensely popular after their OSU days were over, and Hicks remains so today as an affable and successful member of the Columbus business community. Parker died in 2005.

Stringer's popularity soared after his death from complications of a heat stroke he suffered on a Minnesota Vikings' practice field in 2001, although he was enormously popular among those who were fortunate to know him during his playing days in Columbus. Stringer, a powerful Ohio State offensive tackle from 1992 to 1994, was like a big, cuddly, 335-pound teddy bear, always smiling, always treating friends and fans and teammates as he would have wanted to be treated himself. He was the regular guy who became a star and never changed.

"He was a fun guy," former OSU teammate Steve Tovar later said. "We took it for granted. It was just him. Every time I saw him, he had a smile on his face or was trying to make people laugh."

After Stringer died during Vikings training camp at the age of twenty-seven, the outpouring of affection for him was incredible, in the Twin Cities, in Columbus, and back in his hometown of Warren, Ohio.

The cross section of testimonials was overwhelming. People from all walks of life described him as modest, unassuming, generous, and kind. Teachers spoke of a man who was great with kids, who listened to their stories like he was one of them. He signed autographs, shook hands, posed for photographs. He brought them pencils, t-shirts, notebooks, and even tickets to Vikings games. Neighbors said that he had sat on his porch the previous Halloween with a big bowl of candy and allowed each child to take a generous portion he referred to as a "Korey handful."

Vikings coach Dennis Green called him "one of our gifts" and said that whenever a player got released, "Korey spent a lot of time [with him] just making him feel good about himself." Minnesota teammate and former OSU star Cris Carter said there "was not a more well-liked player on our football team . . . not a player that anyone enjoyed spending more time with than Korey."

At his funeral, his wife, Kelci, talked about what a "real" person he was, with no phony personalities or fronts, a guy who was genuine and sincere.

"I caught myself thinking the same thing about him," former OSU teammate Raymont Harris said. "You lose someone like that, it's a devastating loss." Back in Warren, most of his friends, family, and acquaintances were Ohio State fans, but they were even bigger Korey Stringer fans. Steven Arnold, an assistant coach at Warren Harding High School when Stringer played offensive tackle there, did as good a job as any in explaining to reporters at the funeral why Korey was so popular everywhere he played.

"A lot of guys who make it to the big time forget where they came from, but not Korey," Arnold said. "He was always back here, always involved with the people in this town."

In fact, he had been there a month before he died.

"Myself and a friend were sitting in my living room a few weeks ago, talking about what we could do to get one of our local pee-wee football teams some equipment," Arnold said. "Korey stopped by during our conversation, and when we stopped talking, he said: 'Wait a minute. Don't go anywhere. I'll be back.'

"Korey went out to his truck, came back about a minute later and he's got this check in his hand. It was the check he got for playing in the Pro Bowl—his first-ever Pro Bowl—and he signed it over to us. I couldn't believe it. I won't say how much, but it was a lot of money. He called me the other day from camp to make sure I was getting the best equipment for the kids, too."

Stringer probably died too young for first-name recognition, but make no mistake about, Stringer was as big of a hero as any who ever wore an Ohio State uniform.

Call him Korey. Just Korey.

# 23

# Fallen Heroes

It all started at a Fiesta Bowl that would determine the 2002 national champion. Maurice Clarett, a brash freshman running back who had always shown a willingness to speak his mind even when it wasn't wise to do so, started popping off to reporters about how unfair it was that he wasn't allowed to attend a murdered friend's funeral back in Youngstown, Ohio.

It was a reporter's dream and a coach's and fan's nightmare. Clarett wasn't some guy who figured to spend the title game waving towels and giving noogies to unsuspecting equipment guys on the Ohio State sidelines. He was the team's biggest star. He should have been locked in on the favored Miami Hurricanes, thinking about what he would have to do and how he would have to do it to achieve the school's biggest win in thirty-four years. Yet there he was, firing verbal darts at OSU officials, saying things that made fans who were *desperate* to win this game very, very nervous. They couldn't help but see him as an arrogant kid who was going to blow it for who knew why.

"They jerked me," Clarett said, referring to the school officials who wouldn't let him go home for the services. "I guess football is more important than a person's life to them, so that's why I'm just ready to get the game over and go back home."

Get the game over? Had he really said that?

The next day was media day, where all of the players had to be made available for more interviews per Fiesta Bowl rules. But instead of retracting his earlier statements or at least softening them, he let 'er rip again.

But of course he did. This wasn't some senior offensive lineman willing to go out on a limb and say what "a fine team" Miami was. This was Maurice

Clarett, the human distraction, a guy with no filter between his mouth and his brain. His candor was as refreshing to some as it was maddening to others. He wasn't about to let anyone tell him what he could and couldn't say. Reporters loved him. He drove fans crazy.

"I filled out the paperwork," he said. "So they can't lie about that. I won't sit here and let them lie about that. It's on file. I talked to the coach, and he pointed me in the direction of the compliance lady [Heather Lyke Catalano], and the compliance lady said she'd get back to me in my room. But she never called me back in my room, and she never called me back on my cell phone, so that's the real reason I was mad. Of course, they're going to make themselves look better than me. They make me look like I'm stupid."

The irony is that Ohio State won the game, in part because of him. But Clarett's descent had started, and it gradually picked up momentum until it was a full-blown free fall.

He filed a false police report claiming that more than $10,000 in clothing, CDs, cash, and stereo equipment was stolen from a car he borrowed from a local dealership and was suspended from school for the 2003 season; tried to go to the NFL before its rules would allow him to; smeared OSU in a national magazine; and was drafted and then cut by the NFL's Denver Broncos. Then exactly three years from the day he called university officials liars at the Fiesta Bowl, with the Buckeyes back at the same bowl, although not in the national title game, the estranged former Buckeye was accused of using a gun to rob a couple in an alley behind a downtown Columbus bar.

Clarett was only one troubled young man in a world overrun with them, but some Ohio State fans took it personally. They still do, even though he was given a seven-and-a-half-year sentence in the Toledo Correctional Institution for robbery, carrying a concealed weapon without a permit, and resisting arrest. When a man's sins involve their favorite football program, forgiveness doesn't come easily.

Never in the long history of Ohio State football has one player so rewarded and so distressed the OSU faithful as Clarett has. At one time, he was Public Enemy No. 1, ahead of Jim Harbaugh, Walter Smith, Charles Woodson, Marcus Ray, and all of the other Michigan blabbermouths so adept at getting under the Buckeyes' skin. He was higher on the list than

Jim Plunkett, Tom Harmon, Charles White, Anthony Davis, Tshimanga Biakabutuka, and all of the others who had beaten the Buckeyes with their talent. The animosity for him has faded some now, but there is no denying that Clarett is still the program's No. 1 anti-hero.

He *was* good. In his first college game, a 45–21 win over Texas Tech, he had 175 rushing yards, 30 receiving yards, and three touchdowns, and was the first freshman running back to start OSU's season opener in the modern era. In his third college game, a 25–7 win over No. 10 Washington State, he carried 31 times for 230 yards, a 7.4-yard average. He had 119 yards in 20 carries in a 14–9 win over Michigan, and also caught two passes for 35 yards, including the Buckeyes' biggest gainer of the game. He played that game with a painful stinger to his shoulder that had caused him to miss the Illinois game the week before and took one hit on a 17-yard run in the second quarter that doubled him over in pain, even though trainers had packaged him like a piece of fine crystal. He kept playing.

He scored the winning touchdown against Miami in the title game, a 5-yard run in the second overtime. He also made a huge defensive play in that game, ripping the ball away from Hurricanes' safety Sean Taylor, who was in the process of intercepting a Craig Krenzel pass in the end zone. He finished the season with 1,237 yards rushing on 222 carries, even though he had missed a game.

Hard as it is to believe that the fans could learn to hate this guy, they came to see him as the enemy for multiple reasons: he didn't respect the program and tried to get it in trouble with the NCAA, sued the NFL to try to get away from the program, and soiled the program with his actions and his antics. The irony is that Ohio State couldn't possibly have won that 2002 title—the one Buckeye fans waited thirty-four years for—without him. That was a season of close games and Clarett was arguably the best player on the team.

But when you look back on that remarkable freshman season now it's not hard to see how this happened. When he wasn't actually on the field stirring memories of Hop Cassady, Eddie George, and Archie Griffin, Clarett really didn't fit in. He didn't live on campus. He wasn't close to his teammates. He always said what he felt, even when it made his coaches and teammates uncomfortable, even when it had more to do with "me" than "team."

He said he didn't "have that much affection for Ohio State," and he meant it. He made it clear he saw through the glad-handers who liked him only because he was an OSU football player. He never hesitated to express his disdain for the system he had to use to get to the NFL.

Seven games into his freshman season, Clarett told *ESPN the Magazine* that turning pro after the season has "got to go through your head," even though the NCAA had a rule against it and school officials worked overtime trying to make it sound as though the writer had baited him. Those of us who knew Clarett knew better.

No baiting was ever required in a Clarett interview. He usually said what he thought, and he thought the school and its well-heeled supporters were using him. If he had been good enough to go to the NFL out of high school and it had been legal to go to the NFL out of high school, Clarett probably already would have been there. For Clarett, like many athletes with professional sports aspirations, college sports was merely a means to that end.

A few weeks before that national championship game, Clarett used the school's pre-bowl-game interview sessions to say how bad the OSU fans could be.

"I just feel like it's cool to play football, but it should be left at that," he said. "It kind of gets on your nerves. People are kissing your butt all year and then like overnight . . . I always think back to [former OSU quarterback] Steve Bellisari. People were pretty much kissing his butt all year when he made great plays, and as soon as he made a mistake it was like . . . 'We don't like you.'"

In some ways, Clarett was both too smart and too dumb for his own good. He was the square peg in the round hole, a street-smart kid who didn't care for the rules and didn't always follow them, the kind of person who had been declaring his early eligibility for the NFL draft in other ways for years.

Before the 2005 draft—he sued the NFL to be included in the 2004 draft and won his case but lost on appeal—he sat down for an interview with Tom Friend of *ESPN the Magazine*. He supposedly wanted to set the record straight and let NFL personnel directors know he wasn't to blame for all of his problems at OSU. There were many shots at the school in there, which some thought was the only reason he did it. When I read it, I kept trying to imagine an NFL general manager reading it and suddenly slapping his palm to his forehead in shock over his sudden realization that Clarett would be just about the perfect player to have on his team.

In it, he said OSU coach Jim Tressel had told him that one of the conditions for his return to the team after his suspension was a daily 6 a.m. workout, and the story made it sound as if this was unfair because Clarett isn't "a morning person." He spoke of the cushy jobs that the coaches got for him.

"I did show up at first," he said. "But I was like, 'This is boring, I ain't doing this.' I used to go watch 'em hang drywall or something. I'd just hang out, go to McDonald's, come back, watch, leave, be gone. I made a couple grand."

As could be expected, none of this went over well in the Ohio State community, and it probably didn't sit well with most NFL personnel types, either. The picture he painted of himself didn't fit the image of the kind of hard-working guy they were looking to draft.

He was surprisingly drafted by Denver in the third round after he had been expected to go a few rounds later. He was drafted after his junior year under the NFL rule he challenged, the one that said a player must wait three years after graduating from high school to declare for the draft, after he had sat out two years. He went to the Broncos' camp overweight and out of shape. After unimpressive workouts and problems with his coaches, he was cut without ever having played in an NFL game. Four months later, he was charged with robbery.

By the time Clarett was finally sent to prison, most Ohio State fans were glad to be rid of him. They were tired of reading stories about him and hearing his accusations against the university. When he started writing a blog from prison—*The Mind of Maurice Clarett*—and I wrote a column about it, the groans from some quarters were so loud that it was almost impossible to sleep.

But the entries seemed to show a man determined to change his ways and earn another shot at a pro football career. After being incarcerated for three and a half years, he received his early release in August 2010, and he played that fall for the Omaha Nighthawks of the United Football League. He said he appreciated the opportunity that he was given. He returned to Columbus and enrolled at Ohio State in hopes of getting a degree in gerontology.

Clarett played for the Nighthawks again in 2011, although he made more news with his Twitter account and his blog than he did with his legs, criticizing new OSU coach Luke Fickell—who coached him on special teams when he was a freshman—during and after a loss of 24–6 to Miami.

"You can't make the janitor the principal overnight," he tweeted. And "Luke needs to take his talent to Toledo." And "Luke was a coach of mine and is a friend. He's a good coach but not a good Head Coach for OSU right now. I can separate my emotions #truth." He also plugged a blog, which he titled "Fickell not ready for prime time."

Among the numerous e-mails I received after that, this one probably best represented how the fans viewed this latest development:

"Exactly how many readers—or fans—do you think are interested in anything Maurice Clarett might tweet? I am so disgusted that his name keeps getting resurrected, as though he should always be revered in Columbus."

Regardless of where Clarett's football skills take him, it's doubtful he will ever be revered by many Ohio State fans. He helped give them their most prized possession in over three decades, that 2002 title, but he seems like the generous spouse caught cheating once too often. It's hard for them to forgive and forget.

Before Clarett, OSU had another high-profile fallen hero. Art Schlichter didn't commit crimes against the program but against himself and others, and consequently he has been viewed more sympathetically by the program's supporters. Despite the ugly stain he left on the program for his gambling addiction, most fans hoped that he could turn his life around even as his troubles continued to mount.

Schlichter is Ohio State's career leader in passing yards—he had 7,547 from 1978 to 1981—and was so good that he was the fourth pick in the 1982 NFL draft. He came to OSU from Miami Trace High School, an hour's drive down I-71, with a cannon arm and more press clippings than any one man can carry. He started the season opener against Penn State as a freshman—Rod Gerald, the returning starter was moved to wide receiver—in a dramatic moment that had been a closely guarded secret by Woody Hayes.

The Buckeyes lost that game 19–0, but it was a sign that Woody knew what he had, even if he didn't know quite how to use him. It was Schlichter's interception in the Gator Bowl that year that led to Woody's punch of Charlie Bauman and his firing, which in some ways was probably a good thing for Schlichter.

"His sophomore season, Ohio State never had a better quarterback," Woody's successor, Earle Bruce, once said.

And it was true. Like Clarett, Schlichter was very good, at times spectacular. His scrambling touchdown run to beat Michigan 14–9 in 1981 is one of those moments still vivid after all these years. A few months later the Baltimore Colts made him the fourth overall pick. An OSU quarterback had never been picked that high, and still hasn't thirty-one years later. But the Washington Court House, Ohio, native quickly went from being a famous quarterback to being a famous compulsive gambler.

He had started gambling while he was in college, both at Scioto Downs, a Columbus-area harness track, and on pro and college games. The habit escalated when he reached the NFL and had more money at his disposal. He had blown his signing bonus by mid-season, and his gambling increased during the '82 NFL strike. By the end of it, he had a reported $700,000 in gambling debts. As his debts piled up further that winter and bookies threatened to expose him if he didn't pay up, he went to the FBI and confessed, and the league suspended him indefinitely. He was eventually reinstated for the '84 season but was released five games into the '85 season when the Colts heard he was gambling again. He never played in another regular-season game, and the downward spiral accelerated.

He was in more than forty prisons or jails from 1994 to 2006, serving the equivalent of ten years, mainly for forgery and fraud for writing bad checks or swindling people out of money in order to feed his addiction. Those close to him estimate that he has lost at least $1 million gambling. Schlichter is a likable guy and a smooth talker. Despite his highly publicized troubles, he was still able to convince people in Columbus to give him money for various trumped up reasons.

It is a tragic story. Schlichter's wife, Mitzi, divorced him. His father, Max, committed suicide. He lost a promising NFL career and many friends because of his addiction, and is still battling his demons.

He tried several times to stop. On April 17, 2000, he spoke to the OSU football team about the dangers of gambling addiction, and on May 16, a

month later, he was accused of stealing a friend's credit cards after spending the night at the man's suburban Columbus home. By the time police
caught up with him, he had already racked up nearly $9,000 in charges
from two withdrawals at an ATM in a local store, and two charges for
money wired via Western Union to Nicaragua and St. John in the Virgin
Islands.

Sad as it is to say, this kind of behavior typified him; at one point,
Schlichter allegedly received $140,000 in advance payments for Final Four
tickets he didn't have. When people who paid in advance demanded
refunds, Schlichter offered to pay them with checks stolen from his father,
leading to unauthorized charges to his father's credit card.

"I don't want sympathy. I don't deserve sympathy," Schlichter said, in a
story in the *Columbus Dispatch* in December 2006. "I just want a chance
to make amends, especially with those I love most."

But a little over four years later, Schlichter was back in the news again,
this time as the target of an investigation by both local and federal authorities centering on a sports ticket scheme that had swindled fifty-five people
out of several million dollars. In 2008, the former quarterback convinced
investors that he could obtain tickets to Ohio State football games, the
Super Bowl, and other prominent sporting events and sell them for a profit.
The money Schlichter collected was instead used to place large bets. One
of the people he allegedly defrauded, the widow of the former chairman of
the board of Wendy's, said she lost millions of dollars and two homes trying to help him and that he pressured her to solicit money for him from her
friends.

He was subsequently arrested and sentenced to ten years in prison, after
he pleaded guilty to twelve counts of theft and one count of engaging in a
pattern of corrupt activity in Franklin County Common Pleas Court. While
awaiting trial on a federal case, he was under house arrest in the Columbus
suburb of Upper Arlington until drug testing in January 2012 revealed that
he was using cocaine. In May, a U.S. District Court judge sentenced him to
ten years and seven months after he pleaded guilty to federal charges of bank,
wire, and tax fraud. The sentences were to run concurrently. At the time of
his second sentencing, his attorney revealed that three mental health spe-
cialists who examined him concluded that he has "significant deficits" in the

frontal lobes of his brain, most likely caused by the fifteen concussions he suffered while playing high school and college football, and noted that that kind of damage can be responsible for impaired judgment.

The theory isn't likely to restore Schlichter's status as an OSU football hero, but the majority still seem to draw a distinction between him and Clarett. By their way of thinking, Schlichter must be sick. He isn't dumb, and that still seems to be the only way to explain his repeated fraud and thievery, particularly in light of the consequences. Normal people wouldn't throw away their families, steal from their friends, and risk a life in prison in order to get a bet down on the Mariners.

No matter how they are judged on a human scale, Schlichter and Clarett remain two of the greatest players ever to wear a scarlet, and, gray jersey. Despite all of their other troubles, it would be a shame if they aren't recognized in that way.

# 24

# The Benefactors

No one owns Ohio State football, even though many people wish they did. In December 2011, *Forbes* estimated the program's worth at $78 million, in part based on its $26 million annual profit.

A lot of rich, powerful people do own a stake in it though, not unlike most precious commodities. Some benefit monetarily from their association—a successful team might spike school clothing or newspaper sales, for example—and others' benefits are more abstract; they're just happy to be a contributing partner in a booming football factory. They enjoy their association, want to help it succeed, and believe that being part of that success enhances their quality of life.

Commercial real estate tycoon John W. Galbreath may have closed a deal or ten because of his association with Ohio State athletics, but it's doubtful that that motivated him. Galbreath was a sportsman. He owned the Pittsburgh Pirates from 1946 to 1985. He bought Darby Dan Farm, ten miles west of Columbus, and developed two Kentucky Derby winners, Chateaugay in 1963 and Proud Clarion in 1967. As chairman of the Greater New York Association in the early 1950s, he supervised the construction of the new Aqueduct race track and the rebuilding of Belmont Park. Galbreath graduated from Ohio University and said he became involved with Ohio State athletics because OSU is the city's team. "You can't live in Columbus and not be a part of it," he once said. He also became involved because of a friendship with Woody Hayes, whom he called "the hardest-working man I have ever known."

Hayes might have said the same thing about him. Galbreath flew all over the world putting up skyscrapers, apartment buildings, factories, and housing developments—in 1986, *Forbes* estimated his and his son Dan's financial worth at $400 million—yet he always found time for Ohio State. He was a member of a group called the OSU Athletic Committee, a panel of businessmen from all over Ohio founded as the Frontliners in the late 1940s to help find and recruit athletes for the school.

Galbreath provided athletes with jobs and, in the case of some of the poorer families, even offered clothes or monetary assistance (which would be illegal today). He helped Ohio State close the deal with Vic Janowicz, the eventual 1950 Heisman Trophy winner, by taking him and his date—along with movie star Bing Crosby—to a Pirates game. The top football prospects also invariably found themselves at Galbreath's 4,200-acre farm, not a bad place for a recruiter to take an impressionable young mind and try to close the sale. Mounted heads of animals bagged on Galbreath's South American and East African hunting parties covered the walls of the main house. There was memorabilia from the Pittsburgh Pirates and trophies from wins in some of the world's biggest horse races. Zebras, bison, rhinoceroses, water bucks, and impalas roamed Galbreath's own game reserve. There were also racing stables, an actual farm—with crops—and an airstrip for his private aircraft.

Galbreath always went above and beyond for the program. Every year on the night before the biggest home game of the season, the real estate mogul hosted a huge party at Darby Dan Farm for the press, athletic officials from both schools, and some of the program's biggest boosters.

As an impressionable young reporter who was tolerated rather than recruited, I was blown away by the food, drink, and atmosphere at the first of these I attended, before the OSU-Oklahoma game in 1977. Woody Hayes and Oklahoma coach Barry Switzer both rose and spoke briefly to the crowd, and a few sportswriters and I ended up drinking with Switzer after about 80 percent of the crowd had gone home. Woody had long since departed, of course, probably to do a little more pregame planning, and it always struck me as funny that even though Switzer drank to the end of the party, his team won the game. To each his own method of preparation, right?

Later it struck me that the potential benefit of having the party before the Oklahoma game might have occurred to someone during the planning stages of the event. Switzer was reputedly a partier. If Woody Hayes were holed up in his North Facility office studying diagrams of off-tackle plays and the opposing coach was out drinking, the Buckeyes might glean some subtle benefit.

If that was the idea—and I'm only half-kidding about this—there are precedents that indicate they should have known better. Hadn't they ever heard the tale about Grover Cleveland Alexander strolling out of the bullpen with a crushing hangover and shutting down the Yankees to win the seventh game of the 1926 World Series? Galbreath surely had. He was a baseball man.

The OSU football program has had hundreds of benefactors and boosters over the years, but probably none as effective or as loyal as he was. And like Galbreath, most of them probably weren't as interested in helping themselves as they were the program.

Former New York Yankees owner George Steinbrenner probably never made a dime out of his devotion to the Buckeyes, but the one-time OSU graduate assistant coach and Rocky River, Ohio, native was one who could always be counted on to support the program when it was needed. He coached high school football in Columbus. His widow, Joan, is an Ohio State grad, and the Joan Zieg Steinbrenner Band Facility in Ohio Stadium is named for her. The Steinbrenners are believed to have donated more than $1 million toward its construction.

The stadium has several names on it besides hers today, most belonging to donors who sponsored one aspect of the Ohio Stadium renovation or another. In light of stricter NCAA recruiting regulations, a big check is the primary means of supporting the program in the twenty-first century.

The local business community has always been willing to help out, both financially and with recruiting support, as well as with its always-helpful advice on play-calling, hirings, and firings. A cynic back in the 1940s had a description of the local fan base that still applies today:

"Everybody in Columbus has two jobs," he said, "his own and coaching the Ohio State football team."

Chic Harley had been out of school only five years when the first enduring local booster group was formed. Ben Ratner, the owner of a Columbus sporting goods and men's clothing store who was a college pal of Harley's, decided to start a club in 1925 to keep all of his jaw-flapping downtown buddies from leaning on his store stock while they were debating football. He wanted to name it the Harley Club and he didn't get his way on that; most of the other twelve members thought a takeoff on the Greek word *agon*, meaning "an assembly met to see games" seemed more appropriate, and the group was named the Agonis Club. It didn't stop his friends from leaning on his stock, either. While membership in the club exploded, his High Street store became a mecca for downtown coaches, particularly during the football season.

"In season," one of these downtown quarterbacks once said, "Ben's place is like a swarm of bees, if bees could holler."

The Quarterback Club was another group that debated football, although its membership was more diverse, taking in factory workers, store clerks, and laborers, as well as the leaders of the local business community. It was created by Karl Pauly, a political writer for the *Ohio State Journal*, to delve more deeply into football strategy, coaching methods, etc., and had a standing invitation for the current OSU coach to speak to the group. Sometimes the coach would bring films of the previous week's game and point out and explain the finer points, which became a topic of debate.

In 1948, screenwriter and novelist Joel Sayre, a Columbus native who grew up in James Thurber's east side neighborhood and later worked with him at the *New Yorker*, offered a good description of the group in a story about Ohio State football in the November 1, 1948, issue of *Life* magazine:

> The Quarterbacks have a waiting list that is pages long, and if any member who has missed two meetings in succession cannot furnish a valid excuse he is mercilessly stricken from the rolls. Meetings are held in a hotel ballroom, commence on the dot of 7:30 p.m. and generally last about three hours. Some members send stooges to the ballroom as early as 6 o'clock to hold good seats for them. At least 15 minutes are devoted to singing football hymns of which Ohio State has several real pulse-racers, particularly Across the Field. To show the team that Columbus was back of it, last year just before the start of the Indiana game, the Quarterbacks formed in two lines that extended from the stadium dressing room to the middle of the playing field,

and as the Ohio State squad passed between the lines every player was given a pat on the back. Strong men choke up and cry over this kind of thing in Columbus.

Much of the financial support, vocal support, criticism, and pressure on the Ohio State coach and athletic director used to come from members of the Agonis or Quarterback clubs. Newspaper reports often mention "the High Street crowd" or the "downtown quarterbacks" and everyone knew to whom they were referring; most of the titans in the Columbus business community belonged to one or both of these groups, and the value of their opinions was not lost on the coaches and the university officials who hired and fired them. Both the program and the city has outgrown this to a large extent—it's not as easy for a handful of influential or wealthy business leaders to wield the kind of influence they did in the smaller, more compact city of sixty years ago—but it didn't go away overnight either. Earle Bruce always maintained that hostile, second-guessing fans weren't his problem in 1987; instead it was the downtown business people who got him fired.

That wouldn't have surprised Esco Sarkkinen, who played and worked in that pressurized climate for more than forty years.

"The Frontliners, we later called them the Committeemen," Sarkkinen said. "They were all very influential, successful people. They were big wheels, the stalwarts of their communities. For the most part they were directly involved in the program. I think they influenced [athletic director Lynn] St. John in a more direct way."

The Frontliners, formed after the Buckeyes suffered a humiliating 58–6 loss to Michigan in 1946, took football devotion to yet another level. The High Street crowd noticed that fifteen of the Wolverines' best twenty-two players were not Michigan natives, and concluded that every Ford and Chevrolet dealer in the country must be talent-scouting for them. They also thought Notre Dame was unfairly using religion to recruit all of the top Catholic players. So OSU Alumni Association secretary Jack Fullen called a meeting of prominent alums and boosters at the Deshler-Wallick Hotel in Columbus on November 26, 1946, to do something about it. The group sought fifty high-powered, well-connected OSU alums from all over Ohio to take on a clear mission: to find and scout good players or to cultivate a close relationship with players the coaches already wanted and convince them to play football at Ohio State.

Del Starkey, general manager of the Columbus Chamber of Commerce, and assistant coach/recruiting whiz Ernie Godfrey took on the task of talking to Columbus-area businessmen who weren't in the group but who might be willing to provide the players with jobs. This was important at a time when the Big Ten wouldn't allow athletic scholarships; players paid tuition and room and board from money made working—or in some cases, not working—at jobs lined up for them by school officials. In the days before the Frontliners, those positions were concentrated in various state office buildings, where the players swept floors and emptied waste baskets for $50 or $60 a month.

The new system worked. The year the group was formed, the coaches landed thirty-three of the thirty-five Ohio prospects they wanted. The Frontliners' work became so pervasive that Clyde Moore, who penned a popular daily feature called "Clyde Says" in the *Columbus Dispatch*, cracked, "Ohio State to get Isotopes! What position does he play?"

Naturally, there were abuses. When Ohio State was slapped with a one-year probation by the Big Ten in 1956 after Woody Hayes told a *Sports Illustrated* reporter he had made personal loans or gifts to some of his "needy" football players from the $4,000 he received annually for his local television show, the Big Ten also found that some players were being paid in season for jobs they weren't doing. Maybe that's why some old-timers snickered when the NCAA suspended three OSU players during the 2011 season for being overpaid for part-time work at booster Bobby DiGeronimo's Cleveland-area company, Independence Excavating. Some things never change, eh?

In the 1956 case, the players sometimes showed up later and worked to repay the "loans," but the arrangements were against the league's rules regarding "unearned financial aid." In part because of this scandal, the Big Ten took a hard look at its situation in 1957 and changed the rule to allow athletic scholarships.

The Frontliners eventually became "committeemen" after the Big Ten decided the original name sounded too predatory, and grew to include Galbreath. By the early 1970s, there were 250 committeemen inside Ohio and fifty around the nation, all doing what they could to get players to go to Ohio State.

"In those days, the downtown quarterbacks met every week," Kaye Kessler, retired sports columnist for the *Columbus Citizen-Journal,* said in 1994. "They were big businessmen, attorneys and legislators, and they always had a lot to say about the Ohio State football team. You have to remember that Columbus was much smaller then, and these guys were very visible around town. And the Frontliners, they were the ones who got the kids their jobs, so they felt they had a say in what went on."

The most coveted players were usually taken care of by the most prominent boosters, as they had always been. Galbreath hired OSU players for various jobs around Darby Dan Farm. Warren, Ohio, hotel man and longtime committeeman Frank Lafferty bragged in the 1974 book *Buckeye* how he got Paul Warfield a job with the state highway department and Van DeCree a job with Republic Steel, but didn't have to do that for Randy Gradishar, the soon-to-be All-American linebacker, because his father ran a supermarket.

"Do we offer other inducements?" Lafferty said. "Well, we're not supposed to do it . . . uh . . . we don't do it."

Thomas Kincaid, who lettered from 1939 to 1941, told author Brett Perkins in *Frantic Francis* that he was offered an excellent position with a Columbus coal company by prominent booster Chester C. Cook.

"He introduced me to all the heads of the departments and told them that whenever I came in, they were to let me work wherever I wanted to in the organization," Kincaid said. "Most of the work was pretty simple. He gave me a certain amount of money each month, which covered tuition. Cook and I remained close for a long time."

The close relationships weren't unusual. Some of the committeemen became lifelong friends with the players they helped recruit. One-time committeeman Chuck McMurray now works with Archie Griffin at the OSU alumni association. Murray and Griffin even talk on a video that is posted on the OSUAA website about how the committeemen and others took the young star at Columbus Eastmoor High School and his parents to dinner at a downtown Columbus hotel, the old Christopher Inn.

"Committeemen, we were very dedicated, because we were happy to know that coach wanted to have some of us involved," McMurray says. "It was enjoyable to be able to sit and talk with the student athletes. But they had to change things because otherwise it would have gotten completely out of control."

Sometimes it does, anyway, often with boosters who aren't officially associated with the program.

In 2011, the actions of Columbus tattoo parlor owner Edward Rife helped create a major scandal that got six players—Terrelle Pryor, Dan Herron, DeVier Posey, Mike Adams, Solomon Thomas, and Jordan Whiting—suspended for the start of the 2011 season for receiving improper benefits. It eventually led to Jim Tressel's resignation as coach and Pryor's early departure for the NFL.

Law officers searching Rife's home for evidence of drug crimes seized memorabilia—Big Ten championship rings, gold-pants charms, and Pryor's 2009 Fiesta Bowl championship trophy—that the players had sold to Rife for cash or traded for tattoos, both in violation of NCAA rules. Rife didn't sell the memorabilia; he was an OSU fan who had an appreciation for the items and enjoyed his friendship with the players.

DiGeronimo apparently did, too. After starting as a committeeman in the 1980s, he supplied players with jobs at his company for years. During the course of its investigation of the Tattoogate scandal, the NCAA determined that DiGeronimo had overpaid several players for their part-time work, including Posey, the team's leading pass receiver. Posey denied it, as did DiGeronimo and university officials. But DiGeronimo had been in the news before; some OSU football players had previously been charged with receiving $200 cash from him while appearing at a charity event for him in Cleveland, the same event where players had appeared without permission in 2006. The overpayments, on top of the Tattoogate scandal caused the NCAA to hit OSU with a "failure to monitor" charge, the second toughest allegation against a program. School officials disassociated DiGeronimo from the program, which made the former booster angry.

"They're trying to put it all on me, the supposedly rogue booster," he told the *Columbus Dispatch*. "They want to get all the heat off them."

In a college football world that seems to have gone wild at times, DiGeronimo obviously wasn't the first to be cast in that role, even at OSU. In 2004, it was reported that a Springfield, Ohio, booster named Robert Q.

Baker gave a job with his Columbus health care company and who knows what else to Chris Gamble, and that an appreciative Gamble even called Baker on his cell phone during halftime of the Fiesta Bowl. Baker also gave quarterback Troy Smith $500, supposedly as an advance payment for work that was to be done at his company, although neither Baker nor Smith ever followed up on it. Sound familiar?

Baker was eventually disassociated from the program and even prohibited from attending future games. At the time, OSU athletic director Andy Geiger described him as part of a seamy "underworld" of overzealous and sometimes dishonest boosters, gamblers, agents, and agents' runners he said exists at every school, an underworld Geiger said he battled daily.

After Smith sat out the Alamo Bowl as part of a two-game suspension for that incident, there was a lot of talk about "boosters" who really aren't—fans more interested in bragging about how they know a player or how they received a call from one at halftime than they are with actually helping the player or the program.

Earl Bruce benefited tremendously from the committeemen's recruiting efforts when he was head coach, but when the news about Baker broke, it didn't take the old coach much time to evaluate the situation.

"*That* guy is no booster," Bruce said, looking as if he were just handed a chunk of limburger cheese. And the same thing could probably be said of Rife, DiGeronimo, or any other Ohio State fan who ultimately ends up inflicting major damage on the football program they profess to love.

Or to put it another way, Robert Q. Baker, Bobby DiGeronimo, and Edward Rife couldn't carry John W. Galbreath's jock.

# 25

# The Rituals

Earle Bruce rocked and yelled and clenched his fist. He nodded and pointed and paced the field, only a few feet from where he once paced the sideline. He clamped his jaw so tightly that his face turned the color of an overripe tomato, his way of letting his listeners know that the words that escaped his lips came from deep inside.

It was Ohio State's senior tackle, one last hit of a tackling dummy for departing seniors before they played Michigan. If anyone can wake up the echoes in Ohio Stadium, the former OSU coach can.

"I am a Buckeye," Bruce's voice boomed into the microphone, as a way of introduction. The crowd screamed so loud that it drowned out his voice, no small feat. "I learned that in 1949 when I came here. I didn't know much about Ohio State then. I know a hell of a lot now."

The year was 1996. Bruce's speech was this ritual at its best or worst, depending on your perspective. Coach Jack Wilce had initiated the "senior tackle" tradition in 1913, as a last-practice-before-the-team's-last-game chance to honor the departing seniors with one last run at the tackling dummy. It turned into an annual rite of passage. For most of its existence, it was a relatively private affair, at times involving only the players and coaches, and later witnessed only by close friends and family members.

But then OSU began to have trouble beating Michigan during the John Cooper era and everybody started looking for ways to shake the Buckeyes out of their doldrums. So in 1994, with Cooper sporting an 0-5-1 record against the Wolverines, OSU athletic director Andy Geiger decided it was time to do something.

"We have all this tradition," he said at the time, "and yet it occurred to me that these players were one, maybe two years old when Archie Griffin played football here. It occurred to me that the things that people talked about, the great traditions, weren't connecting with these guys."

A parade of former players spoke with the team during the daily practice sessions and then the cleanup hitter, 1970 cocaptain Rex Kern, delivered a speech at senior tackle, which suddenly became a public event. Curious as it seems, that senior tackle and the one Bruce spoke at two years later became two of the more memorable events in Ohio State football history.

As Kern's voice reverberated through the old stadium, you could almost see the ghosts stirring. There were more than 20,000 fans in the stands . . . to see the seniors take a run at a blocking sled. Still, the old quarterback made the evening worthwhile.

He spoke of Chic Harley and Jim Stillwagon, of Paul Warfield and John Hicks, of Heisman Trophy winners and butt-kickers. But it was when he talked of his Michigan memories that the current players seemed most attentive.

"I remember when [Jack Tatum] de-cleated Denny Brown, the quarterback for the team Up North," Kern said. "Two series later, Tate was in the same position, firing on the west side, and he gets knocked down. Ron Johnson, the slender All-American tailback, breaks through the line and is going for the score, and Tate gets up off the ground and catches him from behind. That's a great play. That's never quitting.

"I'm gonna tell you who's gonna win the football game tomorrow. It's gonna be the team that makes the fewest mistakes and never quits."

A few feet away, Griffin and trainer Billy Hill couldn't restrain their chuckles. Kern, the football medium, had summoned Woody Hayes from the grave for his pre-Michigan speech. It was loaded with clichés, an enduring monument to corn. Oh, and, uh, Hayes was 16-11-1 against Michigan.

There were several more minutes of vintage Woody, before the former All-American grabbed them with a closing that was vintage Kern.

"In 1970, the crowd elevated us," he said, looking directly at the team's starting quarterback. "Bobby [Hoying], I came up, open end of the stadium, we caught them in man-to-man defense. You've got to seize an opportunity. We called an audible. Bruce Jankowski, 15-yard post pattern.

I threw the football. I landed on my back, and I waited for the crowd to respond. They erupted. I looked in front of me. I was on my back. I saw that ugly helmet in my face, and I said to this guy, not out of boasting, but out of excitement, 'We scored a touchdown, did we?'

"And what I did, I reached down and I saw that ugly helmet and I kissed it, and I said, 'It's finished.'"

The speech was a classic and the crowd went wild. The next day the Buckeyes beat Michigan 22–6, all of which seemed to say that *this* was the way to have senior tackle. So the next year, former All-American linebacker Ike Kelley delivered a good but not-so-stirring speech before another senior tackle/pep rally and . . . the Buckeyes lost 31–23.

Next up: Bruce, who sometimes speaks with such force and conviction that he could probably convince a pacifist to join the army. If possible, the old coach's 1996 speech was even better than Kern's and the crowd was even larger. There may have been 30,000 there this time to see the seniors take a run at a blocking sled.

"Not only do we have [this] tradition," Bruce said, "but I've got a little thing in my hand called the gold pants." The crowd roared. "Hey, guys, I've got eight of them. I want you to get two by kicking the hell out of Michigan."

The crowd screamed its approval. The players were mesmerized. Bruce invoked the sacred name of Francis Schmidt, told them how Schmidt long ago said that Michigan players put their pants on one leg at a time just like the Buckeyes do, and told them how that started the tradition of giving the gold charm to players for beating the Wolverines.

"That coach, Francis Schmidt, beat Michigan 38–0, 34–0, 21–0, 21–0, four years in a row," Bruce said. "And then he lost three." The preacher/coach paused long enough to kiss the tips of his five fingers. ". . . And they kissed him goodbye."

It was priceless, inspiring stuff, and it seemed to reinforce what Kern had started. Then Michigan upset the unbeaten, No. 2–ranked Buckeyes 13–9, and some of the Wolverine players said afterward that they had caught Bruce's spellbinding performance on local TV back at the team hotel and he had inspired *them*. If that were true, it must have acted like a delayed-action time capsule; the Buckeyes dominated Michigan in the first half and came away with only a 9–0 lead, in part because Stan Jackson over-threw Michael Wiley on a sure touchdown pass. And then again, maybe someone showed the Michigan players a tape of Bruce's speech on the side-lines in the second half.

Either way, the days of the big pep rally/senior tackle were over. It was now seen as the problem rather than the solution. So in 1998, senior tackle was again a quiet, team-only affair and the Buckeyes lost to Michigan again, 20–14. In 1999, the ritual wasn't held before the Michigan game at all—they won 31–16 that year—but instead on December 20, before their trip to the Sugar Bowl. Supposedly this was a better way to do it, although if you think about it, it still didn't make much sense. The seniors were hitting the old tackling sled to say good-bye to the same teammates they were going to be practicing with all week after Christmas and the same guys they were going to be playing with against Texas A&M on New Year's night. After the game, they were going to say good-bye to a few juniors who didn't say good-bye at senior tackle, juniors who would be just as gone as the seniors when they entered the NFL draft early that spring.

Remember, when Wilce started this in 1913, there were no bowl games. The last regular-season game was the last game of the season. In those days, that really was the last time those seniors hit the tackling dummy. So in a way the Buckeyes got back in step with tradition in 1999; they were 6-5 going into the Michigan game and weren't invited to a bowl game and sen-ior tackle got moved back to the night before the last game. It was also moved out of Ohio Stadium and back to the Woody Hayes Athletic Center practice field. This time the public was allowed in but not invited.

"We're welcoming," noted senior tackle choreographer Andy Geiger said. "But we're not trying to make it into a Cecil B. DeMille, parting-of-the-seas, let-the-horse-through kind of event."

Although only 400 showed up, they asked for autographs, chatted it up with the players, and generally acted as though they were wandering the grounds of a giant flea market—a strange sight the night before the biggest game of the season. The Michigan players weren't inspired and neither were the Buckeyes. Ohio State lost again.

After Jim Tressel became coach in 2001, the ritual became a private friends-and-family affair, same as it was during Tressel's days on Bruce's staff, and his record against Michigan was spectacular. But when a tradition has been shaped and molded like a ball of Silly Putty, it does create questions of just how much of a tradition it really is.

Ohio State probably has more of these football rituals and traditions than most schools, and some of them are beautiful, some are worthless, and some, like senior tackle, seem almost obsolete. The tradition of giving a little gold pants charm to players that beat Michigan is nice, in part because it hasn't changed at all since Schmidt's day. The Cooper years may have been hard on the membership rolls of the group responsible for ordering and paying for those little charms—for a while, the Michigan Pants Club was about as functional as the Flat Earth Society and the Bull Moose Party—but it did a booming business during the Tressel years. Those little charms are also a good fallback for current players who need money for pizza or high-def televisions—two of the six players (Pryor and Thomas) suspended for the start of the 2011 season for receiving improper benefits sold their 2008 gold pants—and unemployed former players who have bills to pay in a distressed economy. The last pair I saw on eBay sold for $1,000.

Undoubtedly, Script Ohio is the best Ohio State tradition. The signature formation of the Ohio State Marching Band, started in 1936 by then band director Eugene J. Weigel, has actually been honored as the No. 1 college football tradition by several national outlets. Fans of other schools would doubtless disagree. But seeing The Best Damn Band in the Land form in a triple-block O formation and then slowly unwind to form the O-H-I-O while playing Robert Planquette's "Le Regiment de Sambre et Meuse" (a military march written in 1871 and played at graduation ceremonies at the U.S. Military Academy) has been known to raise goose bumps on the arms of even the most cynical sportswriter. I don't think I've spoken with a fan who had just attended his first Ohio State football game who didn't mention it as a highlight, if not the highlight, of his day.

On the rare occasion when a person other than a fourth- or fifth-year sousaphone player dots the i, the moment can be almost as important as the game itself, especially if the opponent is Rice, New Mexico State, or some other non-conference clunker. Woody Hayes, Jack Nicklaus, and John and Annie Glenn are among the i-dotters, and if you watch their performances on YouTube, see their tears of pride and hear the crowd, it's hard not to be moved by the occasion.

Even Weigel would be forced to admit that the inspiration for this great tradition was not all his. A similar floating formation was first performed during the 1932 season by the University of Michigan Marching Band—a set piece—and Weigel said he based the looped "Ohio" script on the marquee sign of Loew's Ohio Theatre in downtown Columbus. Loew's closed the theater in 1969, but the community rallied to save it and today the theater is one of the city's most-treasured jewels. A cynic weary of the city's Ohio State football obsession might suggest that the thought of losing the daily sight of script "Ohio" across from the Statehouse was simply too much for local citizenry to bear.

That same cynic would probably also like to call a moratorium on the playing of "Hang on Sloopy," an OSU band tradition that has always created a lot of head-scratching by nonbelievers. The commonsense crowd thinks there has to be a good reason why the 1960s rock song is played repeatedly at Ohio State sporting events. Was Sloopy a promising fullback who had his career cut short by injury? Was he a rich industrialist who financed the recruitment of high school superstars who weren't sure if Ohio State would provide them with the best, uh, education? Was she Woody Hayes's secret girlfriend? A dog that saved an All-American quarterback from drowing in the Olentangy River? Who was this Sloopy, anyway? And why was he or she hanging on?

In fact, Sloopy was singer Dorothy Sloop, who had no connection whatsoever to the OSU football program. Fact is, there is no deeper meaning to the program's strong attachment to the song. It was recorded by the Union City, Indiana/Ohio pop group the McCoys in 1965 and made it to No. 1 on the national charts in October of that year before it was supplanted by the Beatles' "Yesterday."

OSU band member John Tatgenhorst liked it and created an arrangement for it, band director Dr. Charles Spohn reluctantly agreed to have the band play it, the fans fell in love with it, and it's been a staple of OSU games ever since. In 1985, the Ohio legislature made it the state's official rock song. Apparently, the state's lawmakers didn't have much to do that year. But at least Sloopy connects to fans; the O-H-I-O cheer they do during the pauses in the chorus while using their arms to mimic the shape of the letters has even become a staple at Cleveland Browns and Cincinnati Bengals games.

The Illibuck Trophy, the wooden turtle that goes to the winner of the Ohio State–Illinois game, has no real meaning to even the most devoted fans. The tradition started in 1925 when the schools decided it would be good to start a ritual that would befit the series' competitive history. But why a turtle? As the story goes, a live turtle was chosen because of its long life expectancy, which only makes sense if you believe that the trophy had to be alive in the first place.

But all great traditions have to start somewhere, and this one started at a Columbus fish market, where a live snapping turtle was picked as the embodiment of the rivalry. Illinois won the game that year, and Atius Sachem, the junior honorary society at Illinois responsible for upholding its side of the tradition (Bucket and Dipper has that honor at Ohio State) immediately realized the problem with taking care of a live snapping turtle and advocated the loser getting stuck with it. Nothing doing. Tradition is tradition, I suppose. Fortunately for everyone except the turtle, it died in the bathtub of an Illinois fraternity house in 1927, and a wooden turtle took its place. No one apparently takes unnatural habitats like bath tubs into account when they figure the long life spans of snapping turtles.

Nine wooden turtles have been carved since—the scores of the games are listed on the turtle's shell—and if that wasn't silly enough, somewhere along the line the two societies devised this curious ritual of passing the turtle backwards over the heads of its members as it passed from one side to another. How passing wooden turtles back and forth every year to com- memorate a rivalry that really isn't makes college football any better at either school is anyone's guess, but both sides brag that this is the second-oldest trophy in the Big Ten (behind the Little Brown Jug). At least that live snap- ping turtle didn't give up its life in vain.

There are other Ohio State football rituals that are easier to understand:

The 2,420-pound Ohio Stadium victory bell that has been rung after every home win since OSU beat California on October 2, 1954, is the per- fect punctuation to a victory, although somehow it seems more moving after a win over Michigan than one over San Diego State.

The Buckeye Grove, a stand of trees that commemorates each first team All-American, is a beautiful way of remembering outstanding players while absorbing a little carbon dioxide from the atmosphere. It is located between the southwestern corner of the stadium and Morrill Tower; it's just too bad that's not where it was when the tree-planting ritual started in 1934. The grove, then located near the southeast corner of the stadium, was moved during the stadium renovation project in 1999–2000. But at least it offers fans a chance to do something before the game other than drink beer and eat cocktail weenies at their tailgates.

The team's singing of "Carmen Ohio" in front of the South Stands at the end of each home game is a relatively new ritual, and it probably doesn't rise to the level of "tradition" just yet. When Tressel was hired, he came in talking about "family" and "unity," and in his mind this was one way to foster that. With a bunch of macho football players, however, it was questionable whether this ritual would last.

"One of the best things [about the players] has been their willingness and their openness," Tressel said at the time. "I think they're willing to do anything that makes a little sense. I think they would put their foot down if we said, 'We're going to have a tradition that says we're going to go up to the press box and jump off the back if we win.' I'm not sure they would do that. But they have a willingness to have an open mind."

With the disasters of the previous two seasons still fresh in their memories, the 2001 Buckeyes were willing to try just about anything. A dive off the press box, a night in a bed of snakes, a bag of pork rinds every day for breakfast, even sing.

"Oh, Susanna." "Camptown Races." "La Cucaracha." "Carmen Ohio." What the heck?

"I'll do anything for the team," senior linebacker Joe Cooper said, in a weak monotone. "I'll sing."

It was funny watching them the first few years, players looking up at the scoreboard to read the words and nervously looking around to see if their teammates were singing. But after they won the 2002 national championship, singing didn't seem so bad. Now it seems almost normal.

Urban Meyer said he was "honored to be able to keep a tradition that I believe Coach Tressel started," but admitted that he needed a little help with it after the 2012 spring game, his first as OSU head coach.

"I asked [graduate assistant] Kirk Barton, 'Now where do I go and what do I do,'" Meyer said. "He said, 'You park it right there and look at the scoreboard.'"

Those Buckeye leaves on the Ohio State helmets were embraced right from the beginning in 1967, although not everyone thought the idea concocted by Woody Hayes and trainer Ernie Biggs was such a good one at the time. One UPI reporter described it as "schoolmarm tactics."

"It may never take the place of little gold stars on 'A' papers, but if you're an Ohio State football player, and you're good, you'll get a little Buckeye leaf decal on your helmet," the UPI wrote.

Hayes explained it as "every boy who intercepts a pass, recovers a fumble, blocks a punt, or makes a great play gets a Buckeye leaf on his helmet. So do the top back and top lineman on offense and defense each week."

Tressel tweaked that one a little. After he arrived, only six of the thirty-seven ways to earn a leaf saluted individual accomplishments, and no one received a leaf when the team lost.

This one also has a little oomph behind it. The stickers weren't designed by some doodler in the equipment room but by Milton Caniff, an alumnus and nationally syndicated cartoonist of the popular *Steve Canyon* and *Terry and the Pirates* strips. Several schools copied the idea and now helmet stickers are a common sight in college football.

No one can imagine an OSU helmet without a Buckeye leaf these days, but nearly everyone would like to eradicate the image of car-flipping, mattress-burning rioters east of campus after an important victory. Although this ritual is one that doesn't inspire pride, it has happened sporadically over the years and is understandable: In a metropolitan area of 1.9 million that largely dotes on the Buckeyes, there is a huge twenty-something crowd that knows where to find a party, which is near campus on the night of a big victory. During any given celebration, it's probably safe to say that a high percentage of the revelers aren't students.

Tradition? Well, sort of. The Columbus police seem to have gotten a handle on it lately and that ritual may finally be dying, like the Hineygate party that ended a twenty-six-year run of all home games in 2009 when it lost its place in the Holiday Inn parking lot across from St. John Arena, or shrinking, like senior tackle. But others, like the band's pregame skull session (a band warm-up routine with a pep rally atmosphere) in St. John Arena—the team even stops by on the way to the stadium—seem to be gaining steam, and more are probably on the way.

Ohio State has so many football traditions, good and bad, that it's hard to keep track of all of them. That isn't a bad thing, either. Not every good football program has a long list of traditions and the poor ones never do.

"Michigan doesn't have near the football tradition of Ohio State, I want you to know that," Bruce said a few years ago on one of WTVN's Michigan game-day radio broadcasts. "They have no gold pants to beat the Buckeyes. They have no victory bell that I've ever heard. They have no Buckeye grove to give an All-American a tree, do they? They don't have any of that stuff. They just have football."

And as anyone who has ever passed a wooden turtle over his or her head backwards can tell you, sometimes football just isn't enough.

# 26

# The Secret

To those who knew Woody Hayes and Bo Schembechler, their deep affection for each other has never been much of a secret. To those who didn't, it seems like an impossibility.

The famous Ten-Year War was as much "Woody vs. Bo" as it was "Ohio State vs. Michigan." It was Woody hating Michigan so much he couldn't bring himself to call it by name, referring to it only as the school Up North. It was Bo, one of Woody's former assistants and most trusted associates, coaching with the enemy.

It only makes sense that they must have intensely hated each other, because, well, how else could it be? Bo was a traitor. Woody was an unforgiving hothead. Bo was an Ohio native and took dozens of Ohio players to Michigan. Did I mention that Woody was an unforgiving hothead? From 1969 to 1978, from the time of Bo's hiring at Michigan to Woody's firing at Ohio State, they coached the two best teams in the Big Ten, two teams that were usually in the top 10 nationally, two teams that represented the conference in the Rose Bowl every year.

Woody and Bo as best buds? It seems to defy the laws of nature.

"They couldn't beat me with two Michigan coaches," Woody once said, "so they had to come down here and take a coach that I trained."

Okay, so maybe Woody was just a little bitter over his former assistant coaching at Michigan. Even on his best days, Woody has never been accused of being a gracious loser. But during the ten years they opposed each other, Schembechler described their friendship as "dormant. It didn't change; it was just dormant." And once Woody was no longer coaching, it became clear that their relationship as bitter rivals/old friends was much more complicated than it appeared.

The day after Hayes punched Clemson's Charlie Bauman in the Gator Bowl, the Michigan coach jumped in the car and headed to Columbus to console the now-former Ohio State coach.

Schembechler left Ann Arbor and got as far south as Bowling Green, Ohio, about 125 miles from Columbus, when a huge snowstorm hit and the state highway patrol issued a bulletin advising people to stay off the roads. Bo stopped at a Holiday Inn, called Woody, and told him that he was on his way to see him but that he had to stop in Bowling Green because of the storm. He told him that he would get up in the morning and drive on down.

Woody asked his old rival where he was again and hung up the phone. Three hours later, Woody was knocking on Bo's hotel room door. It was a classic case of one-upmanship—I can make it through the storm and you can't—and probably the last time Hayes treated Bo as a rival.

Acts of friendship after that were numerous though. Schembechler asked Woody to speak to his Michigan team several times in the years following the punch, and surprising as this would seem to the casual fan, Hayes always did it.

"Once he retired, we got together quite a bit and talked quite a bit," Schembechler said. Ohio State fans hated Bo and Michigan fans hated Woody, so it was natural to assume the two men hated each other. But they didn't.

"Several times [Schembechler] would be sick or ill and he would never ever miss a practice," former Michigan defensive back David Key said. "Once he had kidney stones and I swear he passed the kidney stones in the middle of practice just so he wouldn't miss it. But when Woody died, it was such an emotional roller coaster for him, we took two days off of spring drills to honor Woody."

Woody felt the same way about Schembechler, although again that was clear mostly only to those who knew both men well. In 1987, Woody heard Bo was speaking at a luncheon in Dayton. Even though he was in poor health, Woody asked a friend to drive him over there just so he could introduce Schembechler. Bo later remembered how feeble Woody looked leaning on his cane but said he gave a twenty-minute introduction and then stayed for every word of his old friend's speech. Woody died the next day.

Then in his 1989 book *Bo*, Schembechler penned a chapter entitled "Woody and Me" and fessed up:

"I loved Woody Hayes," he wrote. "I am not ashamed to say it. In the 37 years I knew him, he coached me, humbled me, employed me, angered me and taught me more about the game than anyone else could. I guess I was about as close to him as anyone, but to the day he died, I never considered myself his equal."

But not every sports fan reads every book, so the image that Woody and Bo were enemies persisted, even though Bo would occasionally be caught saying something nice about his old rival. The Ten-Year War, remember? Then in 2003, Schembechler wrote the foreword to a book called *I Remember Woody* in which he lavished more praise on the old coach and closed with "I miss him a lot."

Probably not until all of the publicity accompanying Schembechler's death, the day before the 2006 Ohio State–Michigan game that matched No. 1 against No. 2, did the full extent of their relationship begin to hit home with the public.

Schembechler spoke at a Michigan press conference that Monday and was complimentary of his former boss. They went way back; Bo had been a graduate assistant coach on Woody's first Ohio State staff in 1951, and after a stint in the army and jobs at three other schools, he returned to Hayes's staff for five more years.

"I escaped from Columbus when I got the head-coaching job at Miami [University]," Schembechler said. "But I had a wonderful experience there because I coached for Woody when Woody was really Woody. He was the most irascible guy that ever lived and the worst guy in the world to work for. But I wouldn't change that experience for anything in the world because . . . I learned a lot."

The day after he died, Dave Dowdell, a retired OSU policeman, told the *Columbus Dispatch* how he had been Bo's bodyguard for several of his games as Michigan coach in Ohio Stadium, was his escort at Hayes's funeral, and was given permission by then university president Edward Jennings to take Schembechler to the Ohio State ROTC building, where he could spend a few moments in Hayes's office. Dowdell said Schembechler walked around in silence, looking at the memorabilia, then sat down at his desk where Hayes had scattered papers and notes for a book he was writing. He was in the midst of a chapter entitled "Bo" when he died. Dowdell said Schembechler "shed a few tears in the office that day."

Two days before Bo's death, HBO Sports had interviewed him for a documentary (*Michigan vs. Ohio State, The Rivalry*) that was released a year later. In it, the former Michigan coach was sitting there, talking about Woody in hushed, almost reverential tones.

"I was his best friend," Schembechler said. "And he was a great friend of mine."

Another clip shows an ailing Hayes paying tribute to his old foe. "And after that Woody went home and died," Schembechler said.

So the idea of Woody and Bo as more of an episode of *Friends* than a battle scene from *Braveheart* is no longer much of a secret and becomes less so every day. A couple of years ago, then Stanford coach Jim Harbaugh relayed a story that his dad, former Michigan assistant coach Jack Harbaugh, had told of the day that Woody was fired.

"I remember my dad telling me that when they fired Woody, Bo came into the staff meeting sobbing into his arms, saying, 'They got the old man. They finally got him.' It was a crushing day for Bo, realizing the love he had for Woody and that their legacy was tied to each other."

A secret?

Not anymore.

# 27

# Gospel Writers

There is a story about Jim Schlemmer, a longtime sports editor for the *Akron Beacon-Journal*, that old writers swear is true.

Schlemmer was supposedly standing in the old press box at Ohio Stadium before an Ohio State football game one fall Saturday when he looked down at his watch and smiled.

"Well, they should be going down the aisle right now," he said.

One of the other writers looked at him quizzically. "Who?"

"My son," Schlemmer said.

The other sportswriter was aghast. "Your *son*? You aren't at your son's wedding?"

Schlemmer smiled again.

"If he's dumb enough to get married on Ohio State game day," he said, "then that's his problem."

The rotund writer covered the Cleveland Indians for forty-five years and was the founder of the Soap Box Derby in Akron in 1935. But he had a special place in his heart for Ohio State football ever since his college days when he was the sports editor of the student *Ohio State Lantern*.

By all accounts, Schlemmer was quite a character. Another story about him that has made the press box rounds involve his drinking too much one night while covering Indians spring training in Tucson. He stripped down to take a shower at his hotel, opened the front door instead of the bathroom door, and ended up standing outside in the parking lot, as the door to his room slammed shut. He supposedly hid in the bushes the rest of the night—thankfully, this was Arizona and not Wisconsin—until he was able to flag down one of his cronies and get him to retrieve a key from the front desk.

Schlemmer was hardly the only character who knew his way to the Ohio Stadium press box over the years, and he sure wasn't the only one who thought OSU football was special.

Paul Hornung also covered the sport from his days with the student *Lantern* and for most of his fifty-one years (1930–1981) with the *Columbus Dispatch*. Sometimes he seemed to have more allegiance to the program than to his newspaper, and his willingness to become a shill for the program didn't always make him popular with the other writers. He became so close to Woody Hayes that he would sometimes be admitted to the OSU locker room after games—while the rest of the writers huddled outside like pariahs. But he was such a soft-spoken, well-meaning gentleman that it was difficult, if not impossible, for his peers to dislike him, even if they didn't respect him for his occasional disregard of journalistic principles.

I replaced Hornung on the OSU beat in 1977, and before my first day of practice at the old North Facility, my boss, Dick Otte, told me to make sure I asked trainer Billy Hill for injury information after practice. But when I asked Hill if anyone had been hurt in practice, he looked at me as if I had just asked for combination to the wall safe in his home.

"I can't give you that," Hill said. His words were accompanied by a look of disbelief. This kid really was new. "The old man doesn't like it. If he says it's OK that's fine, but we've never done that before."

So I went down the hall and knocked on the door of Woody's little office, thinking an ugly scene was about to unfold. Would Hayes treat me like one of those offending downs markers he had been known to attack? Would he try to turn me into a human pretzel? No one said this journalism stuff would be easy, I guess.

"I asked Billy if anybody got hurt during practice and he said I had to ask you if it was OK." I winced, waiting to be buried in an eruption of molten lava.

"Awwww, I don't give a shit," Woody said, crinkling his face into a look of disgust. "Tell Billy to give you the information."

I probably couldn't have looked more surprised if Woody had handed me a $100 bill. At the time, it seemed impossible to believe that Hornung might not have even asked Woody for injury updates all these years, but the longer I knew both men the more likely it seemed to me. Hornung was probably more worried about info getting out that might somehow hurt the program than Woody was. To a guy only a few years out of journalism school, it all seemed very strange.

After Pauley—that's what his *Dispatch* coworkers called him—retired, he wrote a book on Ohio State football. I was asked to write a review of it, an uncomfortable task given that I really liked the guy and he had been my coworker. It was a nice book, but it included none of the good insider OSU football stories Hornung had told me while he worked there. I politely pointed this out in the review and then mentioned to him on the phone later that everybody would have enjoyed reading those stories.

"They never will," he said. "Those are private. I will take them to my grave."

He also didn't mention Dick Beltz's name in his account of the '35 OSU–Notre Dame game, even though Beltz's fumble had cost the Buckeyes the game. Hornung told me that he had purposely left it out so as not to embarrass him, another sign that he had a good heart, if not a journalist's or historian's sense of duty. Hornung's act of kindness was apparently misplaced. In a 1995 interview, Beltz said that it took him a while to realize it, but that mistake "was only four or five seconds in a lifetime" and he didn't think it should be treated as though it were a disgrace. As badly as Hornung wanted the Buckeyes to win, it was probably difficult for him to believe that this might not be the defining moment in a seventy-year-old man's life. Deep down, Hornung may have even resented the fumble that had cost his Buckeyes an important game.

It wasn't unusual for collegiate programs to have boosters in the news media in the old days, although Hornung was clearly near the top of his class in that respect. The press contingents were much smaller in those days and newspaper writers had much more access to the players and coaches than they do today, which in turn created friendships and relationships that wouldn't be tolerated by today's editors.

Si Burick from the *Dayton Daily News* covered Ohio State as long as Hornung did over roughly the same period of time and, like Hornung, rarely missed a game. Hayes also considered the longtime Dayton sports editor a friend, even though Burick wasn't reluctant to criticize the coach in print when he deserved it.

After the Buckeyes lost a national championship in the 1976 Rose Bowl, losing to a UCLA team it had already beaten previously, an angry Hayes refused to let his players meet with reporters and wouldn't even make himself available for a few questions. In an open letter to his old friend, Burick took Hayes to task:

"Dear Woody: This is man to man, not boy to boy. You and I have known each other for almost 30 years, through good times and bad, through fat years and lean. You'll be 63 come Feb. 14. That's a grownup age, Woody. "

Burick wrote that no one had ever asked him to be a good loser and eventually nailed it with this line: "Your unwillingness to face the media, Woody, or let your quality kids do so, embarrassed your school and the Big Ten Conference."

Like Hornung, Burick was a good guy who considered Ohio State football important. Journalistically, his way was much better and his loyalties weren't misplaced. He worked for his newspaper, not Ohio State.

"He never missed a game, even when his health was bad and I mean bad," retired OSU sports information director Marv Homan said. "He even had a driver bring him here. He dragged himself to all the games, home and away."

During the 1940s, '50s, and '60s, several writers besides Burick, Hornung, and Schlemmer did that. Kaye Kessler was Hornung's counterpart on the *Columbus Citizen* and eventually the *Columbus Citizen-Journal*. While he didn't challenge Hayes, Kessler wasn't his personal PR man the way Hornung was. Tom Keys, the *C-J*'s sports editor and another writer who attended most games, once explained that if Hayes said he didn't want to see something you saw at practice in the paper and you put it in, you would probably never be allowed at practice again. Unless a local reporter was changing professions or at least changing beats, he didn't have much choice but to adhere to Hayes's rules.

For years, John Dietrich of *The Plain Dealer* and Jack Clowser of the rival *Cleveland Press* were also regulars at all OSU football games, home and away. Homan said he used to get a kick out of the running feud the two friends had during the Woody years over his ground-oriented style of play.

"John was with the *Plain Dealer* and it had a Sunday edition and the *Press* didn't," Homan said. "John always joked that he liked Woody Hayes's football because the clock didn't stop much. He used almost all running plays and because of that, John had a little more time to devote to his story. Jack would complain of the lack of passing . . . you know they actually argued about that. Jack always accused John of defending Woody just because of the quick playing times. There was a lot of good-natured banter, but I think there was something to it."

The level of trust between coaches and reporters has dissipated over the years. In 1919, OSU coach Jack Wilce closed practices before the Michigan game that year and the *Ohio State Journal*'s Walter Chamblin said that the squad practiced "behind gates closed tighter than prison doors." But reporters were allowed in and some of them even described the "secret" workouts in some detail. Several of the reporters had been around for a while, which must have helped; *Columbus Dispatch* sports editor Harvey A. Miller held that position from 1903 to 1924 and was a regular at almost all of the games for most of those years. The most unusual arrangement belonged to center Fritz Holtkamp, who served as a correspondent for the *Dispatch* and reported details from practice under the name "Wahoo."

Many famous sportswriters beat a path to Columbus to cover games over the years. The *Chicago American*'s Harold Johnson came to see Chic Harley in 1919. New York writers Grantland Rice, Damon Runyon, and Allison Danzig covered the 1935 Notre Dame game in Columbus. *The Chicago Tribune*'s Wilfrid Smith was also there to see the Buckeyes and Irish in '35, and he was in the Ohio Stadium press box quite often over the years. So was Chet Smith from the *Pittsburgh Press* and in later years, the *New York Times*'s Gordon White.

But the local guys were the ones who mostly spread the gospel to legions of Ohio State fans. Bill McKinnon succeeded Miller at the *Dispatch* and covered the team for many years at the same time Lew Byrer was at the *Citizen* and Bob Hooey was at the *Ohio State Journal*. All three were local institutions.

Hooey was a big man who loved to eat, a dapper dresser who was something of a playboy in his early years. An old reporter described how "he always kept, in the bottom drawer of his desk, a couple of 'spare' columns on timeless subjects, ready to be grabbed and put into type on those days when he came to work on a grim morning after."

Maybe that explains a famous Hooey description of Chic Harley on the wall in the media center at the Woody Hayes Athletic Facility:

"If you never saw him run with a football, we can't describe it to you. It wasn't like Red Grange or Tom Harmon or anybody else. It was kind of a cross between music and cannon fire, and it brought your heart up under your ears."

It's great stuff . . . but Hooey didn't write it. Humorist James Thurber, who went to the same Columbus high school as Harley and was also in school at OSU during the Harley years, wrote it for the New York newspaper *PM* in 1941, and Hooey used it in a column in 1947 as if he wrote it, possibly fishing it out of that bottom drawer of his desk. Hooey died in a car crash in 1949, on his way home from picking up his tickets to fly to the 1950 Rose Bowl.

When it came to Ohio State sports, Byrer was an expert. He became sports editor of the *Citizen* in 1918, the year before Harley returned for his senior year, and he retired in 1959 when Woody Hayes was on the sidelines. He went to high school in Shelby, Ohio, and played pro football with the Shelby Blues; he enjoyed talking about how he played football against the great Jim Thorpe. He worked on newspapers in Shelby and Marion, Ohio, before the *Citizen* hired him. When he became sports editor a year or so later, he was reminded that his appointment was only temporary, and he joked in a 1949 column that "I'm still on that temporary assignment. Someday, I hope they make it permanent."

Byrer was mentioned in a syndicated story about OSU coach Francis Schmidt by *Syracuse Herald-Journal* sports editor Joe Williams in a vignette that showed that Schmidt wasn't distrustful of reporters the way later coaches were. Williams wrote about how he was allowed to wander into the Buckeyes' locker room and found literally hundreds of Schmidt's plays hanging on the walls.

"We were mildly astonished at the easy informality of the place," Williams wrote. "Apparently total strangers are not discouraged from strolling into the dressing room and digesting the Schmidt masterpieces at length.

"We commented on this to Lew Byrer, the able local gazetteer. Mr. Byrer shrugged his shoulders . . . 'Nobody knows what they mean anyway, and I doubt if even Schmidt does.'"

Byrer knew his subject, and by extension, his readers did, too. Without him and others like him, Ohio State's rich football history would be little more than a long list of scores, dull records, and grainy pictures.

## 28

# A Season from God

The 2002 season had been in the past for only about thirty minutes when senior linebacker Matt Wilhelm tried to make sense of it in an interview tent outside the Fiesta Bowl where the BCS national championship game had just been played.

"We're just a team of fate," he said.

Fate?

Oh, boy. Normally, that tired junk doesn't get past the mental stop sign in a reporter's brain. Probably ninety-nine out of every one hundred times those words slip out of an athlete's mouth, the thought never makes it to the printed page. And it shouldn't. It's mostly nonsense. The phrase has been uttered in various ways millions of times, both by members of championship teams and by the poor wishful souls who want to be, dreamers who seem to believe they can talk their way into sports immortality. Some call themselves a team of fate. Others say they're a team of destiny. Those who chance to lose to one of these fortuitous teams regard fate as an obscenity. They have another, less magnanimous name for it. They call it luck.

The 2002 Buckeyes were indeed lucky; most unbeaten teams are. But if you watched all of the games, this was one of the few times where it almost seemed as if there might actually be something to all this "fate" and "destiny" garbage, that the season really might have been an act of divine providence.

On a cool January night in the desert, a fantastic, if improbable dream came true in maybe the greatest game in school history—Ohio State 31, Miami 24, in double overtime.

A national championship, thirty-four years and a bazillion heartaches after the last one. A 14-0 season that was played on a tightrope ended in a win that was two fourth-down overtime conversions and a late pass interference call away from ending.

When a brutal deadline night for reporters had passed and they gathered for a few postgame beers to ponder what had just occurred, one sentiment was almost universal.

"Can you believe that *this* team just went 14-0?"

Well, uh, no. There had been other Ohio State teams that seemed more likely to run the table, teams that had more talent and entered the season with more experience. But the comment wasn't meant to degrade the Buckeyes, but rather to marvel at the accomplishment. Winning fourteen games without a loss is a remarkable achievement, regardless of the strength or weakness of the schedule. Even when a team is loaded with great players, even when everybody thinks it has an excellent chance to win every game, it can almost always count on finding just enough of a pothole somewhere to knock it off course.

OSU fans will never forget the 28–24 loss to Michigan State in 1998 that shouldn't have happened, the pothole that spoiled what might have been a national-championship season. They remember the loss to Michigan in 1996, the loss to USC in the 1980 Rose Bowl, and the tie game with Michigan in 1973.

But 2002 was different. If anything, those hidden chuckholes seemed to have the opposite effect. When these Buckeyes seemed headed off course, when they seemed about to plunge off a steep cliff, the chuckhole sent them back toward the road and another victory.

Fate? Sometimes it sure seemed that way. Luck? Sometimes it sure seemed that way, too. Some would say that any team that wins as many close games as this one did, that won at Cincinnati in part because the Bearcats dropped two passes in the end zone, that won at Purdue on a 4th-down, 37-yard touchdown reception in the final two minutes, that had to go to overtime to beat Illinois, that won in overtime in the title game, is like a gambler who inexplicably keeps picking the right number on a roulette wheel.

Fate isn't an easy concept to come to grips with. It implies that an invisible force of some kind is pulling things along, following some celestial script that we can't see but we know must be there. It implies that things happen that are somehow out of our control. It says that life can be preordained, that sometimes events occur for some mysterious but precise reason we can't explain.

There are those who would also say that teams make their own luck, that good things happen when teammates care about one another, when they work toward a common cause and when they play together. Craig Krenzel's 37-yard touchdown pass to Michael Jenkins didn't just happen; if Krenzel had underthrown it or if Jenkins had dropped it, the Buckeyes would have lost the game.

Sometimes, it pays not to engage in too much analysis. Sometimes, it's better not to spend too much time studying, to accept good fortune without asking why. This was a beautiful season by anyone's standards, one with enough memories to last a lifetime. The close games and tense moments only served to make it much more special.

One reason it was special: There wasn't even a hint of what was to come in the beginning. The team was ranked No. 13 in the Associated Press preseason poll, and no one, not even the Ohio State players themselves, was talking about a national championship. There were twelve returning starters off a 7-5 team. Krenzel, a junior, was favored to succeed Steve Bellisari at quarterback after starting the final two games in 2001 when Bellisari was suspended, but Scott McMullen and freshman Justin Zwick figured to offer him serious competition for the job. Sophomore Lydell Ross was expected to start at tailback; freshman Maurice Clarett was still just a promising recruit, listed behind Ross and Maurice Hall on the depth chart. The view from the beginning was remarkably different from the view in 2012.

The Buckeyes deviated from the script in the opener and rewrote it the rest of the way. Clarett started against Texas Tech, the first freshman running back to do so at Ohio State in the modern era, and he responded with 175 rushing yards, 30 receiving yards, and three touchdowns, including TD runs of 59 and 45 yards. The 45–21 win over Tech hiked their ranking to No. 8.

The Buckeyes hammered Kent State 51–17—no surprise there—and quickly moved up to No. 6. Then came No. 10 Washington State, favored in some circles to win the Pacific-10 and owner of a 7–6 lead at halftime.

But the second half of the game brought the OSU football that Tressel learned from Earle Bruce, who learned it from Woody Hayes, who learned it from, well, maybe Moses. Part the defensive line and march right through it. And when you're on defense, make the other guys feel like they've just been swamped.

"That second half was Ohio State football," Wilhelm said. "The offense moving the ball, keeping the defense off the field. The defense going out there, confusing a great quarterback and getting three-and-outs, getting interceptions—that's Ohio State football."

No one was sure how the senior linebacker recognized it exactly, given that the program had a 21-15 three-year won-loss record. But the game read like a history book. An interviewer asked an assistant coach about Clarett and his answer contained references to Eddie George. Head coach Jim Tressel brought up Keith Byars. After the opener, Clarett had been compared to Archie Griffin. George . . . Byars . . . Griffin. Something was going on here. Had we passed through a time warp?

"One thing about Maurice Clarett, it's a little bit like when we had Keith Byars here," Tressel said. "He wore on you. In that first quarter you might get him down for 2 and the second quarter you get him down for 3 and in the third quarter you couldn't get him down. He's that kind of guy."

The difference was that Clarett was a freshman playing his third college football game. Clarett's 31 carries for 230 yards—a 7.4 average—made you rub your eyes. This wasn't what fans in the old horseshoe had gotten used to seeing the past few years.

And then again, the following week the Buckeyes played Cincinnati in Paul Brown Stadium—on the road against an in-state opponent for the first time since 1934—and the impressive performance the week before seemed light years away. Clarett missed the game because of arthroscopic knee surgery, but that shouldn't have been a problem; these weren't the Big East Bearcats of today but the Conference USA Bearcats, and the No. 6 Buckeyes were 17-point favorites. But UC led 19–14 entering the fourth quarter, before a Mike Nugent field goal and Krenzel's scrambling touchdown put OSU ahead 23–19 with 3:44 left.

What followed would have a tremendous impact on this storybook season. Bearcats quarterback Gino Guidugli got four shots from the OSU 15-yard line in the final minute and receivers Jon Olinger and George Murray, on respective first and third downs, both dropped passes in the end zone that could have won the game. Finally on fourth down, Wilhelm made a desperate leap at a slant pass intended for LaDaris Vann and tipped it into the air, allowing safety Will Allen to intercept it in the back of the end zone. There were twenty-six seconds left.

"Once Will Allen caught that ball," safety Mike Doss said, "I just looked to the heavens and said, 'Thank you, Jesus.' He was with us out there on that drive."

If Doss had known at the time that one of those plays might have cost the Buckeyes a national championship, he might have prayed all night.

The next week was easy; Clarett returned and OSU beat Indiana 45–17. Then the Buckeyes had another subpar effort at Northwestern. This time it was three lost fumbles by Clarett that gave the 25-point underdog Wildcats a chance before OSU held on and won 27–16. Following a rout of San Jose State, Ohio State trailed 14–13 entering the fourth quarter at Wisconsin. This time, the Buckeyes used a 9-play, 88-yard drive to take the lead—a conversion attempt failed—and wide receiver/cornerback Chris Gamble's interception of a Jim Sorgi pass in the end zone to avoid a Badgers' upset.

The last time the Buckeyes won at Wisconsin, they had danced on the W in the center of the field. This time, they knelt down and said a prayer of thanks for the 19–14 win. Beginning to see a pattern here?

Gamble was the star again the following week in another close call against Penn State. The Buckeyes were trailing 7–6 in the third quarter when Gamble—the first player to start on both sides of the ball for Ohio State in thirty-nine years—intercepted a Zack Mills pass and zig-zagged 40 yards for a touchdown. The Buckeyes, now No. 4 , were 9-0.

Minnesota was a breeze the following week, but at Purdue the Buckeyes, up to No. 2 in the BCS standings, needed an almost-miracle finish to keep the streak alive. Clarett went out of the game early with a shoulder stinger, and the running game fell flat in his absence. They were down 6–3 when Gamble returned a punt 22 yards to the Purdue 46 with 3:10 left. It appeared to be their last shot. On 3rd and 14 from the 50-yard line, Krenzel passed to tight end Ben Hartsock for a gain of . . . 13 yards. Fourth down and one.

Krenzel went to the line intending to throw for the first down. Hartsock was his first choice and he was covered, so he looked deep to Jenkins, who was running a takeoff route with one-on-one coverage by Antwaun Rogers. Krenzel fired a rainbow into the wind and Jenkins caught it for a touchdown. The deep pass was a gamble, but it worked.

"It feels like we're almost kind of destined," Jenkins said.

Only Illinois and Michigan stood between the Buckeyes and a national title shot now. Only. The Buckeyes' road struggle continued at Illinois on a cold, windswept day, with the Buckeyes missing Clarett because of his sore shoulder. The Illini's John Gockman kicked a 48-yard field goal on the last play of regulation to tie it 16–16 and send OSU to its first-ever overtime. The Buckeyes got the ball first and Maurice Hall scored from eight yards out to put OSU up, and then Tim Anderson knocked down Jon Beutjer's fourth-down pass to the end zone that could have tied and sent the teams to another round of overtime.

Afterward, there were no plausible explanations for what was going on, how the Buckeyes always seemed to be living on the edge but never fell off.

"We're 12-0, you know?" Wilhelm said. "Who cares [why]? We're winning ballgames."

Onto the Michigan game, one where many a national title hope had died. But not this time. Clarett was back—he gained 119 yards in 20 carries—and so was the defense. Hall scored the winning touchdown with 4:55 left, and the defense forced turnovers on Michigan's last two possessions to hold on for a 14–9 win, and the No. 2 Buckeyes were somehow 13-0 and on their way to the Fiesta Bowl for the BCS national title game.

The possibility of that seemed like pure fantasy back in August. There was that tortuous thirteen-game schedule, an inexperienced quarterback, a second-year head coach who still hadn't proved himself at the Division I level, a team where the most talented players appeared to be freshmen, and a recent reputation for losing big games.

Really? A shot at the national championship?

Even now that the dream had become tangible, the odds still seemed unbelievably long. Miami was the defending national champion. It had a thirty-four-game win streak. It was an eleven-point favorite at game time. But as you watched the game unfold, as you watched the OSU defense put the squeeze on the Hurricanes, you weren't even sure this was that much of an upset. It was just an extension of a magical, if improbable, Ohio State season, more of what we had seen week after week after week.

Miami running back Willis McGahee takes the handoff and wham, he's on the ground. Quarterback Ken Dorsey drops back to pass and bam, he is chewing on a dirt sandwich. There were mean, angry bodies in the Miami backfield, aggressive, hostile guys who spent the month chewing on rusty nails instead of reading the Hurricanes' press clippings.

Fate? I don't know. Defense wins championships, and the OSU defense had been fantastic all year. Without stifling defense, Krenzel could never have won the game with that spectacular pass to Jenkins at Purdue. Without it, there would have been no win against Michigan. And against Miami it was at its best, holding the powerful Hurricanes to 11 rushing yards in the first half.

OSU's defensive linemen—Kenny Peterson, Will Smith, Tim Anderson, Darrion Scott, Mike Kudla, and David Thompson—were dominant against a team that was used to scoring at will. Dorsey, sacked only eight times all year, was sacked four times. He was even knocked out of the game for a play in the second overtime after a brutal hit by Wilhelm. Miami turned the ball over five times, including once when Maurice Clarett ripped the ball from the hands of cornerback Sean Taylor after an interception.

Even so, Ohio State seemed to have lost it all in the first overtime. An incomplete fourth-down pass from Krenzel to Gamble in the end zone was the Buckeyes' last gasp. Miami players and fans had even begun storming the field in celebration.

Fate can be wily. A field judge had thrown a late flag. Pass interference on Glenn Sharpe. OSU's dream wasn't dead after all.

In the second overtime, Clarett scored on a 5-yard run, and then Buckeyes put up a goal-line stand that ended when linebacker Cie Grant rushed Dorsey into a bad pass on 4th and 1 that fell incomplete.

That fateful flag on the pass interference call in the first overtime would never be forgotten by Miami fans, but to the Buckeyes it just seemed like a continuation of a season-long fairy tale.

"I wasn't surprised," Wilhelm said. "I really believe we're a team of fate."

# 29

# The Greatest Games

I n my first year on the beat in 1977, I covered what seemed certain to be regarded as one of the greatest games in school history. Oklahoma and Ohio State, two of the sport's traditional powers, had never met on a football field. The Sooners were ranked No. 3 and the Buckeyes were No. 4. The game lived up to its advance billing, with Oklahoma finally winning 29–28 on Uwe von Schamann's 41-yard field goal with 18 seconds remaining.

In the weeks immediately following the game I learned that no matter how exciting a game is most fans don't think much of it when their side loses. A game historians regard as a "classic" is taken out with the trash very quickly by most of those on the losing side.

Afterward, the typical exchange about the game between an OSU fan and me would go something like this:

ME: "That was one of the best games I have ever seen."

FAN: "What was so good about it?"

ME: "No, I mean it was exciting."

FAN: "What do you mean?"

ME: "You know, two great programs, lots of scoring, decided by a long field goal at the end . . ."

FAN: "Yeah, so?"

Over the years, I have since discovered that programs with Ohio State's history have so many huge games that it is almost impossible to compile a top 10 or even top 20 "greatest" games list that means anything. There are so many big ones that the author of such a list is guaranteed to embarrass himself by leaving some of the best ones out. If you break them down, it's possible to compile lists of the most exciting games, the most significant games, the most historic games, the biggest wins, the most gut-wrenching losses, and even the best games that were OSU romps, i.e., games that wouldn't qualify for the list in any way other than fan satisfaction.

Most of us define greatness by games that we remember, contests that we witnessed or that have at least occurred in our lifetimes. Recent helps. Yesterday is even better. By that standard, the No. 6 Buckeyes' 31–26 win over No. 8 Arkansas in the 2011 Sugar Bowl (which was later vacated because of NCAA violations) and No. 8 OSU's 26–17 win over No. 7 Oregon in the 2010 Rose Bowl might be regarded by some as two of the greatest wins in school history, even though neither would likely make a real top 20 list as this chapter will show.

This works the other way, too. An old fan who was there the day that Chic Harley called time, changed his muddy shoe, and kicked the extra point to beat Illinois 7–6 in 1916 would swear that was the greatest Ohio State game ever; most of today's fans wouldn't put it in their top 50, if they were even aware the game had been played. Numbers provide the best way to show the futility of this process. Since 1930, the Buckeyes have played fifteen teams that were ranked No. 1, winning five of those games. OSU was ranked itself in eleven of those games and in the top 10 in nine. It has played eighty-eight games while being ranked No. 1, and in eleven of those games the opponent was in the top 10, and in twenty-seven of them the opponent was ranked in the top 25. It has played ninety-two games in which both teams were ranked in the top 10. Heck, beginning with the 2002 BCS national title game against Miami on January 3, 2003, the Buckeyes have been a part of five No. 1 vs. No. 2 battles. The past twenty years alone could provide a top 10 list of "greatest" games.

The two most famous games in school history have their own chapters in this book: the '35 Notre Dame–Ohio State game was judged the best college football game ever by many of the reporters and fans of that era, and the '50 OSU-Michigan game, the Snow Bowl, was famous mostly because of the teams involved and the blizzard conditions they played in.

The obvious question, then, is where to go from there? The Buckeyes have played in five national championship games in the last twenty years, the only official ones in school history, so they should be on any list. The case can be made that the 31–24 double-overtime 2002 title game win over Miami was the biggest win, the most exciting, and also one of the most historic, because it was the first of the school's national championships won in that quasi-official format. It was also huge because Ohio State had gone thirty-four years without a national title, the longest drought since OSU first started winning those mythical honors in the 1940s.

But was that really more important than the No. 1 Buckeyes' 27–16 win over No. 2 USC in the 1968 Rose Bowl, which clinched the national title? And what about previous title-clinching wins: in 1957 (over Oregon, 10–7, in the Rose Bowl), in 1954 (over No. 17 USC, 20–7, in the Rose Bowl), and in 1942 (over the Iowa Seahawks, 41–12)? Few today would argue that a wartime victory over a team they probably never heard of would be one of the best in school history. But Iowa Pre-Flight was a team of college and professional athletes getting advanced flight training before being sent overseas during World War II. The Seahawks were coached by legendary former Minnesota coach Bernie Bierman and carried a 7-1 record when the Buckeyes beat them and claimed the crown. The Seahawks had already beaten Minnesota, Michigan, and Nebraska and had lost only to Notre Dame. The win didn't happen in a made-for-television extravaganza the way that the 2002 title game against Miami did, but if the Buckeyes had lost, they wouldn't have been the '42 champs, so it accomplished the same thing.

Okay, we've got five "official" national title games, four unofficial ones, four top-two team matchups, the two most famous games in school history and . . . uh, we're up to fifteen without choosing any of the classic OSU-Michigan games that most of us know have to be there.

But how can any of those games be judged more significant than that 7–6 win over Illinois in 1916 that was truly the big bang of Ohio State football, the beginnings of the monstrous football animal that we know today? Before that, interest in the program was steady, but underwhelming; after that upset, fans began to pack little Ohio Field on High Street, and three years later plans would be hatched for Ohio Stadium. What if they had lost *that* game? For all we know, today's Buckeyes might be playing flag football in a cornfield.

Those 1916 Buckeyes also had to upset favored Wisconsin 14–13—keep in mind there were no rankings in those days—and Northwestern 22–3 in the last game of the season to claim the school's first Big Ten title, a milestone that stands on its own. And when most of those same players beat Michigan for the first time in 1919, many fans of that era called that the single most important game in school history. At the time, the two schools had met on fifteen occasions and Michigan had won thirteen and tied two. The Buckeyes' 13–3 win in Ann Arbor that year was the beginning of college football's greatest rivalry. Many of the OSU fans who attended that game were still talking about it thirty to forty years later, and it was regarded as one of the program's biggest wins of all time, at least until all of those players, fans, and reporters died.

Another contest that was huge at the time but is mostly overlooked today was Red Grange's final collegiate game, played against Ohio State in the Horseshoe on November 21, 1925. From here, it looks like just another 14–9 loss to Illinois. From there, it was huge. It drew national attention because Grange was the sport's biggest star, and there was much national intrigue over whether he would or wouldn't turn pro.

Attendance was 84,295—at the time the largest crowd to attend a sporting event in this country—and Grange did turn pro, after a dramatic day in which he gained 113 yards in 21 carries, completed nine passes for 42 yards, returned three punts and one kickoff, and intercepted two passes—the second on the game's final play.

Then came the real drama. First, Illinois coach Bob Zuppke took Red on an hour-long taxi ride around Columbus and tried to convince him that playing pro football was a bad idea, which was a waste of time. Then when Grange returned to his hotel, he found the place jammed with reporters and fans—star-struck women in particular—and he climbed down the hotel fire escape, sneaked off, and caught a cab to the railroad station, where he would catch a train for Chicago and sign with the Bears the next day. It wasn't necessarily one of the most exciting games in school history, but for many reasons, it was one of the most exciting days.

So trying to come up with a top 10 or even top 20 list of the greatest games is a futile exercise. It might be fun to do, but the exclusions are bound to be ridiculous. Even if you break down that big list into several smaller ones, the games that are chosen are strictly a matter of taste and depend mostly on how much weight is assigned to history, excitement, stakes, etc.

Two recent OSU-Michigan games would be on my lists: the 2006 game that pitted No. 1 Ohio State against No. 2 Michigan with a berth in the BCS title game on the line, and the 2002 game that got OSU into that title game against Miami and gave the Buckeyes their first national championship in thirty-four years.

Of the two, the 2006 game rates higher because it not only had two unbeaten teams with everything at stake but also was one of the most exciting games ever witnessed in Ohio Stadium, a 42–39 OSU victory. It was the only time the two rivals had ever been ranked No. 1 and 2 when they met and even spurred calls for a rematch in the BCS title game. Many times great matchups don't result in great games, and that one did.

But the other one was more memorable to me, not so much because of the competition, but because of the scene before, during, and after the game. I remember walking across the northeast stadium lot after parking my car and experiencing something different: the air felt as if it were carrying an electric charge. The team parted the crowd as it made its walk from the marching band's skull session in St. John Arena to the stadium and people displayed a remarkable intensity in cheering them on. The atmosphere was static-charged and a little scary. After the players passed and I resumed my march to the press entrance on the stadium's west side, the charge in the air was still noticeable. Was this nervous energy? There had been so much frustration over the Buckeyes' failure to win a national title in so many years and the fans seemed poised at the edge of an emotional precipice. Beat Michigan, play for the national title. Win that game and relieve all that frustration, all that maddening angst. It seemed as if thousands of tense, excited fans were leaking energy and maybe they were. After the Buckeyes won 14–9 in an exciting game, the place exploded, probably as much from relief as joy. Unless the Buckeyes go another twenty-five years without a national title, something tells me that scene will never be experienced in and around Ohio Stadium again.

So our list has passed 20 now, and many of the best games still aren't on it. Those obvious to me include No. 2 OSU's 50–14 win over No. 4 Michigan in 1968 and the revenge game, No. 5 OSU's 20–9 win over No. 4 Michigan in 1970. After the Buckeyes were upset by the Wolverines in 1969, the '70 game was one of the most anticipated games in school history. There is also a 21–7 win over Michigan in 1942 that moved the Buckeyes into position to win the national title against Iowa Pre-Flight the following week.

There were two huge games against Iowa in 1957 and in 1985. In the first one the No. 6 Buckeyes rode the legs of fullback Bob White for a 17–13 comeback victory over the No. 5 Hawkeyes that helped OSU eventually win the national championship. In the second, the No. 8 Buckeyes knocked off the 7-0 and No. 1 Hawkeyes in a steady downpour in the Horseshoe. Keith Byars delivered an emotional speech before that one in which he knocked over food trays, broke a water glass against the wall, and kicked over chairs, and a sophomore linebacker named Chris Spielman made nineteen tackles and had two interceptions.

The 1954 game against No. 2 Wisconsin was both memorable and significant, because it set up No. 4 OSU's run to the national title. The Badgers were leading 7–3 and driving when quarterback Jim Miller faked a handoff and tried a quick pass to the flat; Hop Cassady stepped in and intercepted it at the 12-yard line and streaked 88 yards for the touchdown in what some call the finest display of broken field running in school history. Momentum shifted dramatically, and the Buckeyes went on to a 31–14 win and captured the No. 1 spot in the polls.

And on the flip side, what about the 17–16 loss to No. 3 USC in the 1980 Rose Bowl, when the Buckeyes were ranked No. 1? They led 16–10 only to lose the title when the Trojans put together an 83-yard, fourth-quarter drive. The game was a classic, but it wouldn't make a lot of fans' lists because OSU lost.

The first-ever meeting between Ohio State and Texas on September 10, 2005—think '77 OSU-Oklahoma—also deserves to be on the list both for its historical significance and because it was a fantastic game. The No. 4 Buckeyes charged back from a 10-point lead and led by 6 with five minutes left, but lost when Longhorn quarterback Vince Young led a 67-yard drive. The clincher was Young's 24-yard touchdown pass to Limas Sweed with 2:37 left that gave No. 2 Texas a 25–22 decision. I had learned my lesson by then, though; I didn't tell *any* fans I thought that game was a classic.

Three more games that are historically significant also deserve mention: a 5–0 win over Ohio Wesleyan on October 7, 1922—that was the first game in Ohio Stadium (the stadium dedication game against Michigan was played two weeks later), a 10–7 win over Pittsburgh in 1985 that marked the first night game in stadium history, and the 17–15 loss to Clemson in the 1978 Gator Bowl when Woody Hayes punched Charlie Bauman on the OSU sidelines and was fired. It's not one that OSU fans want to remember, but there's no choice in this matter; on a list of significant games, it would have to rank near the top.

And then there are those games that are etched in memory even though they aren't that important in the great scheme of things, games that didn't involve two high-ranked teams and had little bearing on a championship.

In 1980, the Buckeyes were No. 7 and on their way to the first of six consecutive 9-3 seasons when unranked Illinois came to town. The Buckeyes jumped out to a 28–0 on one of Art Schlichter's best passing days (17 for 21 for 284 yards and four touchdowns). But Illinois came charging back in the second half, and when it was over Illinois quarterback Dave Wilson had set an NCAA record that stood for eight years with 621 passing yards. Wilson completed 43 for 69 passes and six touchdowns. Two costly Illinois turnovers—a fumble inside the OSU 10 and an interception in the end zone with 3:06 remaining—preserved the Buckeyes' 49–42 victory in one of the most entertaining games ever witnessed in the old horseshoe.

It's funny, but when I told several OSU fans what a terrific game it had been in the days following the victory, every one of them agreed.

# 30

# Former Saint Tress

Jim Tressel used to be a saint. For a few years after he succeeded John Cooper as Ohio State head coach in 2001, his apparent canonization was confirmed nearly every day in the flood of e-mails that reached the *Columbus Dispatch* on any topic even remotely connected to him. A columnist who dared imply that Tressel wasn't being totally truthful about something—let's say the coach had cunningly suggested a woeful San Jose State team would provide his Buckeyes with a difficult challenge—might just as well have suggested St. Francis of Assisi was guilty of murder. Tressel was above reproach. If he did it, it must be right. If he said it, it must be true.

The transformation from mere mortal to saint didn't take long. Tressel said all the right things when he arrived from Youngstown State, espousing the importance of family, academics, integrity, and beating Michigan at a time when the fans were tired of player arrests, academic failures, and annual losses to the Wolverines. When his first two teams beat Michigan and the second one went on to win the 2002 national championship, his football canonization was complete. Tressel won, he cared about his players, he ran a clean program, he made the fans proud. Some people, many people, believed he was the second coming of Woody Hayes.

Tressel's pristine image first began to fade, not when some of *his* players also got in trouble, which they did, but when his Buckeyes began to lose some games fans thought they should have won. Supporters fire off a machine-gun spray of excuses for every conceivable kind of problem and/or irregularity when a team is winning. Losing is a mortal sin.

In the eyes of his biggest fans, Tressel could still do no wrong and still can't, although he officially lost his halo in March 2011, when university officials revealed that he had committed a major NCAA violation. It was the beginning of a sequence of events that eventually led school officials to ask him to resign, which he did on Monday, May 30, 2011.

Tressel's downfall started with an e-mail. Columbus attorney Christopher T. Cicero informed him in April 2010 that two of his players had broken NCAA rules by selling championship rings, gold pants pendants, and uniform parts to the owner of a local tattoo parlor who was under FBI investigation for serious criminal activity. Tressel didn't relay this information to any of his supervisors until after OSU officials discovered it in his e-mails nine months later.

He claimed Cicero had asked for confidentiality, and that assertion proved the basis of his initial defense: Tressel said he didn't report it because he didn't want to compromise the investigation and was afraid that if he did so it might jeopardize his players' safety. Many of his devoted followers bought it, even though his explanation didn't seem to make sense. He had had numerous chances to tell OSU officials what he knew but didn't, even after the school discovered that six players were involved and then announced that five of them would receive five-game suspensions for the 2011 season in December. He even signed a compliance document with the NCAA in September saying that he knew of no such violation by his players. The *Columbus Dispatch* later reported that Tressel didn't even stick to his claimed confidentiality in the beginning. When he received the information, he forwarded it to Ted Sarniak, a hometown mentor to quarterback Terrelle Pryor, one of the players involved. A public records search later showed that after Tressel received that e-mail from Cicero warning him of possible NCAA violations on April 2, 2010, the OSU coach exchanged seventy-seven calls and text messages with Sarniak and spent four and a half hours on the phone with him, including an eighteen-minute conversation on December 21, two days before Pryor and the others were suspended. So was confidentiality really that important to him or did Saint Tress lie?

While the Tressel loyalists remained true to him, the divide between them and his critics widened. Some called for his dismissal and others didn't, but his immaculate image had been sullied even for those who were on his side. The majority now saw him for what he was—not a saint, but a human being. That doesn't mean Tressel isn't a good man; in some ways, he may have done more for his players, for the community, and for the university than any coach in school history. But the days when at least 80 percent of the Buckeye Nation would refuse to believe he could be guilty of anything more serious than helping an old lady only halfway across the street in order to get to church on time are over. Some of his most vocal critics went so far as to call him a hypocrite and a fraud.

Athletic director Gene Smith and school president E. Gordon Gee tried hard to preserve his squeaky clean image even when they confirmed Tressel's guilt and announced the school's self-imposed punishment, a two-game suspension (later increased to five because Tressel supposedly wanted to serve with the offending players), a $250,000 fine, a public apology, and a requirement to attend an NCAA rules compliance seminar. The press conference proved to be an embarrassment, seeming more like a tribute to Tressel than a rebuke for what he did. Smith said "we trust him implicitly," a curious statement given that his coach had refused to tell him what he knew about the incidents even months after the fact. Gee went beyond that, performing verbal cartwheels in an effort to keep Tressel's halo intact.

"As Gene said, this university is very committed to this coach," Gee said. "This university president is very committed to this coach. . . . He has had success on the football field, and we applaud that. He has had great success working with young people, and we applaud that. But I think equally important, he has had great success building the character and reputation for this university, and I'm entirely grateful for that.

"He and his great wife, Ellen, chaired the campaign for our library, one of our most important aspects of this university. He has supported our academic and medical center. . . . [He] has focused on hunger, has focused on our troops. He made a trip to Iraq in 2009. I have had the occasion to spend time with his young people, and he teaches them devotion to one another, to larger purposes, to the good of others, to the state, to our country, and to the common good."

When Gee was asked whether he considered firing him, the popular president tried to make a joke that he came to regret.

"Are you kidding?" Gee said. "I'm just hopeful the coach doesn't dismiss me."

It demonstrated the level of respect Gee had for Tressel; under the circumstances, it also seemed more than bizarre. The scene came off more as a celebration of Tressel's career than a censure for his deception. The only things missing were some drunk baseball players spraying champagne all over the place, a grinning network analyst standing next to him, and maybe the governor or the president stepping out of the shadows and handing a sheepish-looking Tressel a trophy the size of the Stanley Cup.

It was the kind of tribute many today still bestow on Hayes, which again makes some of those Hayes-Tressel comparisons seem relevant. As mentioned earlier, Hayes had his own little brush with the rulebook in 1955. The Big Ten and subsequently the NCAA put the program on one-year probation in 1956, in part because Hayes had made personal loans or gifts to some of his "needy" players out of the $4,000 he received annually from appearing on a local television show. It was a clear violation of conference and NCAA rules, although Hayes never acknowledged that he did anything wrong.

A few days after Tressel resigned, golf legend Jack Nicklaus was asked at the Memorial Tournament, the Columbus PGA Tour stop that Nicklaus founded, what Hayes would have thought of this fiasco.

"I think Woody would have ended up doing exactly the same thing," Nicklaus said.

The quote had been in the newspaper only a few hours before my phone rang. When I answered it, there was fire on the other end. After my ears stopped burning, I identified the caller as former Hayes player, two-time All-American Jim Stillwagon.

"Woody Hayes would *never* have done that," Stillwagon said. "He may have done other stupid things, may have beat the shit out of us in practice and stuff like that, but he's saying that Woody would have signed that document and lied about this? That's bullshit. Woody's values are why he was so successful. People who hated him respected his values."

There were several more sentences to Nicklaus's quote: "but I think that maybe he wouldn't have had a news media that, no matter what happens, [it] gets on the news. " And "I think Woody would have protected his kids.

He probably did protect his kids. Woody was a good man. I think Tressel is a good man." And "well, obviously, the cover-up was far worse than the act."

But Stillwagon had seen enough. He said he had heard former Buckeye coach Earle Bruce, say basically the same thing as Nicklaus. It was more than he could stand.

"To bring [Woody] out of the grave to justify Tressel's stupidity is bull-shit," Stillwagon said.

Long before the scandal cost Tressel his job, these Tressel-Hayes comparisons used to make me wince. I would try to envision Tressel in that gray sweater vest pushing his car across the Michigan state line into a gas station in Toledo, and the ridiculousness of it would make me laugh. And can *anybody* envision a wild-eyed Tress tearing up downs markers, ripping the bill off an unlucky baseball cap, or stomping the life out of an innocent wristwatch during practice?

When sportswriters of the future seek out entertaining old stories about how Tressel posted his incredible 9-1 record against Michigan, it probably won't take long to collect and compile them. A couple of his former players might reminisce about how Tressel always made them watch twice as much tape during Michigan week. Another might talk about the time Coach Tressel reminded him of the importance of special teams. The best story, the one in which Tressel takes his starting quarterback aside and stresses the value of good decision making, probably won't be turned into a full-length feature film. This isn't exactly the stuff of legends.

Several years ago, I asked safety Nate Salley if Tressel seemed at all different during Michigan week.

"There is nothing that really jumps out that he does different," he said. "Just like everyone else, he's just a little more excited."

And how could Salley tell that?

"Just the way he speaks," Salley said. "Walking into the meeting room yesterday, we're talking and we're like, 'Hey, are you ready to go?' and he had this big, old grin on his face and he's like, 'Yeah, but we can't be ready to play now.'"

A grin? A few feet from Salley a longtime Ohio State official was talking about how an irritated Woody once ordered him to get a photographer so he could snap some photos of the overflowing toilets in the OSU locker room; Hayes said those dastardly Michigan officials used to fill them with you-know-what every year.

No, Tress and Woody aren't the same guy. They never have been. Tressel was always a little too corporate, a little too smooth, a little too religious to be the tempestuous, sometimes grandfatherly, sometimes maniacal Hayes. While he was coaching, few thought of Woody as a saint, football or otherwise, even though charitable acts and unannounced hospital visits to strangers were part of his daily routine. Tressel's perfect image seemed to have been honed by an expensive public relations firm almost from the day he arrived.

During his first few years in Columbus many people knew the image but weren't sure exactly what was behind it. Just about all of the reporters who covered the team were in this camp, even though they were around Tressel two or three days a week. In those days, their questions to Tressel found little spontaneity. All of his answers seemed prepared, and if a question surprised him, he rarely answered it. He always said precisely the right thing or he talked and talked and said nothing at all. He seemed less robotic and more genuine in the later years of his tenure, interacting with reporters and even occasionally uttering a phrase he might regret later, although his weekly press conferences during the season were still masterpieces of obfuscation.

Regardless of whom the Buckeyes were playing or how well they were expected to do in the game, there was rarely even the slightest change in Tressel's demeanor. He loved Bruce and considered him a mentor, yet Bruce and Tressel are as different as two people can be. It is impossible to forget the sight of the energy-emitting Earle, looking as if he were about to explode at the team hotel on the morning of the '79 Michigan game. It is just as difficult to envision Tressel in that condition as it is seeing him push his car over the Michigan state line to avoid buying gas. If Tressel had exploded during his tenure at OSU, it would have happened only because somebody slipped a hand grenade into his suit coat while he was smiling and nodding. And if he had survived the blast, he would probably have calmly described it as an "excellent explosion," said he "has always had respect" for people who make hand grenades, and might have even added, evenly and without a change in tone, that "we all come to Ohio State to participate in excellent explosions like this."

His coaching style was successful . . . and matched his personality. In Tresselball, as his system came to be called, turnovers were worse than bad—they were destructive. Horrifying. Turnovers and Armageddon were first cousins. He was usually content to let the other side make a key error or two, then capitalize on them and win a close game. It was a boring concept, yet also an effective one. If Tressel's constant refrain about the punt being the most important play in football caused a spike in the state's mental-illness cases, if his emphasis on turnover reduction threatened a statewide narcolepsy epidemic, it also produced plenty of victories.

But as with any Ohio State coach who doesn't win them all, Tressel couldn't remain outside the range of cannon-fire forever, especially in a coaching sense. Before the 2006 national championship game, he was the unofficial king of college football. He seemed to win every big game, beating both Michigan and his bowl opponents with amazing regularity. OSU fans wouldn't brook even the mildest criticism of him. He was Saint Tress with a capital S.

Even when something negative occurred—the grisly fall of Maurice Clarett, for example—the soot blew right past him and landed on someone else. Those sweater vests he wore seemed to be woven from Teflon fibers.

By the time he resigned, the Teflon had long since worn thin. When his teams started to lose big games, many fans began to tire of his conservative style and wanted more than his stock answers. When the offensive line underachieved, they wanted to know why the line coach wasn't fired. When the offense sputtered, in part because of unimaginative play calling, they wanted to know who was the responsible one, the offensive coordinator or the head coach. When Tressel explained it by spending over a minute not explaining it, his lack of candor made people mad.

It is remarkable—and crazy—how many fans advocated getting rid of him in 2009 after the home loss against USC and the upset loss at Purdue five weeks later, even though his teams had played in three national championships, won one, and were in the midst of a run of four consecutive Big Ten championships, a run that eventually reached six.

The plunge in reputation was deserved—and wasn't. While there is no denying that the favored Buckeyes were embarrassed by Florida in the 2006 title game, they had no business even being in the title game in 2007, where they suffered another rout at the hands of LSU. They had lost to Illinois the week before the Michigan game and should have fallen out of the running, but were abruptly thrust back into the mix when other teams ahead of them also lost. Once they got to the bowl, the game was suddenly billed as a chance for them to atone for the previous season's blowout, and they weren't good enough to live up to that. That wasn't Tressel's fault as much as that of the flawed BCS system that put his team in the title game. The Buckeyes followed that with a nationally televised 35–3 disaster against No. 1 USC in the Los Angeles Memorial Coliseum in September 2008, lost to No. 3 Texas 24–21 in the Fiesta Bowl on a Colt McCoy touchdown pass with sixteen seconds left, and then lost to USC 18–15 in 2009, this time in Columbus. When Purdue upset the Buckeyes on a day when Pryor committed four turnovers, Tressel no longer looked like such a gridiron genius. He had gone from a guy who always wins the big games to one who never wins them.

A coach's reputation is never stationary, though. It rises and falls like a share of stock. After Tressel's coaching reputation underwent a steady slide from that 2006 title game to the loss to the Boilermakers, in the ensuing weeks the market started to turn. Tressel stopped trying to deliver on recruiting promises made to Pryor to turn him into a pro quarterback and went back to the basics. The Buckeyes began to run the ball more than they threw, and the wins followed, culminated by an unprecedented sixth consecutive win over Michigan that gave them their sixth conference title in nine years. Their Rose Bowl matchup with pass-happy Oregon seemed to set the stage for another public display of old and outdated vs. glitzy and new; instead, it proved that things probably had never been as bad as they had appeared. Pryor turned back into the spectacular composite running-passing machine everyone had slobbered over when he was coming out of high school. The flashy sophomore completed 23 of 37 passes for 266 yards, with two touchdowns and one interception, and added 72 yards rushing on 20 carries. The Ohio State defense bottled up the Ducks' wide-open offense and the Buckeyes won 26–17. If this were old vs. new, old won, validating the Tressel concept and sending the Buckeyes up to No. 5 in the final polls.

Tressel could never regain the unqualified support he had had early in his tenure—a 31–18 loss to Wisconsin in 2010 that spoiled an unbeaten season for his No. 1 team ensured that—but he still had come a long way back. He had that Woody Hayes thing working in his favor, and truthfully, his conservative brand of football might have been what Hayes would be doing had "three yards and a cloud of dust" made it to 2011.

There are other similarities, to be sure. When *Forbes* magazine named Tressel the most underpaid coach in college football in 2008, he seemed surprised. At the time, he was making $2.6 million a year, or about a million less than when he resigned; Hayes, by comparison, went for years without accepting a hike in his relatively modest $43,000 annual salary.

When Tressel was told how *Forbes* came up with this ranking, he took exception with the magazine's methodology. It was based on a metric that compared a coach's wins (with a bonus for BCS bowl victories) for the previous three years to the average in wins and salary, and Tressel never believed that a coach's success should solely be based on winning. His late father, Lee, was a winning football coach at Baldwin-Wallace, and Tressel said he never saw his dad in those terms.

"The way I saw it, living with him, was that his success was the difference he made in lives," Tressel said. "And that's what we hope we can do. And we take it seriously."

That is the Tressel that reminds you of Hayes, and the one his supporters love. The two men may be no closer than a priest and a pirate in temperament, but they did share one important trait: both cared deeply about their players.

In 2004, OSU defensive coordinator Mark Dantonio took the head coaching job at the University of Cincinnati, and was honored at a luncheon put on by the Touchdown Club in his hometown of Zanesville, Ohio. Both Dantonio and Tressel spoke at the luncheon, and Dantonio, now head coach at Michigan State, said that it was because of Tressel that he had decided to pursue a head coaching job.

"I took the job at the University of Cincinnati basically for one reason, to try and do some of the things that Jim Tressel was able to do at Youngstown State and Ohio State," Dantonio said. "That doesn't mean winning football games. That means impacting young people in the community.

"That's really why I took the job, because I've seen him be able to change people's lives and make a significant impact on young people. I really felt like that's his ministry and that's got to be my ministry, and I think that's why you coach."

It was one of the things that sold OSU athletic director Andy Geiger when he hired Tressel to replace John Cooper. The program had had some academic difficulties, discipline problems, arrests, etc., and Tressel came to OSU from Youngstown State stressing how important it was for the Buckeyes to be "a family." In his introductory press conference, Tressel said his father taught him that "there's only one reason to miss class, and that's because of a death in the family—your own." He said doing your best for the "group" is the key to everything.

Woody would have loved that stuff and the fans sure did. Before Tressel's first game, he gave his players the words to "Carmen Ohio," the school alma mater, and told them that they would all be singing together in front of the south stands at the end of every home game. It is accepted as part of tradition now; at the time, it raised some eyebrows, particularly among the older players. While it may have seemed like an *Ozzie and Harriet* concept in a *Modern Family* world, many people liked it. After the chaotic last days of the Cooper regime, it seemed as if the "family" and all of its trappings were exactly what a bickering, divided, underachieving team needed. Then when Tressel's Buckeyes beat Michigan that first year, the first time in Ann Arbor since 1987, and followed it up with another win over Michigan and a national championship in year two, everyone was certain: Tressel's methods worked. The good old days were back and so was Woody. He had just assumed a new guise.

In the days before the 2002 title game, a Phoenix columnist described Tressel as "OSU's cornball coach," and it's not hard to see why many saw him that way. He wasn't the cool kid worried about the latest trends. He didn't swear. He rarely showed anger. He didn't share his religious beliefs in press conferences or official university functions, but they were impossible to miss. He always wore a W. W. J. D. (What Would Jesus Do) band on his wrist and occasionally spoke at religious events, but never as the Ohio State football coach. There is a chapter called "Faith and Belief" in his 2009 book *The Winners Manual: For the Game of Life* in which he explained:

> Obviously when it comes to sharing my faith and my life, some venues are easier than others. I make sure when I talk about my faith that I'm not speaking on behalf of Ohio State but I'm there on my own

behalf. I present it as what I happen to believe. Seldom do I speak
about my faith unless I've been invited.

The spiritual side of him was often in evidence, though, and Tressel
seemed determined to present an almost perfect image, one reason the news
media came down on him so hard when it was discovered that he had lied
to the NCAA and withheld information from his bosses. Critics who had
never believed the image responded with a stream of "I told you so's," pointing to NCAA troubles during Tressel's Youngstown State days and previous
incidents involving Clarett and Troy Smith at OSU. When the NCAA
investigated Clarett for receiving improper benefits in 2003 and Smith was
suspended for receiving $500 from a booster in 2004, Geiger almost exclu-
sively handled those public relations nightmares. Tressel had few comments
and was rarely made available for questions, which irked his critics. They
surmised that school officials would go to any length to keep from losing a
winning football coach, and that the high-principled coach could look the
other way with the best of them.

This was confirmed for them again when, after the six players linked to the
tattoo parlor were suspended for receiving improper benefits, the NCAA permitted them to postpone their suspensions and play in the Sugar Bowl, and
Tressel willingly used those players against Arkansas. In this case, it wasn't
clear he had much choice; bowl officials, Big Ten commissioner Jim Delany,
Smith, and others had lobbied for their bowl eligibility. Still, when three of
the players (Pryor, running back Dan Herron, and defensive end Solomon
Thomas) starred in the 31–26 OSU victory, it appeared the Buckeyes had
gotten away with something and Tressel had gone along with it.

He had tried to calm the public outcry before the game by requiring the
suspended players to agree not to turn pro if they wanted to play in the
game, but the move didn't have much effect on the perception. Many saw
Tressel as trading his principles for a chance to finally beat an SEC team.
Fair or not, the criticism illustrated the high standard that had been created
by Tressel's saintly image.

The school's announcement the following March that Tressel hadn't been
forthcoming with his knowledge of the violations as his contract required
shoved the debate over his motives into high gear. Was he *really* worried

about their safety? Had he kept quiet about it because he didn't want to spoil what figured to be a terrific season? Or—and to many who know him this seems more likely—had he done this because he saw it as part of his higher mission, to "save" kids from their destructive behavior and channel them back on the road to productive lives?

This again sounds like Woody, a curious mixture of good intentions and arrogance, of integrity and deception, of strict adherence to the law and a blatant disregard for the rules because, well, he believed he was being called to a higher mission and he knew better than the NCAA or anyone else what was best for his kids.

Maybe that's why many of his fans still believe he can do no wrong, even though he is no longer on the sidelines. (On February 2, 2012, he accepted a position as vice president of strategic engagement at the University of Akron.) While there is much to like about Tressel, it would be interesting to see how those same fans would feel about him if he hadn't taken a high-profile program even higher, and presided over probably the most successful ten-year period in the program's history.

It is clear now that Tressel was never the saint many considered him to be. In some ways, he now seems almost as enigmatic as Woody Hayes. But those determined to find a way to reconcile the spiritual Tressel with the deceptive Tressel, those intent on making sense out of his positive acts and the events that led to his downfall, must ultimately face this undeniable fact: most Ohio State fans never would have thought of him in those saintly terms if it weren't for all the winning.

# 31

# The Flock

There is no such thing as a typical Ohio State fan. There are longtime alums who attend every home game, and short-time enthusiasts who have never ventured within a mile of the main campus. There are corporate titans who make huge donations to the President's Club to secure season tickets rights, and store clerks who couldn't afford tickets even if they were given a rare chance to buy them. There are no-lifers who sweat blood over every lost fumble and want to see somebody, anybody, everybody fired after every loss, and casual fans who somehow find a way to go on living even when the Buckeyes lose to Michigan.

All Ohio State fans are not created equal, and they represent a wide range of intensity and/or lunacy. There are great fans, good fans, bad fans, apathetic fans, and lunatics. There are kind-hearted souls who welcome opposing fans into the stadium with a smile and a nod, and obnoxious idiots who scream obscenities at the quarterback, the coach, and even a kindly grandmother who dares to wear opposing colors to the 'Shoe.

Sometimes even the most civil fans are hard to recognize. They might turn scarlet when an Ohio State player inexplicably tries to field a punt on the 3-yard line and fumbles it away; they just don't hang over the railing and rain abuse on him when he leaves the field the way the idiots do. They might tell their friends that the dope calling the plays on the OSU sidelines should be changing tires or washing cars for a living; they just don't write long, vicious letters about it to every news media outlet this side of Indianapolis. At an Ohio State program where success is sometimes seen as an inalienable right, the lines between the civil and the not-so-civil sometimes blur, often when alcohol is involved. But there is no denying that the

249

Buckeye Nation is too large and too diverse to be described with sweeping generalizations.

It's been almost a dozen years ago since I first tried to sort Ohio State fans into recognizable groupings. Some things have changed since then—John Cooper was fired and replaced by Jim Tressel, who resigned and was replaced by Luke Fickell, who was replaced by Urban Meyer—but most of the categories haven't changed much and are still as valid now as they were then.

Here's an updated version of that earlier list:

**The Tresselites (10 percent):** This crowd thinks Tress did a fantastic job, is the spiritual leader of the free world, and is underappreciated by the majority, who don't realize the program will soon be living in a dumpster without his inspired leadership. They occasionally surprise their friends and coworkers by asking if Tressel could be rehired.

**The Loyalists (10 percent):** They say if you're a true OSU fan, you owe your loyalty to the current coach—whoever he is, even if he has run the program so far into the ground that the OSU School of Agriculture is considering cultivating corn on one of the Buckeyes' grass practice fields. Their number is cut in half when the team suffers through a rare losing season. Loyalty has its limits.

**The Silent Majority (50 percent):** These sensible folks are happy with a 10-2 and 11-1 seasons and can even accept a 9-3 year or two without suffering a nervous breakdown. They would love to go 12-0 and win the national championship, but they also thought it was great that the restaurants around Columbus weren't as crowded the Saturday night after that devastating loss to Michigan State in 1998. They didn't break out into a cold sweat at 3 a.m. wondering if Mike Brewster was going to turn pro early. They also don't have a deep appreciation for a high school defensive back from Yeehaw Junction, Florida, whom recruiting experts say is the sixth-rated cornerback prospect in the nation and might make OSU one of his official visits.

**The Coach Haters (20 percent):** They didn't like John Cooper because he lost to Michigan, made a hot tub commercial, and sounds as if he had been on Stonewall Jackson's staff at the Battle of Fredericksburg. They didn't like Tressel because he a) lost two national championship games, b) didn't pass enough, c) wouldn't fire his offensive line coach, d) didn't pass enough, e) didn't finish in the top 10 in last year's recruiting rankings, and f) didn't pass enough. They couldn't fathom why OSU athletic director Gene Smith bothered to keep a coach who won only one national title in ten years. They didn't like Luke Fickell because he had never been a head coach before he got the job, didn't pass enough, didn't win a Big Ten championship with a mediocre team, and, uh, didn't pass enough. And they already don't like Urban Meyer, even if they're not sure why. Their admiration for any coach seldom extends beyond the first loss, if it gets that far.

**The Woodys (5 percent):** They haven't watched a game in years but use holiday get-togethers, neighborhood picnics, and backyard barbeques to bore everyone with stories about how the Buckeyes used to win the national title just about every other year when Woody Hayes was coaching. If you aren't receptive to this line of thinking, be wary of flying spatulas, baseball caps, wristwatches, and turkey legs.

**The Nouveau Riche (5 percent):** They moved to Ohio from Pittsburgh or Atlanta. They have tickets because their company grosses $50 million annually and can afford to contribute enough money to OSU to have a President's Club membership. They think it's a crime that they can't buy more tickets when the school is wasting thousands of tickets on students. They are more worried about whether they have anything to wear to the next game than whom the Buckeyes are playing.

The list is obviously tongue-in-check, but there are elements of truth there that are recognizable to all of us. Which group dominates the radio talk shows, letters-to-the-editor columns, and Internet message boards depends in part on whether the team is having a terrific season (is undefeated) or a horrendous one (has lost a game).

When Cooper's teams were having trouble beating Michigan, my inbox at the newspaper was swamped with comments from those claiming that "if only OSU could beat the Wolverines, I would be happy no matter how the Buckeyes did in their other games."

When Tressel's teams started winning the Michigan game with regularity, the tone of the e-mails suddenly shifted. Then the writers demanded to know why the Buckeyes lost to USC or Texas or Purdue, and rarely mentioned Michigan.

As inconsistent as these positions seem, they probably didn't come from the same people. As a season ebbs and flows, different vocal minorities step forward and dominate the inboxes, the air waves, bar discussions, and chat rooms. The "just one Michigan win would make me happy" crowd falls asleep in the easy chair with a full belly, fat and happy after gorging itself on the latest victory. The "yeah, but" crowd steps to the forefront and starts squawking. That may be one reason the Ohio State fandom often seems so unreasonable; it is so large and diverse that there's always somebody out there who isn't happy and lets everyone know about it.

There are some extremists out there though. When Columbus landed a National Hockey League franchise and chose the name Blue Jackets, the cry went up from some quarters that it was totally unacceptable, that there might come a time when fans would rise to their feet in a local sports arena and yell "Go, Blue!" Some fans even protested blue being one of the team colors, as if that were an act of sacrilege. Some said they would never attend a game in an arena with blue seats.

When Paul Keels was named to succeed Terry Smith as the voice of the Buckeyes in 1998, it got out that he had once broadcast Michigan football games. For some, this created a crisis of global proportions. It didn't matter that Keels was a Xavier graduate who had done University of Cincinnati football and basketball on the radio for seven of the previous nine years, or that his resume included broadcasts of the Cincinnati Bengals, Detroit Pistons, and the USFL's Michigan Panthers in addition to his six years on the Michigan football broadcasts. It didn't even matter that he had been an OSU fan as a kid growing up in Cincinnati. The fact he had done Michigan games on the radio was a maize-and-blue letter he couldn't remove.

As soon as Keels got the job, he appeared on Kirk Herbstreit's local radio show and had to defend himself. Some of the callers reacted as if Herbstreit had put on Saddam Hussein.

"The first caller right off the bat said he wanted to let me know that it made him sick that somebody from Michigan would be doing Ohio State games," Keels said at the time. "I said 'I'm not from Michigan.' And he said, 'Then somebody who worked for Michigan.' And I said, 'I didn't work for Michigan; I worked for a radio station.'"

Twelve years later, Keels is popular with Buckeye fans, but it took a while. Some just couldn't get past the idea that he called Michigan football games, even if he was doing it to earn a living. Presumably, he should have gone on welfare or even starved to death. But then again, these are probably the same people who think an Ohio kid who goes to Michigan to play football has committed a heinous crime against his friends and neighbors and that he has no right—none—to go to the school of his choice if Ohio State wants him. There are no shades of gray in their world. There is only one gray and it goes with scarlet.

Herbstreit knows this better than anyone. He is a former starting quarterback for OSU and a former captain. The Dayton native's father, James, played football for the Buckeyes and was a captain in 1960. Kirk worked for a Columbus sports talk station after graduation and eventually landed a job at ESPN as a college football analyst.

That's also when he began to have problems. Some Ohio State fans couldn't accept the fact that his job required objectivity, or that he wasn't a human PR machine for the program that spawned him. The longer he was at the network, the more vocal his critics became. Finally, Herbstreit and his wife, Allison, sold their suburban Columbus home and moved to Nashville. He said he had contemplated such a move for three off-seasons and finally decided it was time to move on.

"Nobody loves Ohio State more than me," he said. "I still have a picture of Woody Hayes and my dad [a former OSU player] in my office, and nobody will do more than I do for the university behind the scenes. But I've got a job to do, and I'm going to continue to be fair and objective. To continue to have to defend myself and my family in regards to my love and devotion to Ohio State is unfair."

What made it especially difficult for him was that he believed that it was a small percentage of OSU fans that had forced the move.

"From a sports perspective this is rough," he said. "I love Ohio State. Love the [Columbus] Blue Jackets. Love the [Cincinnati] Reds. Those are my hobbies. I don't like moving. I love living here. I don't want to leave. But I just can't do this anymore. I really can't keep going like this. Eighty to ninety percent of the Ohio State fans are great. It's the vocal minority that make it rough. They probably represent only 5 to 10 percent of fan base, but they are relentless."

The fact this lunacy seems to have become more common in recent years doubtless in part reflects the increasing number of outlets available for people to express their opinions. But it has become obvious in recent years that there are a lot more OSU fans in the all-football, all-the-time category than there used to be, and that interest in OSU football today is higher than it has ever been. Like the hungry plant in the musical-comedy *Little Shop of Horrors* ("Feed me!"), the monster that is OSU football just keeps getting bigger.

A few years ago, retired OSU sports information director and broadcaster Marv Homan told me that he doesn't think there's any doubt that interest in Ohio State football is at an all-time high and growing in intensity.

"I think the Internet is a big factor in that because now regardless of where you live, you can keep abreast of things so much easier than you once could," he said. "No matter where you live, there's no real reason to feel detached from it."

If there is a reason at all to feel that way, it's probably socioeconomic, that is, fans without the connections to get tickets to always-sold-out Ohio Stadium or those who couldn't afford to buy them if they did. But if those fans can't pay $75 to attend a regular-season game, they can usually come up with $5 for a spring-game ticket. The Buckeyes drew an estimated 76,000 to the 2008 Scarlet-Gray game, then set a national record when 95,722 fans watched the spring scrimmage in 2009. They drew 81,112 to the 2012 spring game that was Meyer's first as coach; Alabama, coming off its second national title in three years, was the only other school within 22,000 of that with a spring-game attendance of 78,526.

Prior to the 2008 spring game, I followed a gawking, meandering family of five Ohio State fans across a footbridge over the Olentangy River, and it reminded me of how diverse the Buckeye Nation is. Mom, Dad, and their three kids all wore some form of scarlet and gray, although it wasn't hard to tell they weren't regular visitors to that upscale neighborhood on football Saturdays.

There wasn't one $150 football jersey or a $50 OSU t-shirt among them. There was no pricey Buckeye jewelry. Mom wore generic scarlet sweatpants without a stylish emblem. Dad was wearing one of those foam OSU hats with the screen backs that you can pick up at a truck stop for $6 or $7. The kids' t-shirts had that generic discount-store look.

But clothes don't make the fan. The kids were excited. A boy of about eleven was pointing at the giant stadium and jabbering constantly. Dad was grinning and trying to find a way to squeeze his answers into his son's relentless chatter. Another boy of about six was walking so fast that Mom kept trying to rein him in, lest he beat them to Ohio Stadium and break something before they got there.

It was an intriguing snapshot, and based on a quick perusal of the stadium's west parking lot, it was also a fairly common one. While the season ticket holders are decidedly upscale, that doesn't mean that they are better fans than those who are thrilled just to get into the stadium for a few hours to watch a spring scrimmage. These fans love the Buckeyes, hate Michigan, and love/hate the coach as much as those who have had season tickets since the fall of Wes Fesler. Their emotions burn just as hot inside them.

After that shocking 28–24 loss to Michigan State in 1998, the flood of e-mails I received showed how important these games are in some people's lives.

"Leaving for dinner out, I watched the local news to see what happened," wrote one OSU fan from Baton Rouge, Louisiana. "I saw the final score and . . . I just felt sick to my stomach. I felt like my best friend had died, and that 'it just wasn't right, wasn't fair, etc.' Then I'm thinking 'It's just a game. I'm a grown man and I should be able to go on and have a good weekend.' For some reason, however, I couldn't let it go.

"The upset haunted my thoughts, my sleep and my appetite. I was depressed!! . . . I don't like the way I'm talking. . . . I don't even know who I'm feeling more sorry for, myself, the players or the fans."

Another e-mailer said he felt "like someone died" and other messages with titles such as "Tragic Loss" and "Wearing Black" provided an excellent gauge of the emphasis many place on OSU football success. To say that perspective was in short supply that week would be a huge understatement, and it happens a lot, especially after losses.

The fans do sometimes get a bad rap though, particularly when it comes to being poor winners. After the win over Michigan in 2002 that sent the Buckeyes to the national championship game, one of the cable news channels served as my alarm clock that Sunday morning, waking me during a segment that offered a report about "rioting in Columbus, Ohio."

Against a backdrop of burning furniture, broken windows, and torched cars, the news reader intoned "Fans in Columbus, Ohio, celebrating Ohio State's win over Michigan and perfect 13-0 season, rioted last night, burning mattresses, turning over cars and breaking into stores. . . . The win put the Buckeyes in the BCS national championship at the Fiesta Bowl . . ."

Unfortunately, that wasn't what it was. The riot wasn't about football. It was an excuse to party, like New Year's Eve or Halloween, a reason for many people who weren't even fans to go crazy and drink lots of beer. It was a reason for the party crowd, a fairly large group in a metropolitan area with 1.9 million people, to descend on campus that night for what they knew was going to be the party of the year.

By the time I had left the area around 9 p.m., all the "celebrating" was pretty much finished. The tailgaters had gone back to Bexley, Bucyrus, Bellaire, and Barnesville, and the folks who had gone to the Horseshoe suffering from a serious case of high anxiety already were sleeping it off. Some students were still walking the streets, drinking beer in some cases, and spitting up a mouthful of "Go Bucks" in others. Some had already congregated in the houses near campus that have become a natural gathering place since "progress" has destroyed most of the campus-area bars.

The area immediately south and east of the student rental properties on the campus fringe is riddled with crime, and a win over Michigan gave local hooligans a cover. Instead of their regular Saturday night activities—slashing the neighbor's tires, smashing empty beer bottles against the wall of the local elementary school, or breaking into some poor sap's garage and stealing his lawn mower—the thousands of legitimate drunken revelers made it easy for them to blend in.

So they went down to campus and "celebrated" the win over Michigan by looting some stores, starting fires, and turning over a few cars, and the next thing you know, a college professor was being quoted in the newspapers about how fan violence is an extension of the violence on the field. A sociology professor/author was on television talking about a game the home team had to win and how "the long tradition of hatred between the two schools" helped him predict a major disturbance.

Burning mattresses and looting became an enduring symbol of the overexuberant Ohio State fans, when in fact it wasn't the fans on the streets east of campus nearly twelve hours after the game ended so much as some drunken students, cross-town party-goers, and neighborhood criminals. It took a couple more "celebrations" over a period of years before the police finally got these disturbances under control.

The fanaticism of OSU football fans is a fact though. As a group, they are considered one of the most loyal fan bases in sports, but they can also be among the most demanding and the most unreasonable. A place has to work to cultivate a reputation as a "graveyard of the coaches," and many of today's Buckeyes fans might be even less patient and more demanding than they were when coaches' bodies were regularly planted there.

It's always a little scary to venture into my electronic mailbox the first few days after an Ohio State football loss. It's like a trip to the dark side. The anger practically smothers you. It could be a place invented by Stephen King. There's lots of name-calling, finger-pointing, and probably even some uncontrolled weeping, although e-mail can't confirm that the way the smeared ink on a paper letter does. The deep sense of betrayal is disturbing, as if a lost football game has robbed some of these poor souls of the last sliver of joy in their miserable existence. There are reasonable, intelligent people in there, too, people who offer their observations without the rage and revulsion, many of whom doubtless care just as deeply about Ohio State football as the others. Their voices tend to get drowned out by the shrill ones, though.

After the Buckeyes lost to USC 18–15 in 2009, some fans were already convinced that sophomore quarterback Terrelle Pryor should be sent to the bench. If he wasn't Public Enemy No. 1 for some Ohio State fans, he was at least No. 2 or 3. His brief journey from top recruit in America to promising Ohio State quarterback to 6-foot-6 bull's-eye showed how impatient some OSU fans can be.

Did Pryor insist on throwing against USC when he should have been running? Did he make a bad judgment on the pass where he was called for intentional grounding? Was his inability to move his team 30 yards or so in the final 1:01 for a tying field goal an ominous sign?

"I have no idea what to make of Mr. Pryor," one fan wrote. "He sure does not look like the most sought-after recruit in the country two years ago. Either he is not all he was cracked up to be, or he is pathetically coached. I don't buy the 'only a sophomore' talk anymore."

After Pryor fumbled four times, lost two, and threw two interceptions in a 26–18 loss to Purdue later that season some fans gave up on him entirely, convinced that he would never be a good college quarterback.

"I get the impression Pryor couldn't complete a pass if no defense was out there," one critic wrote.

Some of the criticisms couldn't be printed anywhere but a pornographic website. The hysteria was disquieting. The anger made me squirm.

Pryor's performance against Purdue sent the OSU offense skidding back to the days of Woody Hayes—he attempted only 17 passes in each of the Buckeyes' last three regular-season games—but the team won five in a row and the anger gradually dissipated. Then he went back to the future in the Rose Bowl against Oregon, or at least to a future that nearly everyone had foreseen for him when he was recruited. He turned back into the dangerous either/or Pryor that coaches saw in their dreams.

After the Buckeyes' 26–17 win, he was not only the game MVP, but again the favorite player of most of the fans. With such a phenomenal quarterback back for two more seasons, some were even giddy that a national championship appeared within reach again.

The 2010 season was more of the same. Pryor was a hero until the Buckeyes lost to Wisconsin; he was seen as part of the problem after that. His December suspension with his five OSU teammates for receiving improper benefits dropped his stock even lower; beating Arkansas with a big game in the Sugar Bowl again made him a hero. That changed when Tressel quit. As the most visible of the six suspended players, Pryor immediately found himself blamed for costing the coach his job. A later report that he had signed autographs for a local photographer for cash, perhaps for as much at $20,000 to $40,000, put him back in the fans' crosshairs and he stayed there when he announced that he planned to forgo his senior season and enter the NFL supplemental draft.

Were those different fans than the ones who were on his side earlier? Probably. And then again, maybe they weren't. Pryor's rise, fall, rise, and fall again is a microcosm of football life at OSU.

"When you get right down to it, I don't know that the fans have changed a heck of a lot," Homan said. "They've always been a little impatient here. But I certainly think that because of the availability of so many talk shows, they have more means of venting their frustrations or feelings now than ever before. People were unhappy before, but there wasn't the chance to immediately communicate and make that known all over the place. I think that discontent, even though it almost might be of a temporary nature, breeds even more discontent."

Football losses have never gone down easy at Ohio State. My files include a few early *Columbus Dispatch* clippings that hint at fan unrest. Some fans were furious with OSU coach E. R. Sweetland for booting three key players from the team for training violations. Others were angry with the suspended players for being so undisciplined.

The furor came after the Buckeyes had lost two games in a row, a crisis some saw as an almost unspeakable horror. The year was 1904.

# BIBLIOGRAPHY

Brondfield, Jerry. *Rockne: The Coach, The Man, The Legend.* New York: Random House, 1976.

Cannon, Ralph. "Harley to Horvath." *Esquire,* September 1945, 92–94.

Claassen, Harold. *Ronald Encyclopedia of Football.* With statistical compilations by Steve Boda Jr. New York: Ronald Press Company, 1960.

Cohen, Richard M., Jordan A. Deutsch, and David S. Neft. *The Ohio State Football Scrapbook.* Indianapolis: Bobbs-Merrill, 1977.

Cromartie, Bill. *The Big One.* Atlanta: Gridiron Publishers, 1994.

Danzig, Allison. *The History of American Football, Its Great Teams, Players, and Coaches.* Englewood Cliffs, NJ: Prentice-Hall, 1956.

———. *Oh, How They Played the Game: The Early Days of Football and the Heroes Who Made It Great.* New York: Macmillan, 1971.

Davis, Jeff. *Papa Bear: The Life and Legacy of George Halas.* Blacklick, OH: McGraw-Hill, 2004.

East High School. *100 Years of Excellence, East High School 1898–1998, Columbus, Ohio.* Columbus, OH: Central Ohio Graphics, 1998.

Emmanuel, Greg. *The 100-Yard War: Inside the 100-Year-Old Michigan–Ohio State Football Rivalry.* Hoboken, NJ: John Wiley and Sons, 2004.

Grange, Harold E. *Zuppke of Illinois.* Chicago: A. L. Glaser, 1937.

Greenberg, Steve, and Dale Ratermann. *I Remember Woody: Recollections of the Man They Called Coach Hayes.* Chicago: Triumph Books, 1997, reprinted in 2004.

Greenberg, Steve, and Laura Lanese. *Game of My Life: Ohio State: Memorable Stories of Buckeye Football.* Champaign, IL: Sports Publishing, 2006.

Halas, George. *Halas by Halas.* With Gwen Morgan and Arthur Veysey. New York: McGraw-Hill, 1979.

Harper, William L. *An Ohio State Man, Coach Esco Sarkkinen Remembers OSU Football.* Columbus, OH: Ariel Press, 2000.

Hayes, Woody. *You Win With People!* Columbus, OH: Typographic Printing, 1973, reprinted in 1975.

Homan, Marv, and Paul Hornung. *Ohio State: 100 Years of Football.* Columbus, OH: Ohio State University, 1989.

Hornung, Paul. *The Best of the Buckeyes.* Columbus, OH: Zimmerman & Leonard, 1982.

————. *Woody Hayes: A Reflection.* Champaign, IL: Sagamore Publishing, 1991.

Hunter, Bob. *Buckeye Basketball, Ohio State University.* Huntsville, AL: Strode Publishers, 1981.

————. *Chic: The Extraordinary Rise of Ohio State Football and the Tragic Schoolboy Athlete Who Made It Happen.* With Marc Katz. Wilmington, OH: Orange Frazer Press, 2008.

————. "Harley's Absence Calls Top Five List Into Question." *Columbus Dispatch,* November 22, 2002.

————. "Harley Should Be Honored With Statue at Horseshoe." *Columbus Dispatch,* March 5, 2003.

————. "Legend Loses Step to Time, Years Have Clouded Memories of Chic Harley, OSU's First Superstar." *Columbus Dispatch,* August 27, 2000.

————. "OSU Football Fans Fall into Categories." *Columbus Dispatch,* November 24, 1998.

Hyde, David. *1968: The Year That Saved Ohio State Football.* Wilmington, OH: Orange Frazer Press, 2008.

Hyman, Mervin D., and Gordon S. White Jr. *Big Ten Football: Its Life and Times, Great Coaches, Players and Games.* New York: Macmillan, 1977.

Jones, Johnny. *Now Let Me Tell You.* Columbus, OH: Dispatch Printing, 1950.

Kinney, Harrison. *James Thurber, His Life and Times.* New York: Henry Holt, 1995.

Levy, Bill. *Three Yards and a Cloud of Dust: The Ohio State Football Story.* Columbus, OH: Nicholas Ward Publishing, 2004. First printed in 1966 by World Publishing.

Lombardo, John. *A Fire to Win: The Life and Times of Woody Hayes.* New York: Thomas Dunne Books, 2005.

Madej, Bruce. *Michigan, Champions of the West.* With Rob Toonkel, Mike Pearson, and Greg Kinney. Champaign, IL: Sports Publishing, 1997.

McCallum, John, and Charles H. Pearson. *College Football U.S.A., 1869–1971: Official Book of the National Football Foundation.* Greenwich, CT: Hall of Fame Publishing, 1971.

McClellan, Keith. *The Sunday Game: At the Dawn of Professional Football.* Akron, OH: University of Akron Press, 1998.

Michelson, Herb, and Dave Newhouse. *Rose Bowl Football Since 1902.* New York: Stein and Day, 1977.

Morgan, David Lee, Jr. *More Than a Coach: What It Means to Play for Coach, Mentor, and Friend Jim Tressel.* Chicago: Triumph Books, 2009.

Ohio State University Archives. *The Makio, Yearbooks for 1915–1930.* Columbus: Ohio State University.

Ohio State University–University of Illinois football program. "Tributes to Chic Harley." October 10, 1953, 22–23.

Park, Jack. *The Official Ohio State Football Encyclopedia.* Champaign, IL: Sports Publishing, 2001.

Perkins, Brett. *Frantic Francis: How One Coach's Madness Changed Football.* Lincoln: University of Nebraska Press, 2009.

Perry, Will. *The Wolverines, A Story of Michigan Football.* Huntsville, AL: Strode Publishers, 1974.

Peterson, Robert W. *Pigskin: The Early Years of Pro Football.* New York: Oxford University Press, 1997.

Pickenpaugh, Roger. *Buckeye Blizzard: Ohio and the 1950 Thanksgiving Storm.* Baltimore: Gateway Press, 2001.

Pollard, James E. *Ohio State Athletics, 1879–1959.* Columbus: Ohio State University Athletic Department, 1959.

———. *History of the Ohio State University: The Story of its First Seventy-Five Years, 1873–1948.* Columbus: Ohio State University Press, 1952.

Porter, David L., ed. *Biographical Dictionary of American Sports—Football.* Westport, CT: Greenwood Press, 1987.

Rea, Mark. *The Die-Hard Fan's Guide to Buckeye Football.* Washington, DC: Regnery, 2009.

———. "Harley Leaves Legacy, But Meets Sad Ending." *Buckeye Sports Bulletin* 24, no. 9 (November 6, 2004): 30–31.

———. "A Talent Never to be Forgotten." *Buckeye Sports Bulletin* 24, no. 7 (October, 23, 2004): 24–25.

Roberts, Howard. *The Big Nine: The Story of Football in the Western Conference.* New York: G. P. Putnam's Sons, 1948.

———. *The Chicago Bears.* New York: G. P. Putnam's Sons, 1947.

Smith, Robert. *Illustrated History of Pro Football.* New York: Madison Square Press, 1970.

Snook, Jeff, ed. *What It Means To Be A Buckeye: Jim Tressel and Ohio State's Greatest Players.* Chicago: Triumph Books, 2003.

Snypp, Wilbur, and Bob Hunter. *The Buckeyes: A Story of Ohio State Football.* Huntsville, AL: Strode Publishers, 1982.

Thomas, Robert D., ed. *Columbus Unforgettables: A Collection of Columbus Yesterdays and Todays.* Columbus, OH: Robert D. Thomas, 1983.

———. *More Columbus Unforgettables: A Further Collection of Columbus Yesterdays and Todays.* Vol. 2. Columbus, OH: Robert D. Thomas, 1986.

Thurber, James. "If You Ask Me." *P.M.*, October 22, 1940.

Tootle, James. *Baseball in Columbus.* Chicago: Arcadia Publishing, 2003.

Tressel, Jim. *The Winners Manual: For the Game of Life.* With Chris Fabry. Carol Stream, IL: Tyndale House Publishers, 2008.

Vare, Robert. *Buckeye: A Study of Coach Woody Hayes and the Ohio State Football Machine.* New York: Harper's Magazine Press, 1974.

Watterson, John Sayle. *College Football, History, Spectacle, Controversy.* Baltimore: John Hopkins University Press, 2000.

Wilce, John W. Biographical Files. Ohio State University Archives.

———. *Football, How to Play It and How to Understand It.* New York: Charles Scribner's Sons, 1923.

———, as told to Norman H. Dohn. "My 16 Years at Ohio State." *Columbus Dispatch Sunday Magazine*, November 14, 1954.

Willis, Chris. *The Columbus Panhandles, A Complete History of Pro Football's Toughest Team, 1900–1922.* Lanham, MD: Scarecrow Press, 2007.

Wilson, Kenneth L. (Tug), and Jerry Brondfield. *The Big Ten.* Englewood Cliffs, NJ: Prentice-Hall, 1967.

WOSU. Brent Greene, producer. *The Birth of Ohio Stadium.* Columbus: television documentary, 1999.


Microfilms and hard copies of the following newspapers and magazines were also consulted extensively:

*The Chicago Tribune*

*The Columbus Citizen*

*The Columbus Dispatch*

*The Dayton Daily News*

*The New York Times*

*The Ohio State Journal*

*The Ohio State Lantern*

*The Ohio State Monthly*

*The Ohio State Quarterly*

# INDEX

# ABOUT THE AUTHOR

Bob Hunter has been a sports columnist for the *Columbus Dispatch* since 1993 and began covering Ohio State football for the newspaper in 1977, the year before the last of Woody Hayes's career. He has authored or co-authored six other books, including two on Ohio State football. The most recent, *Chic: The Extraordinary Rise of Ohio State Football and the Tragic Schoolboy Athlete Who Made It Happen,* was published in 2008. A graduate of Ohio University, Hunter is married to the former Margie Monahan and has three grown children, Amy, Bryan, and Rob. He is a native of Hamilton, Ohio.